Human Rights Education and the Politics of Knowledge

Around the world there are myriad non-governmental organisations (NGOs) using human rights education (HRE) as a tool of community empowerment with the firm belief that it will help people improve their lives. One way of understanding these processes is that they translate universal human rights speak using messages and symbols which make them relevant to people's daily lives and culturally resonant. However, an alternative more radical perspective is that these processes should engage individuals in modes of critical inquiry into the ways that existing power structures maintain the status quo, and control not only how we understand and speak about social inequality and injustice, but also act on it.

This book is a critical inquiry into the production, distribution and consumption of HRE and how the discourse is constructed historically, socially and politically through global institutions and local NGO practice. The book begins with the premise that HRE is composed of theories of human rights and education, both of which are complex and multifaceted. However, the book demonstrates how over time a dominant discourse of HRE, constructed by the United Nations institutional framework, has come to prominence and the ways it is reproduced and reinforced through the practice of intermediary NGOs engaged in HRE activities with community groups.

Drawing on socio-legal scholarship it offers a new theoretical and political framework for addressing how human rights, pedagogy, knowledge and power can be analysed between the global and local by connecting the critical, but well-trodden, theories of human rights to insights on critical pedagogy. It uses critical discourse analysis and ethnographic research to investigate the practice of NGOs engaged in HRE using contextual evidence and findings from fieldwork with NGOs and communities in Tanzania.

Joanne Coysh is a Postdoctoral Research Fellow with the Institute for Reconciliation and Social Justice, University of the Free State (SA), a tutor at the University of Warwick (UK) and a freelance participation and learning consultant working with international NGOs. Her research focuses upon learning processes for equity and social transformation.

Routledge Research in Human Rights Law

Available titles in this series include:

Developing the Right to Social Security – A Gender Perspective
Beth Goldblatt

The ECHR and Human Rights Theory
Reconciling the Moral and the Political Conceptions
Alain Zysset

Resolving Conflicts between Human Rights
The Judge's Dilemma
Stijn Smet

Business And Human Rights in Africa
History, Politics, Context, and Emerging Trends
Uché Ewelukwa Ofodile

The Right to Food
From Sovereignty to Security
Kirsteen Shields

Forthcoming titles in this series include:

Jurisdiction, Immunity and Transnational Human Rights Litigation
Xiaodong Yang

Extraterritoriality and International Human Rights Law
The Spatial Reach of African Human Rights Treaties
Takele Soboka Bulto

The Law and Practice of the European Social Committee
Francesco Seatzu & Amaya Ubeda de Torres

Human Rights Education and the Politics of Knowledge

Joanne Coysh

Routledge
Taylor & Francis Group
LONDON AND NEW YORK

First published 2017 by Routledge

2 Park Square, Milton Park, Abingdon, Oxfordshire OX14 4RN
52 Vanderbilt Avenue, New York, NY 10017

Routledge is an imprint of the Taylor & Francis Group, an informa business

First issued in paperback 2018

British Library Cataloguing in Publication Data
A catalogue record for this book is available from the British Library

Library of Congress Cataloging in Publication Data
Names: Coysh, Joanne, author.
Title: Human rights education and the politics of knowledge / Joanne Coysh.
Description: New York: Routledge, 2016. | Series: Routledge research in human rights law | Includes bibliographical references and index.
Identifiers: LCCN 2016035259 | ISBN 9781138779112 (hbk) | ISBN 9781315769493 (ebk)
Subjects: LCSH: Human rights—Study and teaching. | Non-governmental organizations.
Classification: LCC K3240 .C695 2016 | DDC 323.071—dc23
LC record available at https://lccn.loc.gov/2016035259

ISBN: 978-1-138-77911-2 (hbk)
ISBN: 978-0-367-07598-9 (pbk)

Typeset in Galliard
by Keystroke, Neville Lodge, Tettenhall, Wolverhampton

Contents

Acknowledgements

This book has been a long journey and I would like to thank all those who have believed it should be written and encouraged me to do so. As a practitioner and someone who designs and facilitates processes, writing about ideas is not always easy but it is a necessary skill to capture and theorise about what may be happening in real life – as a process of praxis in itself.

This book would not have been able to take the shape it has without the support, guidance and input from staff and colleagues at the University of Warwick, in particular Professor Andrew Williams, whom I thank for his intellectual leadership and contribution to my PhD, Professor Ann Stewart and Professor Abdul Paliwala, who takes an avid interest in how HRE can be used to shape society in Tanzania. I would also like to thank Professor Andre Keet at the Institute for Reconciliation and Social Justice, who contacted me about my work and has provided much needed support since.

Because I spent twelve months in Tanzania with my family in order to conduct the research I am incredibly thankful to all those people who assisted in making it happen and helped along the way. In particular, I would like to thank all the staff at the Legal and Human Rights Centre in Dar es Salaam, where I was provided with office space, resources and logistical support, especially Anna Henga and Felista Mauya who allowed me to share their office and put up with my constant questions about the English translation of Kiswahili terms. In saying this, I could not have managed without the valuable assistance of Jofrey Pima, who travelled with me to the rural areas and helped to translate workshops. He was a great travelling companion and demonstrated consistent hard work and a commitment and interest in the community. I wish him all the best in his future career. I especially want to thank Mama Helen Kijo-Bisimba for her advice and support. It is unlikely that without her encouragement I would have gone to Tanzania. She is both a friend and inspiration in terms of her commitment and tenacity in working for the interests of the people in her country.

I would also like to thank Scolastica Jullu and the staff at WLAC, Zameer Noorali and the Peace Club students, Justa Mwaituka, the staff and children at KIWOHEDE. Thanks to Joseph Vere and Mohamed Gulleth from UNESCO who helped to organise and hosted a focus group, and to Samantha Mercer who kindly volunteered her assistance and helped to take notes in the focus group discussions. I was always welcomed in the workshops and communities, and for this I can only thank the Tanzanian sense of hospitality and the people. There are many other friends I made on the journey who helped my family and me to settle and navigate our way in Tanzania. I think about them often.

Finally, I want to thank my family and friends for all their support. In particular, my boys Thomas and Louis for their adaptability, curiosity, love and laughter, as well as their ability to bring me back down to earth and make me see what really matters. And my mum, who has always been encouraging and supportive of my choices, but also for her help for the final amendments and proofreading my work.

I am grateful for being given the opportunity to conduct this research through ESRC funding, without which I could not have dedicated the time to completing this work.

List of Abbreviations

ASP	Associated Schools Project
CEDAW	Convention on the Elimination of All Forms of Discrimination against Women (1979)
CRC	Convention on the Rights of the Child (1989)
CSO	civil society organisation
DHRET	UN Declaration on Human Rights Education and Training (2011)
ECOSOC	Economic and Social Council
FGM	female genital mutilation
HRE	human rights education
ICCPR	International Covenant on Civil and Political Rights (1966)
ICERD	International Convention on the Elimination of all Forms of Racial Discrimination (1965)
ICESCR	International Covenant on Economic, Social and Cultural Rights (1966)
IGO	international governmental organisation
INGO	international non-governmental organisation
LHRC	Legal and Human Rights Centre
NGO	non-governmental organisation
OHCHR	Office of the High Commissioner for Human Rights
RBA	rights-based approach
UDHR	Universal Declaration of Human Rights (1948)
UN	United Nations
UNCHR	United Nations Commission on Human Rights
UNESCO	United Nations Educational, Scientific and Cultural Organization
UNICEF	United Nations International Children's Emergency Fund
WLAC	Women's Legal Aid Centre
WPHRE	World Programme for Human Rights Education

1 Introduction

HRE, the politics of knowledge and social transformation

On 27 March 2013 an estimated 2,000 Maasai women gathered in the village of Magaiduru in Tanzania to protest over a government decision to limit the use of land and natural resources in Loliondo and collectively demand the land be returned to the communities. This 'coming together' was in response to an announcement by the Ministry of Tourism to set aside 1,500 square kilometres of land bordering the Serengeti national park for a 'wildlife corridor'. This will mean that the Maasai who have wandered and used this land as a source of life will be prevented from getting to their pasture land in the corridor. This is because this chunk of land has been leased to Ortello Business Corporation (OBC) for hunting and safari purposes.

'Women are gathering and demonstrating because without land there is no life for them', explains Maanda Ngoitiko, Executive Director of the Pastoral Women's Council (PWC), one of Maliasili Initiatives' partners in northern Tanzania. 'They've been empowered over the years, and have deep knowledge about what is happening and are therefore not willing to sit quietly as their livelihoods are stolen away from them.'

The women collected together their CCM membership cards for the ruling party in Tanzania and handed them back to protest against the party and the decision. They remained in the shade of trees in that spot for 12 days as an act of non-violent defiance. 'We don't belong to any party, our party is our land', said Ms Paraketo, one of the women protesters from Ololosokwan Village, among those on the disputed land.

This conflict between the politics of power and the power of people in Loliondo is ongoing and not the first time that Maasai women have taken matters into their own hands. On 4 July 2009, when Tanzanian police set fire to the Maasai homestead in Loliondo to evict them, eight Maasai villages were burned down, leaving 3,000 people without food, water or shelter. In addition, 54,000 head of cattle were displaced without water or grazing land in acute drought conditions. There were reports of police raping and beating women during the eviction. By August 2009, the burnings had stopped but any Maasai found herding within 5 miles of the OBC lands were arrested. In February 2010, a parliamentary report of the evictions was supposed to be reviewed and discussed, but the ruling political party of Tanzania blocked the report.[1]

Then on 6 April 2010 Maasai women from all over the region gathered in order to protest against the forced eviction. Four hundred women gathered in Ololosokwan. They were threatened with violence by local authorities if they chose to keep marching to Loliondo. The next morning, they decided to keep marching but were intercepted by police in Oloipiri, where they were forced onto trucks under the threat of violence, and were driven back to Ololosokwan. At the same time, women all over the region were walking to Loliondo to protest. Sixty women from Enguserosambu were arrested by Tanzanian police and questioned about their actions. The largest single group was made up of 500 women, who spent the night in the bush outside Wasso. In total, over 1,500 women were able to make it into the city of Loliondo to return 1,833 voting cards to the local government as an act of protest.[2] This was considered a serious political move because it withdrew their support from the political party.

The women were able to organise primarily through mobile-phone contact and through work with local non-governmental organisations (NGOs). On 8 April, the gathering made three demands to the government. First, they wanted the blocked report on the eviction to be reviewed by parliament; second, they wanted the government to discontinue plans to seize village land to create a wildlife corridor that would essentially serve as an extension to the Loliondo Game Controlled Area and would be off limits to people except those with hunting rights; and third, the women wanted to be able to hold a peaceful, public demonstration in Loliondo.

On 12 April, police arrested three employees from the Ngorogoro Non-Governmental Organizations Network (NGONet) for organising the demonstration the Maasai women had held. These arrests drew international attention to the campaign. The Country Director of Oxfam GB said that the detention 'was against the right of citizens to have a voice, and for that voice to be heard was an integral part of democratic society'.[3] A meeting with the District Defence and Security Committee on 19 April highlighted the fragile security situation: that the women had held protests without a permit, a belief that marginalised women did not have the capability of organising a demonstration without external pressure, a concern that civil society organisations (CSOs) were misleading communities and a belief that NGOs should stay out of politics.[4]

In this same period, between 2009 and 2010, I was conducting my own research in Tanzania exploring how NGOs understood and practised the idea of

1 Global Non-Violent Action Database, 'Masai Women Protest Land Seizure in Tanzania, 2009', http://nvdatabase.swarthmore.edu/content/maasai-women-protest-land-seizure-tanzania-2009 (accessed 23 March 2012).

2 Ibid.

3 The Citizen Reporter, 'Oxfam Appeals over Detention of its Staff', *The Citizen* newspaper, Tanzania, 14 April 2010.

4 Handout from Oxfam International during a meeting at the Policy Forum, 29 May 2010.

'human rights education'. In the course of the research many interviewees had expressed a belief that certain groups and communities did not know their rights and needed educating in them. This is a perspective that as always left me with a sense of unease, because my own assumption is that it is the people and communities who live without human rights who understand them better than any outside expert and can demand that those rights must be recognised. If there is anything that demonstrates this point, it is the actions of the Maasai women who, of their own accord, marched in mass protest – they live it, they breathe it, and experience the abuse and struggle for human rights every day. Why, then, is there such an inherent belief that certain groups of people need human rights education and, more to the point, what does this mean?

There is a predominant belief that 'education' is at the root of freedom, but the Maasai women's protests raise important critical questions about what exactly 'learning' entails and the ways that it is shaped by the interrelationship between and contested ideas about knowledge, power and social change. Why, because many of these women had received little or no formal education, is there an assumption they did not understand notions of injustice and inequality and that some professional must have encouraged them to act? What is the influence of the mind in situations of oppression and the willingness to act in resistance? To what extent does the way people understand their reality, their experiences and expectations affect their ability to change it? It is how we experience and give meaning to our realities that can be both a protection against oppression while at the same time an obstacle to liberation. It is the mind that 'adjusts to the body's chains, develops a rationale that makes sense of injustice and order out of chaos'.[5]

Human rights education

This book is an exploration into the complex and critical relationship of how our experiences and expectations shape our ways of seeing, being and doing. It is examined through the lens of human rights education (HRE) which, as a global concept and practice, has grown hugely over the last 20 years, since 1995, when the first United Nations Decade of Human Rights Education was pronounced by the United Nations. The book proposes that it is our experiences and expectations that lead us to make various assumptions about knowledge, power and change, which are fundamentally reflected not only in the ways we understand and interpret human rights but also in how we respond to and engage with them, especially when it comes to learning and how we expect social change to happen.

It shows how ideas about 'education' and 'human rights' are widely contested both in terms of their meaning and the ways they should be approached in

5 T.W. Heaney and A.I. Horton, 'Reflective Engagement for Social Change' in J. Mezirow and Associates (eds), *Fostering Critical Reflection in Adulthood: A Guide to Transformative and Emancipatory Learning*, Jossey-Bass, San Francisco, 1990, p. 86.

practice. They are complex and multifaceted, which means that at any one time they can simultaneously be a way to both reproduce and maintain the status quo and a possibility for social change. Seen from this perspective the aim should therefore be to bring to the surface and expose the practices that are restrictive and oppressive, while at the same time revealing and enabling their emancipatory potential; supporting the possibility for liberating action and freedom.

Because there are so many views about what they mean both in theory and practice, one might assume that constructing a coherent and globally viable model of HRE would be difficult, if not impossible. However, in the decades following the Charter of the United Nations in 1945 and the Universal Declaration of Human Rights in 1948, HRE has graduated from disparate discussions about ways to realise human rights into a centralised, controlled and institutional discourse characterised by the production, distribution and consumption of numerous official texts. These include definitions, obligations and prescriptive implementation guidelines for national governments to follow, many of which have emerged during the last 20 years.

There have been three significant events in this respect. First, the proclamation of the United Nations Decade for Human Rights Education (1995–2004);[6] second, the establishment of a World Programme for Human Rights Education (WPHRE) (2005 ongoing) by the UN General Assembly;[7] and finally, in 2011, after two years of discussions and provisional texts, the United Nations (UN) adopted the UN Declaration on Human Rights Education and Training (DHRET).[8] In this period HRE discourse has penetrated peace building and post-conflict operations and regional development programmes. It has also become a key feature of school curricula and community programmes around the world.

Despite this, there are three problems with the global model of HRE. First is the way that human rights are often presented as self-evident, universally relevant and applicable; second, that institutional knowledge of human rights often positions itself as neutral, universal and non-hegemonic; and finally, the way that HRE appears severed from any idea of history, culture or community and so presents as a factual truth, rather than a plural and dynamic field of thought operating in a complex society. As the discussion in this book reveals, the global model is only one way of seeing, being and doing HRE where in fact simmering beneath the surface what exists are power relationships, and assumptions about knowledge and action, which will influence the possibility of it being a pathway to social transformation.

It is this relationship between theory and social practice that offers a framework through which to analyse the relations that link the institutions and activities of

6 United Nations General Assembly Resolution A/res/49/184 of 23 December 1994.

7 United Nations General Assembly Resolution A/res/59/113 of 17 February 2005.

8 United Declaration on Human Rights Education and Training, General Assembly Resolution 66/137, 19 December 2011.

everyday life with the logic and influences that shape the broader social inquiry. This is an inquiry into the ways that certain assumptions about knowledge, power and social change influence how we conceptualise and act; it examines how human rights knowledge is controlled and explains how certain conceptions and practice dominate over others.

The book reveals how spaces of HRE have become transnational sites of struggle, existing in a permanent relationship of provocation between domination and resistance and caught in a dynamic relationship of power. Understood as a site of struggle, it suggests that while HRE discourse has been used to construct and (re)produce social structures and hierarchies, it can be a space of resistance to (re)construct social relations. Literature about HRE is so often caught up in the distinction between universalism or cultural relativism or different methods and approaches that this has distracted from the most important and determinate relationship, which is the way that power produces knowledge and knowledge produces power.

The context of HRE

In exploring HRE the book focuses upon understanding production, distribution and consumption of the global and local discourse, and the relationship between them. Discourse means not only text and language, but also social practice and interaction which can take place simultaneously. Critical discourse analysis helps to unravel the historical construction of HRE and show how it has been socially constructed. Considered are the ways in which HRE discourse has been used throughout history to construct and (re)produce social structures and hierarchies, or used as a tool of resistance to (re)construct social relations. Viewed from this perspective HRE is essentially a site of struggle. However, while the production and interpretation of HRE discourse are important, also important is the organisation and interaction between the global and the local, institutions and society, theory and practice, and how they shape HRE practice.

Between the global and the local

The relationship between the global and the local is increasingly significant in the way that discourses and ideas circulate today. Focusing upon this relationship does not discount the importance of local level research, knowledge and resources, but is recognition that the local political, social and cultural context cannot realistically be isolated from the broader globalised political, social and cultural spectrum.

The micro and macro relationship is particularly important in the context of HRE discourse, not only in trying to understand what happens to HRE between the global and the local, but also how it is given meaning when transplanted from one context to another. The idea of tracking a concept between the global and the local is partially inspired by the work of Sally Engel Merry, who used this approach to understand the relationship between the different discourses of gender-based violence.[9] Merry claims that viewing the global–local divide as one which separates rights and culture is misguided, and undermines the struggle for human rights. Instead, she argues that it should be viewed as a 'context that defines relationships and meanings and constructs possibilities for action'.[10] Understanding the global–local interface requires attention to transnational cultural flows and their relationship to local cultural spaces.[11]

How, then, do transnational human rights ideas become part of local discourse and penetrate the local consciousness? Merry claims that this takes place through a process of transplantation, which is the appropriation and translation of programmes and ideas from one context to another. A number of academics[12] have also suggested that in order to understand the global–local context, it is 'vital to understand the workings of both the globalized discourse of human rights (itself multiplicitous) and its practice in local settings (how it is interpreted and acted upon in a particular context)'.[13] It is therefore important to understand how human rights dialogue can be affected by the interactions and power dynamics of the different actors involved in the transnational space.

Institutions and society

The second important concern in the formation of HRE discourse is the relationship between institutions and society. This book focuses specifically upon the relationship between the international human rights framework, international and national NGOs, as well as local communities. Why the relationship between NGOs and the community is so important and how this connection is highlighted in the case of informal adult education is explained below.

International organisations, NGOs and CSOs

From the early post-war years, many UN agencies and other international governmental organisations (IGOs) have included NGOs as partners in their programmes. The terrain of international sponsors and the number of international programmes that include NGOs has expanded dramatically in the past two

9 S.E. Merry, *Human Rights and Gender Violence: Translating International Law into Local Justice*, University of Chicago Press, Chicago, 2009.
10 Ibid., p. 9.
11 Ibid., p. 19.
12 It is the field of legal anthropology that has started to gain a foothold in considering the global–local relationship in terms of understanding how human rights works; in particular Sally Engle Merry, Richard Wilson, Marie Benedicte-Dembour, Jane Cowan, Mark Goodale and Shannon Speed.
13 Merry, *Human Rights and Gender Violence*, p. 166.

decades. It now includes not only IGOs, but a complex collection of internationally active governmental, quasi-governmental and private organisations.[14]

The rapid growth in funding by these organisations started in the 1980s, but was particularly notable in the 1990s. This growth was caused by a number of political and social factors, not discussed here, except to note that as a consequence the influence of international organisations upon state policy has steadily increased over the last 30 years. In the field of international development, the interest demonstrated by the United Nations Development Programme (UNDP) and the World Bank in NGOs is a good example. After decades of more or less ignoring them, both institutions began to accept greater participation of NGOs in their programmes.[15] In the 1980s and 1990s these IGOs began to establish a variety of funds and initiatives to support the growth of NGOs. These included the funding of NGO projects; funding and training for attendance at UN conferences; material and technical support for the development of national and international NGO internet networks, and training at numerous workshops, as well as organisational support for a variety of capacity-building programmes.[16]

At the World Bank efforts were also made to increase NGO inclusion in its own financed projects. NGO participation in such projects increased from 6 per cent of all projects from 1973 to 1988 to 30 per cent in the early 1990s and reached 50 per cent of all projects by the late 1990s.[17]

While the mushrooming of international and national NGOs during the 1990s may not necessarily reflect either their success or impact, which is often contested, the growth is evidence of their importance as institutions in the international arena at least. With the post-Cold War wave of democratisation in many countries in the early 1990s, a civil society agenda and rhetoric emerged among bilateral agencies as the new rationale for providing increasing amounts of foreign aid through NGOs.[18]

In addition to material resources, international institutions also provided new opportunities for civil society to participate in political processes at international

14 K.D. Reimann, 'International Politics, Norms and the Worldwide Growth of NGOs', paper prepared for the 43rd Annual Convention of the International Studies Association, New Orleans, 24–27 March 2002, http://isanet.ccit.arizona.edu/noarchive/kimreimann.html#_ftn1 (accessed 15 March 2012).

15 UNDP appointed its first NGO adviser in 1984 and created a special division within UNDP for dealing with NGOs in 1986. Currently, this division is called the Civil Society Organizations and Participation Programme. At the World Bank, relations with NGOs were formalised in 1982 with the creation of the NGO–World Bank Committee. During the 1990s, the World Bank created a new division within its headquarters called the NGO Unit and began hiring NGO specialists at its Resident Missions.

16 The World Bank, *World Bank–Civil Society Relations*, Fiscal 1999 Progress Report, World Bank, Washington, DC, 1999.

17 Ibid.

18 I. Smillie and H. Helmich, in collaboration with T. German and J. Randel, *Stakeholders – Government–NGO Partnerships for International Development*, OECD Development Centre, Paris; Earthscan, London, 1999.

level. As international institutions opened up new channels of access and actively included NGOs in their policy-making process, they encouraged the formation and the growth of new internationally concerned social activists. There was also an equally dramatic expansion in human rights NGOs during this same period, especially in the two years after 1989, coinciding with the end of the Cold War.[19] While HRE organisations have also increased steadily, the growth has not been so dramatic. Nonetheless, by 2004, there was an estimated 300 to 500 national human rights institutions, and the number of national human rights commissions had quadrupled since 1990.[20]

These NGOs are important intermediaries and link the global institutional framework, states and the community. They have an important policy role in the implementation of international norms and standards, which are usually filtered through the state or directly through these third-sector organisations. The advocacy and lobbying of international NGOs tries to ensure that the needs of society are recognised and acted upon by both the state and the international community. In more repressive political environments these become critical in the way they raise external awareness of conditions for communities and people living in these societies.[21] Consequently, NGOs have increasing significance, particularly as important intermediary *translators* which can bridge the global–local divide.[22]

Some, nevertheless, would argue that one of the more negative effects of this expansion has been the 'bureaucratisation of human rights' and see it as a result of larger NGOs acquiring bureaucratic traits. This means that the reproduction of the NGO model has resulted in less creative but more routine modes of leadership, which has not been helped by the requirements of funding organisations to produce three-year strategies and reporting processes based upon prescribed outcomes.

Despite all this, the role of NGOs in HRE has been given relatively little attention in the available literature or institutional texts. This may have to do with the fact that although informal or community-based education was one aspect of the WPHRE, it has never been tackled specifically within the institutional framework, which has concentrated instead upon the design of national action plans at national and policy level within schools. Community-based settings are nonetheless an important aspect of HRE, where many informal HRE spaces can open up as an interface between the global, national and local frameworks. This

19 D. Suarez and F. Ramirez, *Human Rights and Citizenship: The Emergence of Human Rights Education*, CDDRL Working Paper No. 12, 19 August 2004, http://iis-db.stanford.edu/pubs/20682/ramirez_suarez_6.25.2004.pdf (accessed 15 March 2012).

20 S. Cardenas, 'Adaptive States: The Proliferation of New Human Rights Institutions', Carr Centre for Human Rights Working Paper, T-01-04, 2004, in U. Baxi, *The Future of Human Rights*, 3rd edn, Oxford University Press, New Delhi, 2008, p. 93.

21 A further role, not discussed here, is the role of NGOs in service provision, such as healthcare, education and care services, and the relationship between service provision and human rights advocacy work is an important area for further research.

22 Merry, *Human Rights and Gender Violence*, pp. 134–135.

book focuses on this particular aspect by examining the role of NGOs in community-based HRE, mainly in the field of adult education, but it also touches upon other forms of education, often delivered informally and outside the institutional framework. The reasons for concentrating on informal adult education as an important ideological and political site in HRE are discussed in more detail below.

Informal adult education

Historically, adult education has been a site of ideological and political struggle. Studies have shown that in different periods socialists, in particular, have regarded adult education as a source of support for the economic and political struggle to overthrow capitalism and construct a socialist society. The growth of the labour movement in the industrialised countries in the nineteenth century led to active independent adult education programmes for workers, such as Chartist Meeting Halls in England in the 1830s or evening schools in Russia in the 1890s.[23]

After the First World War, Antonio Gramsci contributed to experiments in workers' education programmes through the Factory Council Movement. The aim was to enable workers to gain the intellectual tools they needed for workers' control, viewed as a major step towards socialism.[24] Alternative ideas were considered key to social transformation and a means to challenge the dominant hegemonic ideology.[25] Some capitalists responded by setting up the Mechanics' Institutes, with curricula designed to 'tranquilise the popular mind' and to be 'a sedative to all sorts of turbulence and disorder'.[26] Then, after the Second World War adult education programmes were introduced to 'promote the development of democratic political institutions, to encourage a smooth transition to independence, without the fear of threatening alternatives'.[27]

The regulatory aspect of adult education was most evident in the way it was employed during the colonial project to frame policy, create elites and allies, divide society and serve the interests of the West. Discourse was therefore used to establish a disciplined colonial subject.[28] By framing colonial policies and rhetoric in terms resonant with the local population, the colonisers attempted to hide the true purpose of their ideological project, which was to produce 'the raw materials [needed] in Europe and consumers of the manufactured goods we make in

23 F. Youngman, *Adult Education and Socialist Pedagogy*, Radical Forum on Adult Education Series, Croom Helm, Beckenham, 1983, p. 3.

24 M. Mayo, *Imagining Tomorrow: Adult Education for Transformation*, NIACE, Leicester, 1997, p. 23.

25 Ibid.

26 S. Shapin and B. Barnes, 'Science, Nature and Control in Interpreting Mechanics Institutes' in R. Dale, E. Esland and M. MacDonald (eds), *Schooling and Capitalism*, Routledge, London, 1976, p. 60.

27 Mayo, *Imagining Tomorrow*, p. 34.

28 Youngman, *Adult Education and Socialist Pedagogy*, p. 24.

Europe'.[29] Both regulation and the creation of the human rights subject are key aspects of the critique of HRE in this book.

These colonised people were clearly underestimated, and by the 1970s many colonial states struggling for independence began to construct their own modes of political education, using their contacts and experience.[30] There were clear differences between the individual educational approaches in Europe and the West, which emphasised 'adult education for individual development and self-fulfilment' rather than the more collective development focus characteristic of the colonised states.[31] Adult education became a key site of struggle between domination and resistance, one in which groups opposed to Western colonial policies began to exercise their power and used mass education as a prerequisite to wide spread and sustainable social change.[32]

Community-based adult education is therefore an important location for HRE and, because of its broad social purpose, has often compelled those engaged in it to 'fly below the radar'.[33] However, while it has been used in the past to enable people to adapt and reintegrate into the system, it is also a type of education that can 'empower groups and individuals to confront the system with a view to changing it'.[34]

Informal or community-based adult education is therefore part of a broader struggle for social change worldwide, which has its roots in the ideas of transformative pedagogy and the notion of praxis.

Theory and practice (praxis)

The conception of discourse here is guided by the notion of praxis: reflection and action on the world in order to transform it and where theory becomes a political and transformative activity. Theory and action are inter-reliant in praxis, which means there can be no theory without action, and no action without theory. This is based on the idea that no reality will transform itself and transformation requires the 'critical intervention of the people in reality through praxis'.[35] It involves a

29 Statement of a Governor-General of French West Africa in A. Moumouni, *Education in Africa*, trans. Pn Ott, Andre Deutch, London, 1968, cited in Youngman, *Adult Education and Socialist Pedagogy*, p. 24.

30 Mayo, *Imagining Tomorrow*, p. 56.

31 L. Bowm, 'Adult Education in the Third World', in M. Tight (ed.), *Adult Learning and Education*, Croom Helm, Beckenham, 1983, pp. 38–49.

32 M Mayo, *Imagining Tomorrow*, p. 57.

33 This depends upon context but includes avoiding surveillance or being co-opted into mainstream systems, maintaining connections with the grassroots, remaining a subaltern discourse, or operating 'underground' in conditions of extreme repression.

34 P. Mayo, 'Flying Below the Radar? Critical Approaches to Adult Education', in M.W. Apple, W. Au and L.A. Gardin (eds), *The Routledge International Handbook of Critical Education*, Routledge, New York, 2009, pp. 269–280, p. 269.

35 P. Freire, *Pedagogy of the Oppressed*, rev. edn, Penguin, London, 1996, p. 35.

process of ***conscientização*** (conscientisation),[36] which entails people not only accepting the struggle for humanisation, but also their total responsibility for the struggle itself.[37] Conscientisation, then, is 'the deepening of the coming of consciousness'.[38] It requires working collectively 'to unveil the truths hidden behind ideologies that are more alive when it is said they are dead'.[39]

The idea that people can be active agents in transforming their own world was proposed by Marx and Engels, developed by Antonio Gramsci, and later taken up by Paulo Freire.[40] Freire claims that there are two kinds of educators: the ***activist*** and the ***radical***. The ***activist*** is a person who engages in 'action without the vigilance of reflection' and who has a taste for 'sloganising',[41] perpetuating half-truths and attributing absolute value to the purely relative. The ***radical***, on the other hand, rejects activism and submits their 'actions to reflection'.[42] A transformative pedagogy requires radical individuals rather than activists and should be grounded in reality rather than theory.

According to this position one cannot learn intellectually as it offers no responsibility, no opportunity to make decisions, but 'only gestures and attitudes which encourage passivity'.[43] To separate theory and action is mindless, and leads to what has been described as 'armchair reflection'. Instead, he claims 'that humans transform the world by naming it, dialogue imposes itself as a way in which [humans] achieve significance as [humans]'.[44]

Theory and social practice offer a framework to analyse the relations that link institutions and activities of everyday life with the logic and influences that shape the broader social inquiry. It is an inquiry into the ways that HRE discourse is controlled and explains how certain conceptions and practice dominate over others. This requires an analytical framework that can show the way that the exercise of power and hegemony shape understanding of HRE discourse.

Power, knowledge and ideology critique

The idea that institutions control the formation of discourse in order to regulate society was suggested by Michel Foucault, who claimed that discourse was 'a set of linguistic, polemic and strategic facts designed to produce and sustain an economy of truth' and the site where meanings are contested and power relations

36 A term originally used by Catholic radicals in the 1960s.

37 Paulo Freire's *Pedagogy of the Oppressed* was at the time regarded as a Marxist and revolutionary pedagogy, but has over the years been appropriated and adapted by educationalists and also community development practitioners.

38 P. Freire, *Pedagogy of the City*, Continuum, New York, 1993, p. 110.

39 Ibid.

40 K. Marx and F. Engels, *Selected Works*, International Publishers, New York, 1968, p. 28.

41 P. Freire, *Education for Critical Consciousness*, Continuum, New York, 1974, p. 11.

42 Ibid.

43 Ibid., p. 17.

44 Freire, *Pedagogy of the Oppressed*, p. 69.

determined. It is the through certain disciplinary systems, institutions and social relations that we can see the ways that the exercise of power in society is used to control knowledge and meaning.[45] Discourse is a central part of the struggle for knowledge, through which multiple relations of power function. Harnessing that power to serve particular interests therefore becomes a significant, if not a predominant, role of discourse working within that space. In order to function effectively power relies upon an international discourse of human rights being accumulated, put into circulation and set to work.[46]

Discourse here is taken to mean not only text and language, but also social practice and interaction which can take place simultaneously. It is the discursive orientation of individuals that determines, in part at least, how they make sense of both their own and others' experiences in the world and the types of action they choose to engage in as a result. Therefore, the way in which discursive practices are constitutive of knowledge, and how scientific discourse penetrates fields of knowledge in the formation of the subject,[47] are important because they can reveal truths for what they really are, a socially constructed reality and one particular way of seeing the world.

Examining the different spaces of discourse is an entry point to investigate the ways that transformation takes place, in the past, present and future. It is a way of understanding how shifting discursive practices contribute to the interplay between changes in knowledge, social relations and social identities, as well as the relationship between micro-level instances of discourse and the macro influences.[48] It can also be used as an analytical tool to bring to the surface the hidden and unconscious dynamics of knowledge, power and truth,[49] and how they can influence and forge passive consent which then makes possible the domination of all aspects of society by one single class; in other words, the way that knowledge, power and truth maintain the hegemonic status quo.

The way that power produces knowledge is therefore critical in trying to understand the evolution of the discourse of HRE, conceived here as both being constitutive and constituted by social and institutional practices in a society characterised primarily by relations of domination.[50] The target, then, is not the institutions, theories or ideologies of HRE, but the *practices* and the *conditions*

45 M. Marchand and J. Parpart, *Feminism/Postmodern Development*, Routledge, London, 1995, p. 3.

46 M. Foucault, *Society Must Be Defended: Lectures at the Collège de France 1975–76*, Picador, New York, 2003, p. 24.

47 In N. Fairclough, *Discourse and Social Change*, Polity Press, Cambridge, 1992, p. 38.

48 In particular inspired by the ideas of Norman Fairclough.

49 M. Foucault, *Power/Knowledge: Selected Interviews and Other Writings, 1972–1977*, Pantheon Books, New York, 1980.

50 Foucault and Gramsci applied their theories to localised case studies. Foucault used genealogy to analyse the formation of the subject in hospitals and prisons in France, and Gramsci was looking at educational institutions and the context of socialism in Italy. However, the way they viewed domination and resistance are as relevant in the contemporary global context as they were in their context. Arguably they are more so, given that the boundaries between

that make these acceptable at any given moment,[51] to examine the 'places where what is said and what is done, rules imposed and reasons given, the planned and the taken for granted meet and interconnect'.[52] Doing this reveals not only the ways that HRE can and has been harnessed by some dominant groups to perpetuate a particular cultural form, but also shows how alternative ways of seeing, being and doing HRE could open up spaces for resistance. In this way power and ideology merge into one common objective, which is to understand more about the relationship between domination and resistance within HRE.

Each society, according to Foucault, has its own 'regime' and 'politics of truth', which consist of the types of discourse it accepts and circulates as truth.[53] The critique of truth is that it is what society accepts as true knowledge and thought itself and is intimately bound up with language and inserted into systems of social practice.[54] According to Foucault, it is only through a genealogical type of analysis that one can seek out the different forces at the origin of our taken-for-granted values, concepts and experiences. The analytical task, then, is to show the way in which the historical truth of the discourse of HRE in fact rests upon 'complex, contingent and fragile ground',[55] which introduces a sense of complexity and uncertainty, doubt and reflexivity about its production and claims to knowledge.[56] By rejecting any claim to objectivity and truth, this process instead requires respect for the uncertainty of knowledge claims, on the basis that 'there will always be other perspectives from which to interpret the material under review'.[57] In this sense the notion that human rights are an inherent and a natural 'given' is rejected, and instead they are viewed as a socio-political construction of contemporary society.

According to Foucault, in order to understand the present one must excavate and unpick the social construction of the past. A history of knowledge is claimed to be 'a story of struggle for certain truths', where the outcome is 'constitutive of particular social relations and modes of being' gaining dominance at certain points in time and a consequence of power struggles in which particular realities are privileged and others disqualified.[58] Constructing a *history of the present*

global and local discourses are increasingly blurred and the interpretative struggle has taken on an international scale.

51 M. Mahon, *Foucault's Nietzschean Genealogy: Truth, Power, and the Subject*, State University of New York Press, New York, 1992, p. 129.

52 Ibid., pp. 129–130.

53 Foucault, *Power/Knowledge*, p. 131.

54 See M. Foucault, *The Archaeology of Knowledge*, Harper & Row, New York, 1976.

55 J.D. Marshall, 'Foucault and Educational Research', in S. Ball (ed.), *Foucault and Education: Disciplines and Knowledge*, Routledge, London, 1990, p. 19.

56 S. Ball, 'Intellectuals Or Technicians: The Urgent Role of Theory in Educational Studies', *British Journal of Educational Studies*, 43(3), 1995, p. 269.

57 M. Wetherall, 'Debates in Discourse Research', in M. Wetherall, S. Taylor and S.J. Yates (eds), *Discourse Theory and Practice: A Reader*, Sage, London, p. 284.

58 M. Haugaard, *Power: A Reader*, Manchester University Press, Manchester, 2002, p. 182.

requires analysing how power relations have shaped our ways of seeing and being.[59] It attempts to rupture the dominant discourse by showing how the validation and legitimisation of certain knowledges have produced a particular truth, which really is nothing more than a reflection of social relations saturated with power.[60] In this view, historical developments should not be seen as culminations of historical processes, grand narratives or hidden political designs, but instead, 'manifestations of the balances of power over people, though no one person or collective may have exercised that power or ultimately be held responsible'.[61]

Through this kind of genealogical analysis this book explore the ways that power has been exercised though global institutions and social relation to control the production, distribution and consumption of human rights knowledge and meaning.[62] By exploring the discourse of HRE through the relationships of power not only reveals HRE as it emerged and exists, but also provides a way of looking at it as it should be. A history of HRE discourse is understood as being the result of continual struggles and any knowledge changes are not because new discoveries have been made. Instead, it is when there has been a *shift of forces* which results in a new appropriation of knowledge and, therefore, a new set of interpretations (a new 'truth'). This ongoing and continuous struggle to interpret the truth is what Foucault calls 'the will to knowledge'.[63]

Power analysis

Foucault, however, suggests that there are a few important aspects that one should follow when studying power. First, that power should not be viewed as a single centre, but rather the point is to look at its '*extremities, at its outer limits* at the point where it becomes capillary'[64] where it is 'invested in institutions, is embodied in techniques and acquires the material to intervene'.[65] The task is to study power at the point where intentions are completely *invested in practices* and where it relates directly and immediately to what may be called its *object*, 'the places where it implants itself and produces real effects'.

Second, power should not be seen as something that can be possessed, or transferred. Instead, it circulates, traverses and is 'exercised through networks';[66] individuals do not simply circulate in those networks but at any one time they are in a position to either submit to or exercise this power. They are not 'inert or

59 Ibid.
60 Ibid., p. 182.
61 JD Marshall, 'Foucault and Educational Research', p. 19.
62 M. Marchand and J. Parpart (eds), *Feminism/Postmodern/Development*, Routledge, London, 1995, p. 3.
63 Ibid., p. 76.
64 Foucault, *Society Must Be Defended*, p. 279.
65 Ibid., p. 28.
66 Ibid., p. 30.

consenting targets of power'[67] that is applied to them; instead *power passes through individuals*.

Third, power cannot be deduced as a descending form in order to see how far down it goes; on the contrary we should make an '*ascending analysis of power*, analyse the way in which the techniques and processes of power come into play at the lowest levels'.[68] This book shows how HRE processes are often 'displaced, extended, and modified' but also, importantly, 'how they are invested or annexed by global phenomena'.[69] The critical point here is to stress the interconnection between the macro and micro discourse of HRE; in particular, to examine the relationship between the discourse of HRE in local contexts and practice and the global institutional framework of HRE.

While institutions should be analysed from the standpoint of power relations, Foucault states that the 'fundamental point of anchorage' are the relationships found outside the institution.[70] Power relations, he states, are 'rooted deep in the social nexus, not reconstituted "above" society as a supplementary structure whose radical effacement one could perhaps dream of. . . a society without power relations can only be an abstraction'.[71] Analysing the way that power circulates and shapes HRE reveals not only how it is exercised in order to perpetuate a dominant discourse of HRE, but also how relations of power can open up opportunities and spaces of resistance. Ideology, on the other hand, offers a way of understanding the ways that ideas operate in society through HRE within society in order to (re)produce or (re)construct the dominant cultural form.

Ideology critique

A fundamental interlinked question to ways that power is exercised in shaping the production, consumption and distribution of HRE discourse is whether it serves the interest of the masses or those of a few dominant elite. Hegemony, in the Gramscian sense, is 'a social condition in which all aspects of social reality are dominated by or supportive of a single class'.[72] Different aspects of social life are claimed to be made acceptable to people through the exercise of influence and the winning of consent. In this sense it is important to examine further the ways in which HRE discourse contributes to domination or resistance in society.

67 Ibid.
68 Ibid.
69 Ibid.
70 M. Foucault, 'Afterword: The Subject and Power', in H. Dreyfus and P. Rabinow (eds), *Michel Foucault: Beyond Structuralism and Hermeneutics*, Harvester Wheatsheaf, Hemel Hempstead, 1982, pp. 222–223.
71 Ibid.
72 D.W. Livingstone, 'On Hegemony in Corporate Capitalist States: Materialist Structures, Ideological Forms, Class Consciousness and Hegemonic Acts', *Sociological Inquiry*, 46(3–4), 1976, p. 235.

According to Gramsci, every relationship of hegemony is essentially an educational relationship. The agencies that engage in this educational relationship are the institutions forming civil society and constitute the cultural bedrock of power, in particular the ideological social institutions such as law, education, mass media and religion.[73] In Western society, he claims, sites of education are not neutral but rather serve to cement the existing hegemony and are therefore intimately tied up with the interests of the most powerful groups. It is crucial to secure consent to the ruling way of life which is supportive of, and supported by, the prevailing mode of production.[74] However, hegemony can also be as liberating as it is dominating and viewed as a dynamic space that is constantly changing and open to negotiation and reconstruction. It is incomplete and there are moments when the whole process undergoes crisis; it is in these instances that, Gramsci argues, there is space for counter-hegemonic activity.[75] This relies upon people in civil society engaging in a *war of position*.[76]

'Organic' intellectuals are key to the war of position. These are individuals 'actively involved in society, [who] constantly struggle to change minds and expand markets'.[77] They are viewed as having a critical role, in the fact that they can take a number of possible sides. By siding with the dominant class they serve to mediate the ideological and political conditions of the existing unity. Alternatively, by supporting the opposition or subordinated class aspiring to power, they have the capacity to engage in a *war of position* that enables them to secure alliances to succeed. Finally, if they choose to side with the subaltern group, they can contribute to 'intellectual and moral reform'.[78]

In order to succeed, Gramsci claims that organic intellectuals *must* be politically committed to those they 'teach', otherwise, there can be no effective learning. It is the critical and selective appropriation of existing knowledge, in order to transform it, which constitutes the basis of critique. This requires 'the diffusion in a critical form of truths already discovered, their socialisation as it were, and even making them the basis of vital action, an element of co-ordination and intellectual and moral order'.[79] In HRE it raises the questions about who are the organic intellectuals and whose side are they on?

Ideas about hegemony and ideology are intimately linked; while hegemony is a way of explaining how ideas can dominate, ideology is the underlying concept. Ideology therefore is an important concept for understanding how meaning is

73 P. Mayo, *Gramsci, Freire and Adult Education: Possibilities for Transformative Action*, Zed Books, London, 1999, p. 36.
74 Ibid.
75 Ibid., p. 41.
76 Ibid., p. 36.
77 E. Said, *Representations of the Intellectual: The 1993 Reith Lectures*, 1996, Vintage, New York, p. 4.
78 Mayo, *Gramsci, Freire and Adult Education*, p. 41.
79 A. Gramsci, *Selections from Prison Notebooks*, ed. Q. Hoare and G. Nowell-Smith, International Publishers, New York, 1971, p. 325.

produced, transformed and consumed by individuals and social groups through transcendental processes such as HRE.[80] As a *tool of critical analysis*, ideology 'digs beneath the phenomenal forms of knowledge and social practices and helps to locate the structuring principles and ideas that mediate between the dominant society and everyday experiences'.[81] Similarly, ideology, as a *political construct*, is also important when analysing HRE. It reflects the realisation that in any society certain cultural forms predominate over others, just as certain ideas are more influential than others.

In processes like HRE, where meaning is produced, represented and consumed, the most critical dimension is a reflexive understanding of the interests embodied in the process itself, and how these interests might be transformed, challenged or sustained, so as to promote rather than repress the dynamics of critical thought and action.[82] As a tool of analysis, ideology critique 'informs critical thinking by making it into more than an interpretative tool, and situates critique within a radical notion of interest and social transformation'.[83] This requires breaking through the myths of HRE and exposing how certain orientations or forms of HRE serve the logic of domination, analysing the hidden ideological elements in HRE in order to reveal its social functions. It also involves breaking HRE apart, then reassembling and reframing it, not only to reveal the limits of perspectives and ideas, but also to simultaneously discover 'the new and vital elements in them that could be appropriated for radical purposes'.[84] It calls for reflective consciousness and informs critical thinking by making it into more than an interpretative tool, but something to be considered within the radical notion of social transformation. In this sense an ideology critique of HRE discourse must always remain conscious of the emancipatory potential of the discourse.

Organisation of the book

The first part of the book examines and maps out four theoretical orientations which are identified as significant in HRE discourse. The introductory chapter shows how the relationships between the global and the local, institutions and society, theory and practice are fundamental when trying to understand the production, distribution and consumption of HRE discourse. Throughout the book discourse is seen not only to include the way we talk about things, but also includes text, language, social practice and interaction; discourse as political, in the way it supports, mediates or contests existing socio-political forces that use a particular discursive orientation to validate and sustain their existence.

80 H. Giroux, *Theory and Resistance in Education: Towards a Pedagogy for the Opposition*, Bergin & Garvey, Amherst, 2001, p. 161

81 Ibid.

82 Ibid., p. 154

83 Ibid., pp. 154–155; Giroux applied used ideology critique to examine citizenship education in the United States of America.

84 Ibid., p. 155

The micro and macro relationship in HRE discourse are established as particularly important in trying to understand what happens to HRE between the global and the local, and how it is given meaning when translated from one context to another. It highlights the increasing importance of NGOs as intermediaries between the global institutional framework and local communities, their role as translators within the HRE field and, in particular, their role in defining HRE discourse in community-based settings. Because of its important political and ideological role, and how it has been used in the past, the book focuses specifically upon HRE in spaces of informal adult education rather than schools or formal institutional settings. It emphasises the importance of linking theory with practice, and the notion of praxis, how power and ideology shape HRE discourse, the way it is understood and acted upon.

Chapter 2 then illustrates, by mapping out the diverse conceptions and approaches in HRE discourse, how it is theoretically plural and complex. Despite its diversity, HRE discourse can both plausibly and usefully be organised into four theoretical orientations, according to the arguments advanced both for and against specific conceptions of human rights and approaches to HRE. These are the technical, the interpretative, the critical and the counter-hegemonic orientations. The categories serve as an interpretative framework to help understand the various divergent and competing orientations in HRE and whether one orientation stood out as particularly dominant.

A *technical* orientation is founded upon a rationale that human rights are facts and implies a logical and correlative approach of HRE as transmission. An *interpretative* orientation grounds the argument for believing in human rights upon an assumption that they are common values which can be agreed upon and given meaning in the context and experience of people's lives. This orientation tends to lead to an HRE approach that employs reflective inquiry or deliberation. In a *critical* orientation, while human rights are seen to exist, it is claimed there should be scepticism of institutional expressions of human rights. The fundamental belief is that the authorship of human rights remains part of the experience and suffering of people and so HRE should thus be structured accordingly to provide space for these voices. Finally, according to a *counter-hegemonic* orientation human rights are nothing more than historical, social and cultural constructions that can only be understood by locating them in time and space. They exist to serve a socio-political purpose. Both the critical and counter-hegemonic orientations are, however, connected by a common concern to question and understand the structural root of suffering and injustice with a view to changing it through action. The way they differ is on the question of whether this action does in fact involve the idea of human rights, or should move beyond it. Chapter 2 demonstrates how the meaning of HRE is unclear and that the indeterminate nature of human rights is evidenced by the sheer variety of opinions and perspectives. It reveals how, in theory at least, HRE discourse is ultimately problematic. This interpretative framework is then used to analyse and critique HRE discourse in the following chapters.

The second part of the book analyses the HRE discourse evident in relevant scholarship. Chapter 3 illustrates how the global discourse of HRE grew out of initial discussions and activities of the United Nations in 1945 and the subsequent Universal Declaration for Human Rights in 1948. As the UN framework escalated so did international human rights standards and texts which specifically addressed the relationship between human rights and education. It shows how the language, style and focus of HRE have been adapted over time to suit the socio-political context. Originally, led by UNESCO, it explored ideas relating to education, teaching and human rights. Instead of focusing specifically on international human rights standards, UNESCO stressed the principles of peace and development and the need for a type of education that developed a sense of social responsibility and solidarity with less privileged groups. It stressed the wrongs of war and violence, and the struggle against colonialism and racial hatred. In addition, it identified the significant relationship between economic growth, social development and social justice, the environment and natural resources.

However, the nature of HRE took a distinct turn after 1994 when the term 'human rights education' was first coined.[85] It was from this point onwards that the concept of HRE became increasingly defined, centralised and institutionalised within the UN framework, under the remit of the OHCHR. It was 1995 that signalled the beginning of the UN Decade for HRE and the subsequent World Programme for HRE (First Phase, 2005–2007). Since this time the production and distribution of HRE discourse has become increasingly institutionalised not only in the UN framework, but also into national government policy, through state-sponsored plans of action for HRE.

While Chapter 4 illustrates a continued lack of engaged critique by scholars on HRE, it attempts to provide an analysis of the scholarship available, looking at it in terms of the critical scholarship on the one hand and the practical scholarship on the other. This is in order to consider whether and how HRE scholarship had been influenced and shaped by developments in global HRE discourse. It shows how there was common agreement among the critical scholars about three particular aspects of HRE. First, the limitations of an awareness-raising approach in HRE, especially one focused upon international human rights standards and norms. Second, that HRE is contentious, political and part of an ideological struggle. Third, the idea that HRE has the capacity to bring about social change, but it would require a shift in both the current conceptions and practice of HRE.

It then analyses some of the more common accounts of HRE practice in community-based settings, written by scholars who consider themselves to be HRE practitioners. While the language and descriptions initially seemed to

85 See UNESCO, 'The World Plan of Action on Education for Human Rights and Democracy' (Montreal Declaration), Canada, 1993, www.unesco.org/webworld/peace_library/UNESCO/HRIGHTS/342-353.HTM#one (accessed 19 January 2011); and, UNHCHR, 'Vienna Declaration and Plan of Action', adopted by the United Nations General Assembly on 23 July 1993, A/CONF./157/23, www.unhchr.ch/huridocda/huridoca.nsf/(symbol)/a.conf.157.23.en (accessed 1 February 1993).

indicate an approach to HRE that encourages reflective inquiry and the personal interpretation of human rights, in nearly all cases, HRE processes is informed by a preconception of human rights as facts, either by virtue of a belief in our inherent humanness or as universally agreed facts. As a consequence, and despite all the efforts to make processes participatory and inclusive, the orientation of HRE discourse is predominantly technical. The integration of individual and community experience and knowledge into HRE processes is often only a means through which the idea or principles of human rights can be made contextually relevant.

The third part of the book consists of a case study on HRE in the context of Tanzania. In order to understand the circulation of HRE discourse between the global and the local it is important to consider the way that the global HRE discourse is interpreted and acted upon in communities. The case study provides evidence about how different individuals and organisations can affect both the construction and constructive nature of the micro discourse of HRE. Chapter 5 outlines the significant influence of Julius K. Nyerere upon the nation and his ideas about how 'Education for Self-Reliance' and 'Education for Liberation' could shape an independent nation and society after colonial rule. It also discusses how contemporary Tanzania appears to be very different from that in Nyerere's vision; the high levels of poverty and inequality, and the important but precarious intermediary role of NGOs in navigating HRE discourse. The chapter provides details of the three key sites of observation. These include a series of four workshops on the Maputo Protocol, three meetings on land rights in Kiteto and a three-day workshop for journalists on gender-based violence. It subsequently provides a descriptive account of the findings from the fieldwork research in three parts: first, the different conceptions of human rights, as expressed by interviewees and other participants in the research; second, how they appear to conceptualise HRE; and third, the structure and practice of HRE. It shows that while there appears to be a predominant conception of human rights as inherent, they are commonly referred to with reference to international human rights instruments or national laws. It describes an organised structure of HRE consisting of mass education campaigns and national programmes, as well as the training and supervision of a network of volunteers, who delivered HRE to communities. HRE discourse in Tanzania is not evidently reflective of its socio-political history, but instead NGOs seem to generally adopt a legalistic approach focused upon raising awareness of human rights standards. Experience and knowledge tend to be used in order to give relevance and resonance to human rights. A key aspect revealed in Chapter 5 is the way that the global HRE discourse penetrates local communities through the NGO structure, its networks and practices; even in countries like Tanzania with a strong history of counter-hegemonic activity and resistance.

Finally, the holistic analysis in Chapter 6 draws together the evidence from all the chapters on the theory, scholarship, global and local HRE discourse in order to construct some tentative conclusions about what may be occurring in HRE discourse. Despite the diversity of the theoretical orientations outlined in Chapter 2, it shows how both in the scholarship and in the local context how HRE discourse tends to fall back on the global rhetoric and international human rights standards and texts when engaging with complex social, economic and cultural issues. The main reason for this is the way that HRE discourse is organised and structured. HRE discourse generally operates through an organised network of intermediaries linking the global UN framework to the local community. These intermediaries consist not only of international and national NGOs, but also local-level networks of quasi-professional volunteers.

There is apparent reliance of many NGOs, especially those in developing countries like Tanzania, on international forms of donor finance and resources. A consequence of this was that while in theory NGOs can choose to follow or resist the international human rights discourse, in reality, the financial constraints make them susceptible to the external agendas of funders. While the network of NGO and community-based intermediaries created a potential two-way chain of communication from the international to the local level, in reality it more often involves processes of cultural translation. This takes place in two ways: first, by using individual experience and community knowledge to make the HRE process and human rights both relevant to and resonant with local communities; and second, by reframing experience and knowledge into the language of human rights. Given this evidence, one foreseeable danger is the way that a predominant form of HRE discourse can disempower other more localised cultures and ways of knowing. This then limits and regulates the possibilities of communities and individuals beyond the idea of HRE.

The final chapter outlines the possibilities for HRE as a transformative praxis and how this requires looking at the margins of practice rather than the mainstream. Like Foucault, it advocates situational possibilities, rather than grand theories or totalising perspectives and solutions, which potentially limit our political vision.[86] As one possible way forward, and in order to move beyond a technical and limited orientation, it shows how HRE discourse should invoke the multiple discourses of resistance and action that are connected to pre-existing forms of indigenous knowledge and cultural resources of communities. This requires rethinking HRE discourse to one that is more concerned with unearthing the subjugated knowledges, and founded upon the characteristics of questioning and critique. Supporters of a more radical approach to education call for a revolution of cultural values and educational practices, where the primary goal is the 'liberation of people from the constraints imposed by a class-divided industrial society'.[87] It questions not only the way that HRE is designed and delivered but more importantly the nature of knowledge in HRE.

86 H. Englund, *Prisoners of Freedom: Human Rights and the African Poor*, University of California Press, Berkeley, CA, 2006, p. 202.

87 P.M. Lichtenstein, 'Radical Liberalism and Radical Education: A Synthesis and Critical Evaluation of Illich, Freire, and Dewey', *American Journal of Economics and Sociology*, 44(1), 1985, p. 46.

Conclusion

Given the current neglect in tackling the theoretical foundations of HRE, the hope is that this research will contribute to different understandings about the way in which discourse, power, knowledge and ideology interrelate and contribute to the reproduction and production, reconstruction and resistance to the dominant cultural forms through HRE discourse.

Examining HRE from a theoretical perspective does not discount the inherent value of community-based practice, and the idea that theory and practice are intrinsically linked is the fundamental precept for the notion of praxis. Theoretical reflection is an important aspect of practice. It means that practitioners may avoid falling into an unquestioning mode of transplanting models that have no relevance to people's lives or offering communities false hope of social change through processes which ultimately only reinforce existing inequities.

It is hoped that this book might encourage practitioners to reflect more about the way they work and provoke debate and new ways of doing HRE. Maybe it will advance slightly the process of what Raymond Williams calls the 'unlearning' of 'the inherent dominative mode'.[88]

88 R. Williams, *Culture and Society, 1780–1950*, Chatto & Windus, London, 1958, p. 376.

2 Navigating the field

Orientations in human rights education

This chapter attempts to contribute to the search for a theoretical framework of human rights and learning, which can help to navigate the different ways of understanding and doing HRE. The development of this framework is based upon the fundamental idea that how we plan, design and approach processes of HRE is influenced by number of assumptions that we make about knowledge, power and change. This is because we all have mental models that shape our perceptions, expectations and ways of working. Mental models are deeply ingrained assumptions, generalisations or ideas about how we understand the world; they come from our own experiences and shape the way we act and interact with each other and the world. Specifically, I argue in this chapter that there are four mental orientations: technical, interpretative, critical and counter-hegemonic, each of which is composed of different assumptions about whose knowledge counts, the exercise of power and how social change happens. They provide some insight into why some people and organisations adopt particular HRE strategies, as well as the power relationships and interests reflected in them. This is important because unless we appreciate the ways that our own experiences and expectations influence how we see the world and our actions it becomes difficult to move towards a different way of doing HRE. This framework therefore offers the basic understanding that is needed to develop a more radical pedagogy of human rights.

As an analytical tool it can also help to distinguish between different HRE approaches, mapping them in terms of the potential for maintaining the status quo and social transformation. What matters is the way that particular theories are used to support HRE practice both globally and locally and whether one orientation stands out as particularly dominant.

Technical

A conception of human rights as international norms and standards provides the control and certainty that is required for a technical orientation. This is because a technical orientation in HRE, as I wish to interpret it, relies upon objective notions about human rights, which in turn rest on a number of assumptions about knowledge, human values and the nature of human inquiry. Knowledge is understood here as something objective and therefore should only be described in a neutral fashion. As such, knowledge of human rights is seen as 'situated above and beyond the social realities and relationships of the people who produce and define it'.[1] Objectivity means that knowledge is limited to pre-existing concepts and facts that can be easily translated into operational definitions and precise meanings. The strength of human rights knowledge rests upon its claim to universality; other knowledge unable to rest upon the same assertion becomes discounted and subjugated as mere speculation.[2]

A conception of human rights as facts is based upon two fundamental arguments: the first is that we are all born with human rights; and the second is the (almost) universal acceptance of the principles outlined in the text of the Universal Declaration of Human Rights (UDHR). The next section elaborates on these two key claims.

Human rights as facts

The first argument, that human rights are given by virtue of our inherent *humanness*, is commonly associated with thinkers from the natural tradition of human rights. The second argument, that on paper at least there is almost universal agreement of the principles and values outlined in the UDHR, but also in related human rights instruments, is more generally associated with positivist thinkers. This second argument is often used to give weight to the first which is difficult to express in concrete terms. Both sets of arguments are elaborated in this section.

An assumption that being human endows an individual with certain natural and universal rights derives from the claim that 'all human beings, simply because they are human beings, are entitled to be treated according to certain minimum standards'.[3] Rights are presumed to exist independently of social recognition.[4] This is a claim put forward by individuals who believe in human rights, and traditionally represent the 'heart of the human rights orthodoxy'.[5] Every human being 'has an equal, irreducible moral worth, whatever his or her social utility' and 'regardless of who they are or where they stand, individuals have an inherent dignity and worth for which the state must demonstrate an active concern'.[6]

1 H. Giroux, *Theory and Resistance in Education: Towards a Pedagogy for the Opposition*, Bergin & Garvey, Westport, CT, 2001, p. 178.
2 Ibid., p. 177.
3 C. Beitz, 'Human Rights as a Common Concern', *American Political Science Review*, 95(2) pp. 269–282.
4 Natural rights trace their origin and claim to legitimacy in a certain moral or ethical world view that originates in natural law. The early declarations of rights such as the English Petition of Rights (1627), the American Declaration of Independence (1776) and the French Declaration of Rights of Man and Citizen (1789) are said to be within the natural law tradition.
5 M.B. Dembour, *Who Believes in Human Rights? Reflections on the European Convention*, Cambridge University Press, New York, 2006.
6 J. Donnelly, *Universal Human Rights in Theory and Practice*, Cornell University Press, Ithaca, NY, 2003, pp. 68–69.

The fundamental basis of this argument is that the reality of our identity, situation, society and lives are irrelevant in the existence of human rights – we are all the same, and we all have human rights. It is a claim that is generally based upon a moral belief, at the heart of which is an assumption that each human being is born with 'inherent dignity which should not be denied'.[7] Some argue that this means human rights are 'the highest moral rights' which regulate all other persons and institutions, structures and practices, and as such 'take priority over other moral, legal and political claims'.[8]

A second precept for the claim to universality is that at least as ideal standards 'they are almost universally accepted'.[9] Over half the world's states have ratified various international human rights covenants and therefore undertaken an international legal obligation to implement the rights within; others have expressed approval to the content by signing but not ratifying the content.[10] Because of the abstract and intangible nature of human rights as given or inherent it is difficult to articulate in practical terms. As such, individuals who support this claim often fall back upon the UDHR (and the principles expressed in associated covenants) as a way to illustrate the concrete expression of human rights, arguing these are legitimate representations of universal standards which under the 'right protection will allow communities to thrive'.[11] An acceptance, by states at least, of these international human rights standards has enabled the expansion of human rights which have over the years become increasingly enshrined into international law.

Accordingly, universalism is seen to exist, despite a reality where so few live *with* human rights and so many live *without*. The claim of universality, in as much as those who sleep under bridges have the same rights as those who do not, is in the end challenged by the reality of what it means not to have human rights.[12] The fact that millions of human beings continue to suffer from 'malnutrition, disease, and humiliation, grossly deprived not only of bread and water but of equality and freedom', while others live in relative comfort, can weaken any universal claim about us all being the same into something arguably abstract and meaningless.[13] Nonetheless, many human rights scholars still like to see our common humanity as something that binds human beings despite the massive divisions in our quality of life. Perhaps, however, it is the continuing inequality and injustice that has

7 M.J. Perry, 'The Morality of Human Rights: A Nonreligious Ground?', *Emory Law Journal*, 54, 2005, pp. 97–150.

8 Donnelly, *Universal Human Rights in Theory and Practice*, p. 1.

9 Ibid.

10 Ibid.

11 R.E. Howard and J. Donnelly, 'Liberalism and Human Rights: A Necessary Connection', in M. Ishay (ed.), *The Human Rights Reader: Major Political Essays, Speeches and Documents from the Bible to the Present*, Routledge, New York, 1997, p. 275.

12 Steven Lukes, 'Five Fables About Human Rights', in Ishay (ed.),*The Human Rights Reader*, p. 241.

13 J. Derrida, in C. Douzinas, *The End of Human Rights: Critical Legal Thought at the Turn of the Century*. Hart, Oxford, 2000, p. 197.

caused the human rights orthodoxy to move towards a more deliberative school of thought, where human rights are claimed to be agreed principles and values.[14]

The argument that human rights are facts, in effect, provides no further understanding about the meaning of human rights. Rather they are just presumed to be true. However, while human rights are claimed to be intrinsic, knowledge of them is not. The technically oriented often appear to make an assumption that most people do not know about human rights and require HRE in order to understand their rights and freedoms. A correlative approach therefore is an HRE process that raises awareness of the existence of human rights either as inherent or as concrete international facts. I have called this *HRE as transmission*. It is explored further below.

HRE as transmission

HRE as transmission is plausibly, although not solely, associated with the universal idea of human rights. The notion of ***knowledge*** in a technical orientation is presented as responsive but at the same time fixed and unchanging, in that 'its form, structure and underlying normative assumptions appear to be universalized beyond the realm of historical contingency or critical analysis'.[15] In this sense, proposals for new specific rights are not ruled out within discussion, but often seen as already being met within the broad ideals proposed in the UDHR and associated human rights instruments.

International human rights offer certainty and their definitive nature means they can be ***taught*** as a clear set of predefined standards, and as a way for individuals to make demands and claims against the state. HRE is therefore viewed as an approach where the roles of ***educator*** and ***learner*** are clearly defined and distinguished. They also enable human rights standards to be measured and can be used as a benchmark for state performance. A sustainable transmission approach in HRE relies upon the ability of ***educators*** to separate statements of value from objective facts and methods of inquiry.

HRE as transmission typically comprises a range of awareness-raising activities, including mass media campaigns, using leaflets, newspapers, radio, TV and posters. The aim is to distribute the content of international human rights texts as widely as possible, both among and within states. These processes are concerned with the scale of distribution rather than deep analysis, let alone critique of the content. It is an approach that might typically involve a workshop or training, which focuses upon the communication and distribution of the content in human rights instruments. Normally this is through professionals or quasi-professionals working in communities, but also these HRE processes are targeted at government officials with a view to pressurising them to ascribe to certain human rights standards.

14 Dembour, *Who Believes in Human Rights?*, p. 3.
15 Giroux, *Theory and Resistance in Education*, p. 178.

Questions concerning the legitimacy and production of both the form and content of knowledge are irrelevant in HRE as transmission, and the abstraction of production from the execution of knowledge means that there is very little space made available for reflection or interrogation. Individuals with a technical orientation of HRE have been known to adopt a *banking style* of education, in which the learners are empty vessels waiting to be filled up with the specialist knowledge of the educator.[16] In this sense, learners are viewed as passive consumers and the educators are transmitters or translators of technical knowledge, rather than critically engaged 'negotiators of the world in which they live and act'.[17]

However, attempts by educators to overcome these didactic modes of *teaching* have resulted in them developing more participatory styles of learning that appear to take into account the knowledge and ideas of the learner. I argue that this results in the danger of an essentially one-way transfer of information becoming smoke-screened behind apparent discovery-based, inquisitive and participatory modes of inquiry.[18] The content and process of this approach encourages the individual to be moulded and adaptive, rather than critical and active. It can conceal what has been called the 'hidden curriculum' which in the end some claim 'concretizes and legitimates human powerlessness'.[19] Critics suggest that in some contemporary educational practice the political aims of education are submerged beneath its technical and mythological surface and the 'covert and insidious' hidden curriculum.[20] This teaches us what is assumed to be important and, as such, defines the standard for the dominant culture. The hidden curriculum is the 'dark undercurrent, dangerous and unseen'.[21]

Crucially, in terms of human rights objectives, HRE as transmission serves two purposes. First, it is able to highlight on a broad scale and across society the universality of human rights in terms of both moral values and universal facts. Second, it can increase the general knowledge of both the normative standards and the mechanisms for enforcement, with a view to improving the capacity of individuals to make claims against the state. Knowledge of the law and legal rights is seen as important to enable citizens to channel their disputes within the state structures and to generate solutions for conflict. This is in a world where law has become the privileged site of contestation and regulation and where rights have become an acceptable mode of resistance. This, I argue, perpetuates the notion of individual rather than global justice and one where the court system is presumed to be a viable, legitimate and accessible mode of human rights enforcement. Supporters of a more radical approach to education call for a

16 P. Freire, *Pedagogy of the Oppressed*, Continuum, New York, 1970.
17 Giroux, *Theory and Resistance in Education*, p. 179.
18 This is illustrated in the examples of practice in Chapters 4 and 6.
19 Giroux, *Theory and Resistance in Education*, pp. 179–180.
20 J. Wink, *Critical Pedagogy: Notes from the Real World*, Pearson, Upper Saddle. NJ, 2011, p. 69.
21 Ibid.

revolution of cultural values and educational practices, where the primary goal is the 'liberation of people from the constraints imposed by a class-divided industrial society'.[22] It questions not only the way that HRE is designed and delivered but more importantly the nature of knowledge in HRE.

Other challenges to HRE as transmission focus upon the unquestioning acceptance of the universality of human rights both as given and as agreed. A one-way process of information transfer is often based upon a number of assumptions about the nature of knowledge and what it means to be ***uneducated***. If education is to be more than simply training, it requires 'not only enabling man to know and understand the facts which make up reality, but also know and understand the factors that establish the facts so that [they] can change their human reality'.[23]

HRE as transmission arguably fails to challenge the unequal power hierarchies by encouraging the pursuit of claims through the legal framework and existing state structures. These power structures are left untouched and, as forms of contestation which 'reinforce the centrality of law as a mode of protest', risk re-inscribing the regulatory modes of power which they are struggling against.[24]

It is reasonable to highlight that not all practitioners of HRE ascribe to HRE as transmission, but many implicitly follow it in practice. A consequence of believing in human rights as facts is that it becomes almost impossible to see beyond human rights as an ethical framework. Certainly, it is this technical orientation involving the transmission of facts that drives the development of mass education campaigns and HRE workshops. These often have the purpose of raising awareness of international human rights norms and standards, as well as the mechanisms of enforcement. Knowledge of these principles is understood as a way in which individuals and groups can exercise their rights using the language (international human rights) and system (legal framework) of which they had no knowledge before.

However, as already intimated, the advantages of HRE as transmission are challenged by the counterargument which states that providing people with knowledge of the content of human rights instruments and mechanisms is insufficient. The basis of this claim is that before they have relevance or use, any HRE process should determine what human rights actually mean for individuals

22 P.M. Lichtenstein, 'Radical Liberalism and Radical Education: A Synthesis and Critical Evaluation of Illich, Freire, and Dewey', *American Journal of Economics and Sociology*, 44(1), 1985, p. 46.

23 H. Marcuse, 'Repressive Tolerance', in R.P. Wolff, B. Moor Jr and H. Marcuse (eds), *A Critique of Pure Tolerance*, Beacon Press, Boston, quoted in Giroux, *Theory and Resistance in Education*, p. 179.

24 S. Speed, 'Exercising Rights and Reconfiguring Resistance in Zapatista Juntas de Buen Gobierno', in M. Goodale and S.E. Merry (eds), *The Practice of Human Rights: Tracking the Law Between the Global and the Local*, Cambridge University Press, New York, 2007, pp. 178 and 180.

and groups within society. It is this challenge that is developed more by what I term the *interpretative orientation.*

Interpretative

An interpretative orientation in HRE is defined by the struggle to release the concepts of meaning and experience from the notion of objectivity in human rights. Rather than taking the singular production of knowledge as a starting point (as in the technical orientation), the task is to understand the communicative and symbolic patterns of interaction that shape individual and subjective meaning. Fundamental to this orientation is the idea that the meaning of human rights cannot be removed from the worlds of the social actors who constitute, shape and live within its definitions.

People are viewed, through the use of language and thought, as constantly involved in the production of meanings, as well as interpreting their own experiences and worlds.[25] It is an orientation that is informed by the tradition of positivism, where truth and knowledge are seen as nothing but the products of man, and that man is the ultimate author of knowledge. Knowledge is linked to methods of coming to know and is treated as a specific social act with its underlying social relationships.

This orientation highlights the centrality of communication and interpretation in the production of knowledge and the ways in which it is open to negotiation and change. While knowledge is viewed as something shaped by individuals and subjective meaning, an interpretative orientation can also include processes in which groups can come to agreement through ongoing discussion and negotiation about key themes. In this sense, it is constant negotiation and renegotiation by individuals engaged in consensus-building and the attempt to define the constitutive rules that shape their interactions.[26]

Unlike a technical orientation, the language of human rights is seen as only one way of expressing a world of diversity and plural values. This is considered further below together with its implication for HRE.

Human rights as interpretations

The key argument here is that because human rights are subject to a variety of meanings and open to a multitude of possible interpretations, they should be subject to deliberation. This is necessary if they are ever going to be used as a basis of universal agreement. In this sense, human rights are viewed as political values which will only be adopted and realised if people around the world are convinced that they are the best possible legal and political standards by which to rule society. Scholars who claim human rights are interpretations reject the argument that our

25 Giroux, *Theory and Resistance in Education*, p. 184.
26 Ibid., p. 183.

inherent and common humanity is the sacred basis of universalism, and instead pose the question: why should all human beings be seen 'as possessing the same equal and inalienable rights?'.[27]

Instead, human rights are claimed to be man-made, and this means for many proponents they are founded upon the doctrine of legal positivism. Historically, positivists claim that rights are constructed through law and are a tool for governments, institution builders and reformers, to establish the social conditions necessary for progress. According to positivists, the appeal of moral rights to natural law is no longer tenable as a justification, and the only law worthy of its name is the law posited by the state. As a tool of social engineering, human rights have no place for higher moral principles or individual rights, and talk of natural rights equated to a 'belief in witches and unicorns'.[28]

The perspective that human rights are no more than legal and political standards has led some thinkers 'to insist on the limited scope of human rights', which 'should not be expected to provide anything more than the "thin" principles of procedures'.[29] For traditional positivists, such as Joseph Raz, the existence of human rights is invested in a reciprocal relationship, where one has an interest that is grounded in the duties of others.[30] While Raz acknowledges the existence of some morally fundamental rights, he claims that these 'derive from people's interests in having rights rather than the idea that morality is rights-based'.[31]

It is only the legal and constitutional entrenchment of 'typical liberal rights' that gives human rights a legitimate basis.[32] This is regarded as necessary for the maintenance and protection of 'the fundamental moral and political culture of a community through specific institutional arrangements or political conventions'.[33] The instrumentality of human rights protection is grounded in a certain political culture, or various public or collective goods, which means that some argue the list of human rights should be potentially short, and include only the liberal conceptions of rights.[34] Rights, however, are viewed as dynamic and have the 'capacity to generate new duties with changing circumstances',[35] so the construction of human rights cannot therefore always be predetermined.

The idea of human rights as a political discourse rather than an egalitarian vision is supported by lawyers and politicians,[36] but also anthropologists, like Sally Engle Merry, who claims that human rights are 'part of a distinctive modernist vision of

27 M. Ignatieff, *Human Rights as Politics and Idolatry*, Princeton University Press, NJ, 2001, p. 83.
28 A. MacIntyre, *After Virtue*, Duckworth, London, 1981, p. 67
29 Dembour, *Who Believes in Human Rights?*, pp. 248 and 250.
30 J. Raz, *The Morality of Freedom*, Oxford University Press, Oxford, 1986, p. 166.
31 Ibid., p. 192.
32 Ibid., p. 245.
33 Ibid.
34 Usually limited to those civil and political rights outlined in the International Covenant on Civil and Political Rights (1966)
35 Raz, *The Morality of Freedom*, p. 186.
36 Such as Michael Ignatieff.

the good and just society that emphasizes autonomy, choice, equality, secularism, and protection of the body'.[37] Merry has analysed the consensus-building processes around the Convention for the Elimination of Discrimination against Women (CEDAW).[38] CEDAW, she suggests, has a culturally constitutive role similar to that characterised by law within nation states, although it is the consensus-building processes that have already taken place within the UN framework that arguably give those specific human rights principles legitimacy. According to Merry, the formation of conventions like CEDAW 'takes place in a transnational community that shares ideals of a secular society based on gender equality and women's safety'. For this reason, she views it as 'an instance of transnational consensus building'.[39]

The interpretative or consensus-building processes are prioritised within this orientation because they are seen to give human rights their validity and legitimacy. These are processes that can take place either at the global level through the UN, at the national level through country-wide consultation processes, or at the local level through communities. Ultimately, all these processes involve some degree of reflective inquiry and deliberation. This is discussed in the next section.

HRE as reflective inquiry and deliberation

Reflective inquiry and deliberation are two elements that I claim are independent, but overlapping, HRE approaches within an interpretative orientation. The idea of reflective inquiry, on the one hand, emphasises the social construction rather than the imposed nature of knowledge, and participants are encouraged to explore their own values and either to define problems within the context of their experiences or to relate social problems to the day-to-day texture of their lives.[40] Deliberation, on the other hand, highlights decision-making in the socio-political context, and how discourse should stress negotiation, participation and the importance of values in HRE. It also shows how the relationship between human rights and democracy is regarded as increasingly important. This is evidenced by the frequent use of HRE processes in post-conflict states and UN peace-building missions, where it has arguably become an important vehicle through which to transplant the international norms and standards into the national context and local community discussions.

Reflective inquiry and deliberation can be used in community-based HRE processes to generate agreement among individuals upon a number of substantive and enforceable rights. These can then be legislated or formalised. In a similar

37 S.E. Merry, *Human Rights and Gender Violence: Translating International Law into Local Justice*, Chicago University Press, Chicago, 2007, p. 220.

38 Ibid.

39 Merry, *Human Rights and Gender* Violence, p. 90.

40 R. Barr, D. Barth and S.S. Shermis, 'Defining the Social Problems', *Theory and Research in Education*, 7(1), pp. 1–19, 1979, cited in Giroux, *Theory and Resistance in Education*, p. 185.

way it can also be used to generate cross-cultural agreement among diverse and disparate communities and traditions about what should be the meaning and scope of human rights.[41] In these processes the task is to kick-start an ongoing conversation about how perceptions and interpretations of each cultural tradition support some human rights standards but then also completely reject others. This is in the hope that the exchange process will eventually lead to consensus on which human rights are agreed as universal.

An example of this second approach is the cross-cultural model of human rights proposed by Abdullah An Na'im.[42] This model aims to bridge the gap between international standards on the one hand and the norms and values of the culture on the other. It is based upon the fundamental belief that greater consensus on international human rights norms and standards can be achieved through internal cultural discourse and cross-cultural dialogue. An Na'im argues that the 'credibility and practical efficacy of international human rights standards can be enhanced by increasing their legitimacy in the widest possible range of cultural traditions'.[43] In the end it is argued that because of these processes of engagement with communities and society any resulting principles and standards have validity and legitimacy.

According to this approach the standard itself should be seen to be the product of a commitment to and participation in an internal discourse and cross-cultural dialogue by different cultural traditions of the world.[44] However, reaching agreement on a universal standard is not a simple process. It is something that requires 'a certain degree of political liberty, stability, and social maturity, as well as, technological capabilities that are lacking in some parts of the world'.[45] In the end, the justification for a cross-cultural approach is based upon a belief that universal cultural legitimacy is essential for international standards of human rights. It is the sharing and exchange of knowledge and values through dialogue that enables this to take place. While it is not easy to achieve total agreement in some cases reaching agreement and consensus on universally agreed norms is something that is aspired to.[46]

Approaching HRE as a process of agreement, however, fails to address the ways that power is invested in and shapes the processes of agreement, in addition to the potential outcomes. The 'theory of dominant cultural capital' highlights how systems of meaning, linguistic and social competencies, and elements of style, manner, taste and disposition circulate in society, and where the dominant class is

41 This cross-cultural consensus-building process within human rights was originally proposed by Abdullahi An-Na'im. See A. An-Na'im, *Human Rights in Cross-Cultural Perspectives: A Quest for Consensus*, University of Pennsylvania Press, Philadelphia, PA, 1992.

42 Ibid.

43 Ibid., p. 2.

44 Ibid., p. 39.

45 Ibid.

46 Ibid., p. 430.

viewed as being the most legitimate.[47] According to Pierre Bourdieu and Jean-Claude Passeron educational sites play a crucial role in reproducing the unequal distribution of cultural capital. If we subscribe to this view, then in fact the production of knowledge has very little to do with the negotiated outcomes in HRE processes, and instead relies upon the imposition of meanings and specific modes of behaviour through the social structures.

HRE as reflective inquiry also emphasises the importance of relationships and interactions. However, in an interpretative orientation, knowledge is treated as a specific social act within which there are underlying social relationships. Without a preconceived human rights agenda HRE as reflective inquiry can mean that *learners* are encouraged to explore their own values and to define problems within the context of their own lives or relate them to the daily problems encountered in their surrounding context. However, I am suggesting that those who do adopt an interpretative orientation often believe that human rights principles offer the way forward and use reflective inquiry more often as a way of making the ideas relevant and accepted within a local context.[48]

HRE as reflective inquiry straddles between both a technical and critical approach and illustrates how difficult it is to categorise and define HRE. This is because if the HRE process embarks upon reflective inquiry with a preconceived notion of human rights as facts, it can very often revert to a discussion about international human rights standards and their relevance in that context, hence a technical approach. On the other hand, if the purpose of HRE as reflective inquiry is really to determine the meaning of human rights for individuals in that context and starts from an open discussion of values and ethics it could arguably be viewed as a critical orientation, especially if either the *educators* or *learners* become disparaging about international human rights principles.

The difference between a reflective-inquiry and critical approach, in theory, is the lack of scepticism directed at the international human rights standards and framework in the former. Theoretically, a process of HRE as reflective inquiry can exist independently of the international human rights framework, because its purpose is to engage individuals in dialogue about values and beliefs, duties and responsibilities. Nevertheless, despite it being a theoretical possibility, I question, given the belief in human rights by those with an interpretative orientation, how often there are authentic and open-ended processes of reflective inquiry that take place without reference to human rights instruments or principles?[49]

Ultimately, while HRE as reflective inquiry arguably makes an important contribution to the meaning of human rights themselves, as a theoretical approach it remains trapped within the problematic of what it ignores. By attempting to situate the meaning of human rights in the wider social context it is well intentioned

47 P. Bourdieu and J.C. Passeron, *Reproduction in Education, Society and Culture*, 2nd edn, Sage, London, 1990.

48 This often happens through processes of cultural translation, which I discuss in Chapter 7.

49 This is a question that is revisited in my analysis of HRE discourse in Chapter 7.

but ultimately 'naive and incomplete' in that it fails to move beyond the relativity of knowledge.[50] It does not analyse the history or construction of this relationship or the ideology embedded in it, and it fails to interrogate the ways that such meanings are maintained or how they might actually distort reality rather than understand it. It does not address the way in which power is invested in and shapes the processes of agreement and the potential outcomes, or acknowledge in which way these processes can risk reinforcing existing dominant cultural forms.

HRE as reflective inquiry regularly assumes the validity and legitimacy of the institutional processes, like the UN, which predominantly determines, produces and distributes human rights principles. It therefore unconsciously ignores the way that *hidden power* operates both within the process, as well as in society. This ensures that certain points of view never actually reach the table in the first place and have no place in negotiations. It ignores the ways that power is exercised to control the formation of HRE discourse and how it subjugates particular knowledge forms, both through the structures and institutions that organise the discourse and the classification of knowledge into categories of legitimate and illegitimate.

Henry Giroux argues that adopting a reflective-inquiry approach is a form of 'subjective idealism', which is detached from the troubling concepts of power and ideology, domination and struggle.[51] While it is guided by an objective to promote personal values and experiences, it fails to adequately question the basic social, political and economic structures or arrangements. This means that it can, in fact, serve to strengthen the existing inequalities in wealth, power and participation, because it misses the way in which social relationships shape and are shaped by the political structure of HRE. These are addressed by the third orientation.

Critical

A critical orientation does not discount the meaning and experience of human rights, but instead tries to locate such meaning and action in a social context and how this can place particular constraints and limitations on human thought and action. A critical orientation is based upon the principles of critique and action, but it is dialectical in the way in which it aims to criticise that which is restrictive and oppressive, while at the same time supporting action for individual freedom and well-being.

Such an orientation relies on the capacity of critical thought to reflect upon and reconstruct its own historical origins and to inquire into the process of thinking itself. The purpose is to rupture the ideology that limits how we see and understand life and the rationality upon which a dominant view of the world is based. Those with a critical orientation argue that theory needs to move beyond a conception

50 Giroux, *Theory and Resistance in Education*, p. 186.
51 Ibid.

of social relations at the local level, to one where the local context is seen one part of a broader system of social relations of which it is only one part.

In a critical orientation one person is not viewed as an *educator* and the other a *learner*; instead, everyone is engaged in producing knowledge together. Individuals are claimed to participate in learning as possessors of different types of past knowledge, and the transformative moment in learning comes when an individual can critically evaluate what she/he knows. This means that reflection is prioritised because it is an opportunity to examine, intervene and change life.[52] Fundamental to a critical orientation to HRE is that in order for education to become more than an instrument of integration and conformity, people are required to engage with life in critical and creative ways in order to transform their own reality.

These ideas emerge from theories of critical pedagogy, concerned with understanding and overcoming the ways that a social system steeped in domination legitimises itself through a set of meanings and practice that prevent the development of an open, self-critical community of inquiring citizens.[53] A critical orientation in HRE would therefore be driven by the idea of praxis, linking critique to social action in the hope of creating the ideological and material conditions in which more equitable and just relationships exist.[54] It requires individuals to question the root of knowledge and what they know, and to deconstruct the ways in which knowledge has been shaped by external forces. Some argue that understanding human rights in terms of the broader social struggle highlights the relationship between human rights, knowledge and power. I examine these theoretical claims regarding human rights as struggle and the implications for HRE in more detail below.

Human rights as struggle

The interpretation of human rights as struggle means that some proponents of human rights advocate for a more radical authorship or interpretation of human rights. This is provided by the experiences of suffering and injustice, as distinguished from the production of international human rights norms and standards through systematic processes, which arguably 'normativise' human suffering.[55] A key argument is that the daily lives of the impoverished peoples remain 'unrelated to human rights texts' and that the formulation of international human rights norms only serves to widen the chasm between rhetoric and experience.[56] The problem with the modern human rights paradigm, according to Upendra Baxi, is

52 S. Aronowitz, 'Introduction', in P. Freire, *Pedagogy of Freedom: Ethics, Democracy and Civic Courage*, Rowman & Littlefield, Lanham, MD, 1998, p. 9.

53 Giroux, *Theory and Resistance in Education*, p. 190.

54 Ibid., p. 191.

55 U. Baxi, *The Future of Human Rights*, 3rd edn, Oxford University Press, New Delhi, 2008, p. 7.

56 Ibid., p. 9.

the thought that it could take ***human rights seriously*** without ***taking human suffering seriously***.[57] In contrast, he states, that HRE must begin 'by commissioning a world history of peoples' struggles for rights and against injustice and tyranny', and start with 'the right to be human and to remain human'.[58]

He claims that the language and experience of human rights have become captured and embedded in a 'market-friendly human rights paradigm'.[59] Institutional control over the production, distribution and consumption of human rights is arguably a form of social power, which he states, human rights communities must resist by engaging in the 'perennial struggle with all forms of hegemony, and dominance without hegemony'.[60] Other scholars suggest that the more human rights become an unproblematic part of political and legal practice, the 'more they operate with silent exclusions, ignoring suffering, needs, and interests as long as they do not fit with the scope of their application'.[61] The bureaucratic nature of the UN system means that the global and institutional narrative of human rights is arguably managed by a few elite and alien to the community, who should reclaim their voice of human rights as a central part of their resistance and struggle.

According to a critical orientation the idea of universal human rights is seen to forfeit the cultural understanding of social suffering and alienates human rights discourse from the lived-in experience of our culturally specific and historically constructed humanness.[62] Another perspective is that human rights mirror the 'struggles and concerns of the dominant social groups in society at a particular time' and instead any interpretation should be located in a specific social and historical context.[63]

In a critical orientation the common aim is to engage in a struggle to resurrect and recover the 'sense and experience of human rights', which gives the idea of human rights a human foundation and meaning through the struggle.[64] This calls

57 Baxi highlights the difference between the politics *of* human rights and the politics *for* human rights. The former is used to manage the distribution of power, both nationally and globally, even on occasions through war. Politics *for* human rights arises from the 'voices of the violated' and struggles that 'draw heavily on cultural and civilizational resources': Baxi, *The Future of Human Rights*, p. 50.

58 U. Baxi, 'Human Rights Education: The Promise of the Third Millennium?', in G. Andreopoulos and R. Pierre Claude (eds), *Human Rights Education for the Twenty-First Century*, University of Pennsylvania Press, Philadelphia, PA, 1997, p. 142.

59 Ibid., p. 153.

60 U. Baxi, 'Random Reflections on the Impossibility of Human Rights Education', 1996, available at www.pdhre.org/dialogue/reflections.html (accessed 20 May 2012).

61 K. Gunther, 'Human Rights and Political Culture', in P. Alston (ed.), *The EU and Human Rights*, Oxford University Press, Oxford, 1999, p. 122.

62 T. Asad, 'On Torture, or Cruel, Inhumane or Degrading Treatment', cited in A. Kleinman, V. Das and M. Lock, *Social Suffering*, University of California Press, Berkeley, CA, 1997, p. 285. Also see Upendra Baxi for further arguments of the same nature.

63 I. Shivji, 'Constructing a New Rights Regime: Promises, Problems and Prospects', *Social Legal Studies*, 1999, 8, p. 253.

64 Baxi, *The Future of Human Rights*, p. 7. Also see I. Shivji, 'Constructing a New Rights Regime'.

for a more radical authorship of human rights, situated in the struggles of the most vulnerable, marginalised and poor to be the primary authors, rather than bureaucratic institutions and states. The idea of locating human rights in historical and social struggles can be traced back to Marxism in 1848.[65] While human rights were rejected as 'ideological nonsense' and 'obsolete verbal rubbish',[66] it is a Marxist perspective that provided a new ground for human rights, one associated with democratic socialism, and it was in this context that the right to education was first suggested.

With this in mind, a key question for any critical HRE initiative would be, if it is to be potentially transformative, how can pedagogy adequately represent the 'subversive *might* of peoples' histories, which refuse to be condemned to marginality'?[67] The next section considers the ways in which HRE could respond to this challenge.

HRE as praxis

The prioritising of human rights struggle means providing a space and voice for and engaging actively in it. Individual violations are positioned as symptomatic of broader structural challenges associated with imperialism, capitalism and globalisation; so the international human rights framework is downplayed. As well as acknowledging the voices of experience, the emphasis of a transformative approach is to develop an inquisitive and curious character, a critical mind and reflexive action.

This in turn requires a dialogical process, in which learners engage in critical self-reflection and analysis of their experiences to understand the ways they are given meaning through micro and macro social factors. It is a process of *conscientisation*, which 'forces a choice but does not determine the result: where one may choose to act or to acquiesce and adapt'.[68] HRE actors thus appear as agents of social change, who should be willing to adopt a political position. By acknowledging that the role of the educator and learner are interchangeable, the idea that one knows while the others do not is turned on its head. Instead, education in this sense is the search 'to discover something by the act of knowing which cannot exhaust all the possibilities in the relation between object and subject'.[69] Humility, argues Upendra Baxi, should be the first step in 'dialogical

65 K. Marx and F. Engels, *The Communist Manifesto*, trans. S Moore, Pluto Books, London, 1998.

66 K. Marx, 'Critique of the Gotha Programme [1875]', in K. Marx and F. Engels, *Selected Works*, Vol. 2, Moscow Foreign Languages Publishing House, Moscow, 1962, p. 25.

67 Baxi, 'Random Reflections on the Impossibility of Human Rights Education'.

68 T.W. Heaney and A.I. Horton, 'Reflective Engagement for Social Change', in J. Mezirow and Associates (eds), *Fostering Critical Reflection in Adulthood: A Guide to Transformative and Emancipatory Learning*, Jossey-Bass, San Francisco, 1990, p. 88.

69 P. Freire, 'Literacy and the Possible Dream', in P. Mayo (ed.), *Gramsci, Freire and Adult Education: Possibilities for Transformative Action*, Zed Books, London, 1999, p. 65.

HRE', where sitting at the table as equals applies to states as it does to individuals. 'Collective self-education', he claims, 'is essential to build a true fellowship of learning'.[70]

A critical approach promotes the view that there is no such thing as a neutral education process, and education functions as an instrument which is used to facilitate the integration of generations into the logic of the present system and bring about conformity to it. Alternatively, it becomes the 'practice of freedom'[71] and the means by which men and women deal critically and creatively with their reality and discover how to participate in the transformation of their world.[72] It demands more than attempting to make sense of experiences of oppression or suffering, and asks individuals to critically reflect upon their assumptions that underpin experience, acknowledge these assumptions and take action as a result. For some, transformative learning is seen to 'accompany historical struggles for change',[73] whereas for others it is the process of struggle itself.[74]

Ultimately, it is the struggle towards which 'critical reflections bend and within which contradictions in the social order become apparent'.[75] However, a transformative approach does not create struggle; rather the gradual and conceptual framework for participation is an ongoing social struggle. In this sense, particular problems or issues are dimensions of a totality in which individuals or groups should never be isolated from the larger picture.

While human rights are acknowledged, the formal institutional structures and language are claimed not to reflect the experiences of human rights struggles and suffering. The focus of a critical approach to HRE is less preoccupied with the content of human rights and more with an individual's ethical responsibility to determine their own future. Ethical responsibility means knowing 'ourselves to be *conditioned* but not *determined*' and 'recognizing that history is time filled with possibility and not inexorably determined – that the future is *problematic* and not already decided, fatalistically'.[76] There are overlaps between a critical orientation and the final counter-hegemonic orientation discussed below, although the latter could be considered more radical.

Counter-hegemonic

The starting point for what might usefully be called a counter-hegemonic orientation is that human rights are problematic. It is 'characterized by its lack of

70 Baxi, 'Human Rights Education'.
71 J.L. Thompson, *Adult Education for a Change*, Hutchinson, Beckenham,1980, cited in Mayo (ed.), *Gramsci, Freire and Adult Education*, p. 5.
72 Ibid.
73 Heaney and Horton, 'Reflective Engagement for Social Change', pp. 88–89.
74 For example, Upendra Baxi ultimately suggests this.
75 Heaney and Horton, 'Reflective Engagement for Social Change', p. 89.
76 Freire, *Pedagogy of Freedom*, p. 26.

reverence towards human rights' and the idea that they only exist 'because people talk about them'.[77] Human rights are only one version in a diverse world of various relationships, ethics or philosophies localised in time and space and which show us something about how we live together and our own cultures. It can therefore be attractive to those human rights sceptics or nihilists who are often searching for the value systems that challenge the universal human rights framework and vision.[78]

Makau Mutua, for instance, repeatedly points to the shortcomings of human rights discourse intimating that a more solid emancipatory project is required.[79] He states what is required is:

> a new theory of internationalism and human rights, one that responds to diverse cultures, must confront the inequities of the international order. Human rights must break from the historical continuum expressed in the grand narrative of human rights that keeps intact the hierarchical relationships between European and non-European populations.[80]

This critique of human rights is based on the claim that the 'fictions of neutrality and universality . . . undergird the human rights corpus and belie its true identity and purposes'.[81] The task of a counter-hegemonic orientation is therefore to eliminate the hegemonic conditions that foster human indignity, violence, poverty and powerlessness. For this, human rights need to 'resonate in different corners of the earth', where societies and everyone in them must participate in the construction.[82] The structures must be home-grown and utilise the cultural tools with which the people at the grassroots are accustomed, even if these ideas turn out to 'resemble the ideas and institutions of political democracy, or even borrow from it, they will belong to the people'.[83]

The basic premise of this orientation is that human rights are socio-historical constructions born out of and part of a dominant ideological hegemonic culture aimed at maintaining the status quo and regulating society. Some of the theoretical arguments that support this view are considered below.

77 Dembour, *Who Believes in Human Rights?*, p. 4. In her article Dembour is describing the 'discourse school of human rights' which has a similar character to the counter-hegemonic orientation.

78 Such as Alasdair Macintyre.

79 M. Mutua, *Human Rights: A Political and Cultural Critique*, University of Pennsylvania Press, Philadelphia, PA, 2002.

80 Ibid., p. 7.

81 M. Mutua, 'Savages, Victims, and Saviours: The Metaphor of Human Rights', *Harvard International Law Journal*, 42(1), 2001, p. 3.

82 Ibid., p. 5.

83 Mutua, *Human Rights*, p. 5.

Human rights as socio-cultural constructions

The language of human rights here is recognised as a powerful means through which to express and constitute political claims. While there exist a broad range of views within this conceptual orientation, a common and defining characteristic is an 'awareness of human rights' social construction and 'deep scepticism about their supposed benefits'.[84] The characteristic mistrust of claims to truth means that most of those individuals with a counter-hegemonic orientation tend to be concerned about the imperialistic nature of human rights and doubt the effectiveness of any ethic based upon an individualistic human rights framework. They are often scathing of the role that the law has to play, claiming that it reinforces the neoliberal state power, the ways in which it produces and regulates identity,[85] and how human rights can easily become 'a regulatory discourse, a means of obstructing or co-opting more radical political demands'.[86]

An argument, proposed by Costas Douzinas, is that human rights have become 'ingrained in the new world order', and a lens through which people can understand and speak about the world and their aspirations.[87] This 'colonialism of rights' ensures that the ideas are absorbed into the social nexus and insured against challenge.[88] The main task of human rights, according to Douzinas, is to construct and maintain the legal subject in the position of desiring, in the endless production of human rights. He claims that by removing the idea of human rights from their 'intimate and communal habitat' and putting them into abstract institutional standards 'makes them calculable, exchangeable, and cheap'.[89]

This mass production of global norms, rather than a focus upon communal customs, is argued to have contributed to the legalisation of human rights. According to Gustavo Esteva and Madhu Suri Prakash, the state machinery entrusts deliberations about rights to the legislative organ and, as such, suppresses 'spontaneous bonds between people, both in the small territorial units and in the great social collectives, state control expands by reducing and resisting all forms of local autonomy'.[90] Key to this is the assumption that human rights are historical and social constructs, and 'cultural inventions' rather than the 'natural manifestations given by virtue of our humanity'.[91] Instead, human rights are the

84 Dembour, *Who Believes in Human Rights?*, p. 251.

85 N. Menon, *Recovering Subversion: Feminist Politics Beyond the Law*, University of Chicago Press, Chicago, 2004, p. 205.

86 W. Brown, *States of Injury: Power and Freedom in Late Modernity*, Princeton University Press, Princeton, NJ, 1995, p. 98. Also see W. Brown, 'The Most We Can Hope For . . .: Human Rights and the Politics of Fatalism', *South Atlantic Quarterly*, 103 (2–3), 2004, pp. 451–463.

87 C. Douzinas, *Human Rights and Empire: The Political Philosophy of Cosmopolitanism*, Routledge-Cavendish, Abingdon, 2007, p. 33.

88 Ibid.

89 Ibid., p. 50.

90 G. Esteva and M.S. Prakash, *Grassroots Postmodernism*, Zed Books, London, 1998, p. 132.

91 Ibid., p. 121.

'formal and juridical expression of a specific mode of being and living'.[92] For Esteva and Prakash the abstract concept of *human* is meaningless, because the idea of humanity is intrinsically connected to our natural and cultural environments.[93] In this sense, they affirm Foucault's central concern that the formation of the subject is a key part of any knowledge, which 'cannot be abstracted out of the relation, adopting some divine view from "nowhere". The act of knowing is always performed by a subjectivity specified by locations in cultural time and space.'[94]

However, even in cases where a dominant discourse of human rights is imposed and excludes local understandings, 'social actors no longer think of human rights outside the context of that interaction'.[95] Shannon Speed argues that we cannot afford to assume that human rights struggles are 'inherently contestatory to neoliberal state power'.[96] While the rights discourse is bound up with other discourses and practices of the late stages of capitalism, she claims, that there are still places where 'indigenous people (and others) are appropriating discourses of rights and reformulating them in ways that are radically challenging to the particular forms and logics of power at work in a neoliberal state'.[97] Speed suggests that a critique of human rights as culture offers a more adequate grasp of the complexity of social struggles which involve culture and rights, and the often unanticipated consequences when demands are accommodated or recognised.[98]

The limited relationship between right and law 'is but a window among others' on the world, and an 'instrument of communication and language among others'.[99] Abstracting human rights from its social context, both in terms of their production, distribution and consumption, is claimed to make it a meaningless concept. The phrase *human rights* is claimed not to exist in indigenous cultures, in which the idea that *rights* could be defined by human beings is non-sensical. The idea, as Robert Vachon states, that human rights 'could be defined by a collection of sovereign individuals, is almost ridiculous.[100] Another claim is that human rights are nothing more than 'really strong ethical pronouncements as to what should be done',[101] and asking whether human rights are important is no different to asking the question of whether happiness is important. As such, the

92 Ibid., p. 121.
93 Ibid., p. 124.
94 Ibid., p. 127.
95 Speed, 'Exercising Rights', p. 165.
96 Ibid., p. 180.
97 Ibid.
98 J. Cowan, 'Culture and Rights After *Culture and Rights*', in M. Goodale (eds), *Human Rights: An Anthropological Reader*, Wiley-Blackwell, Chichester, p. 325.
99 R. Vachon, 'L'étude du pluralism juridique: Une approche diatopique et dialogale', *Journal of Legal Pluralism and Unofficial Law*, 29, 1990, pp. 163–173, cited in Esteva and Prakash, *Grassroots Postmodernism*, p. 110.
100 Ibid.
101 A. Sen, *The Idea of Justice,* Allen Lane & Harvard University Press, London, 2009, p. 358.

viability of the particular claim is said to depend on the scrutiny of what is being asserted.[102]

Given the multiplicity of people, texts and institutions, and the variety of practices, struggles and events covered by the term *human rights*, the argument within this counter-hegemonic orientation is that no general theory can ever be sustained or viable. Human rights have no one shaping core and are 'nothing more than the various perspectives on them'.[103] However, an inability to offer concrete alternatives in a world which demands certainty and effectiveness is one problem associated with this orientation. Many sceptics, like Mutua, fail to suggest any viable alternative, which means that they often fall back on the rights rhetoric.[104]

Given this scepticism or rejection of the global human rights rhetoric, I argue that the only suitable approach is a process of ideology critique. This is outlined below.

HRE as ideology critique

The aim of a counter-hegemonic approach is to locate HRE discourse within the broad set of social, political and economic relations, which are then analysed and given meaning by defining them within particular contexts. Discourse is viewed as constructed through the exercise of power, and this approach emphasises 'the need for educators to rethink the cultural and political baggage they bring to each educational encounter'.[105]

HRE as counter-hegemony does examine the meaning of individual experiences and suffering, but takes the critique further than the previous critical approach by considering the ways that these can become distorted because of an unquestioning acceptance of another's values.[106] There are a number of ways that these distortions work. Certain distortions are about the nature and the use of knowledge; for example, the idea that every problem has the right solution with the right advice from the right expert, or that something produced through social interaction becomes viewed as beyond human or social control, such as the law or government.[107] Other distortions are socio-cultural, and involve taking for granted belief systems that are really about relations of power and social interactions; especially those currently prevailing, legitimised and enforced by institutions. One example is mistaking self-fulfilling and self-validating beliefs for those that

102 Ibid, p. 360.
103 Douzinas, *The End of Human Rights*, p. 14.
104 In this respect a discursive orientation subscribes to a post-structural perspective which is deeply questioning and critical of claims to truth and so will avoid making them. It follows a Foucauldian genealogical approach to some extent.
105 Henry Giroux, *On Critical Pedagogy*, Continuum, New York, 2011, p. 75.
106 J. Mezirow, 'How Critical Reflection Triggers Transformative Learning', in Mezirow et al. (eds), *Fostering Critical Reflection in Adulthood*, p. 14.
107 Ibid., p. 15.

are not self-fulfilling or self-validating. So, if we believe that a certain group in society is lazy, unintelligent and unreliable, and treat them accordingly, they may become all these things. It is a self-fulfilling prophecy based upon a false assumption.

Another is the way that the interest of a more dominant sub-group is represented as the general interest of the whole.[108] Educational transformation, for example, is always 'the result and symptom of social transformations in terms of which they are to be explained'.[109] The need to change an educational system does not spontaneously occur as 'if [it] suddenly come[s] to the forefront of human consciousness after having been ignored for centuries'; instead 'there has been a change and that it is this change of which they are an expression'.[110]

Ideology, as it is interpreted here, is the perspectives and interests of the dominant culture, which fails to question the validity of existing social norms and resists any critique of its presuppositions. It is this dominant knowledge that a counter-hegemonic approach attempts to rupture.[111] There must be education in *understanding* as well as education in *sentiment*, which demands reflexivity and integrity in practice. It must 'endow human beings with the power to resist the colonization of the mind by state, civil society, intergovernmental regimes and multinationals'.[112] The restraints that are placed upon knowledge and process within formal education mean that it is difficult to exercise a counter-hegemonic approach. This is because educational institutions command what Michel Foucault called the certificatory power of the state,[113] which make it difficult to identify 'common experiences of oppression and resistance', as well as the agency through which to 'engage in transformative action'.[114] Conventional models of education make independent thinking extremely difficult, because they breed conformity and make resisting the environment risky.[115]

In distinguishing violent revolt from intelligent revolt, Jiddhu Krishnamurti outlines how violent revolt is a mere reaction without understanding, whereas the intelligent revolt 'comes with self-knowledge through the awareness of one's own thought and feeling'.[116] According to this perspective it is only 'when we face experience as it comes and do not avoid disturbance that we keep intelligence

108 Ibid.
109 E. Durkheim, 'On Education and Society', in J. Karabel and A.H. Halsey (eds), *Power and Ideology in Education*, Oxford University Press, New York, 1992, in Heaney and Horton, 'Reflective Engagement for Social Change', p. 96.
110 Ibid.
111 Mezirow, 'How Critical Reflection Triggers Transformative Learning', p. 16.
112 Baxi, 'Human Rights Education', supra note 78.
113 M. Foucault, *Society Must be Defended: Lectures at the Collège de France, 1975–1976*, Picador, New York, 2003.
114 Heaney and Horton, 'Reflective Engagement for Social Change', pp. 93–94.
115 J. Krishnamurti, *Education and the Significance of Life*, Victor Gollancz, London, 1992, p. 9.
116 Ibid., p. 11.

highly awakened'.[117] Others argue that current models of education are based upon exploitation and fear, claimed to create individual barriers to separate and hold one person apart from another.[118]

Education should not, it is claimed, 'encourage the individual to conform to society or to be negatively harmonious with it'; instead, the factors which form the basis of any counter-hegemonic form of learning should help an individual 'to discover the true values which come with unbiased investigation and self-awareness'.[119] Accordingly, any educational initiative should focus upon the capacity of individuals and groups to transform a world that is viewed as becoming increasingly suffocated by the ethics of the market.[120]

While HRE could be viewed as socially constructed, it is also seen as having the potential to be constructive, and as Paulo Freire highlighted is 'always in the process of becoming'.[121] HRE as counter-hegemony is a form of 'anarchy' and about 'learning how to make such power and authority continuously and radically insecure'.[122] It critiques the ways that power has been exercised in order to pursue a dominant ideological agenda, but also looks for new ways and spaces to resist and challenge it through alternative forms of knowledge and cultural resources. It requires completely moving away from the global human rights discourse at both the international and local level, and instead an examination of the various ways in which international and transnational actors pursue their goals.[123] Esteva and Prakash call for a retreat to 'our grassroots experiences [which] continue to teach us that we do not live in a universe, but in a pluriverse'.[124] In this sense, universality is claimed as a minority view put forward by few human rights propagators.

A counter-hegemonic approach to HRE suggests that all knowledge is perspective, so there is never one particular point of view from which to commence an argument. A potential criticism then is it renders all research potentially unsound. Another criticism is that a complete rejection of human rights undermines the hard work and progress of many activists engaged in the human rights movement. However, the main task of a counter-hegemonic approach is to reveal how the dominant culture mediates between its own interests and those of other subjugated cultures, as a form of power, and through the discourse of human rights.

117 Ibid.
118 Ibid., p. 13
119 Ibid., pp. 14–15.
120 Freire, *Pedagogy of Freedom*, p. 24.
121 Ibid., p. 115
122 Baxi, 'Random Reflections'.
123 See M. Goodale, 'Locating Rights, Envisioning Law Between the Global and the Local', in Goodale and Merry (eds), *The Practice of Human Rights*, pp. 3–4.
124 Esteva and Prakash, *Grassroots Postmodernism*, p. 126.

Conclusion

One of the main arguments for the universality of human rights is that the endless manufacture of standards and related texts is evidence that there must be global consensus on their meaning. This is supported by the way that human rights have become entrenched in the institutional rhetoric and policy of international organisations, national governments and community based NGOs. And yet there are many who still argue that the meaning of human rights is unclear and the conceptual understandings plural, blurred and ultimately problematic. The indeterminate nature of human rights is evidenced by the sheer variety of opinions and perspectives: some people view human rights as a natural given; others believe that they need to be agreed as a matter of process; activists often see them as values worth fighting for and embedded in human struggle; while sceptics and nihilists think their existence is part of the hegemonic project and that they only exist because they are talked about in order to serve the dominant cultural form. These various orientations have been sketched out in this chapter.

With this in mind, it is plausible to see that the content, methods or processes of HRE will flow from one's initial orientation and narrative choice. Of course, many, if not most, educators may follow a technical orientation and institutional human rights standards in order to avoid grappling with difficult socio-political or cultural questions.

Baxi, however, gestures towards the 'evangelical militancy' of some within the HRE endeavour, which makes him *anxious* about the place of 'HRE imperialism'.[125] How, then, he asks, 'may we educate the HRE educators, rather than the people they so ardently wish to serve?'.[126] For this purpose, Baxi's question might be reframed to ask 'how can we interpret what human rights education actors do?'. This chapter has provided a spectrum of possible orientations against which practical action can be analysed. To begin this task the next chapter turns to the development of the global discourse of HRE since 1945.

125 Baxi, 'Random Reflections'.
126 Ibid.

3 A global discourse of human rights education

It is not immediately apparent how HRE discourse has responded to the indeterminate nature of its philosophical orientations. Given the diversity, one could expect a range of different responses both at institutional and societal levels. What is evident, however, is that there are at least two distinct levels of HRE discourse: one is the global and institutional discourse of HRE within formal settings and international organisations, in particular the UN. The other is the localised HRE discourse embedded in processes and practice at community level. This chapter considers the evolution or construction of the global discourse.

The UN came into existence in 1945, and was established through the UN Charter.[1] This outlines in the Preamble the UN's fundamental concern 'to maintain international peace and security'[2] and endorses the employment of 'international machinery for the promotion of the economic and social advancement of all peoples'.[3] The UN emerged as an international body with, in theory at least, a wide remit of responsibilities. According to Article One of the Charter, the UN has four purposes: maintaining peace and security; developing friendly relations among nations based on respect for the principle of equal rights and self-determination of peoples, and to take other appropriate measures to strengthen universal peace; to achieve international cooperation in solving international problems and encouraging respect for human rights and for fundamental freedoms for all; to be a centre for harmonising the actions of nations in the attainment of these common ends. This was the first time that the term 'human rights' had been used in an international treaty.

Then on 10 December 1948 the United Nations General Assembly adopted the Universal Declaration for Human Rights.[4] Envisioned as a momentous

1 Fifty nations gathered in the United States to draft and sign the Charter of the United Nations 1945.

2 The Charter of the United Nations, 1945, Preamble.

3 Ibid.

4 General Assembly Resolution 217 A (III), www.ohchr.org/en/udhr/pages/introduction.aspx (accessed 12 January 2011). It was signed by the then 58 Member States of the United Nations representing a range of ideologies, political systems and religious and cultural backgrounds, as well as different stages of economic development. The Universal Declaration is often declared

triumph and proclaimed as a 'common standard of achievement for all peoples and all nations'[5] the Declaration lists a set of fundamental human rights to be universally protected, reaffirmed 50 years later as a 'common language of humanity'.[6] The Declaration stipulated from the outset that:

> every individual and every organ of society, keeping this Declaration in mind, shall strive by teaching and education to promote respect for these rights and freedoms and by progressive measures, national and international, to secure their universal and effective recognition and observance.[7]

By deconstructing the historical and social construction of the global and institutional HRE discourse, this chapter aims to understand how HRE has responded to its multifaceted theoretical roots and assess whether the discourse serves the logic of domination or the interests of society. The establishment of the UN in 1945 is taken as a starting point for the institutional analysis. While there is earlier evidence of HRE in organisations such as Charter Schools and Workers Education Programmes,[8] the United Nations was the first global organisation to forge a formal and institutional relationship between human rights *and* education. This chapter traces the emergence of this relationship within the institutional space, and considers how HRE discourse has adapted to the changing institutional and global social, political and economic climate.

The development of an institutional HRE discourse is discussed in three sections. The first section examines the evidence of HRE in international UN texts and associated documentation, their language and style. The second section shows the leading role of the United Nations Educational, Scientific and Cultural Organization (UNESCO) in the promotion of HRE and the gradual centralisation of the discourse within the UN framework. The final section highlights the most recent developments post-1995, when HRE emerged as a definitive institutional concept with accompanying world programmes, guidelines and documentation. Each section also outlines the broader socio-political context and how this may have influenced and shaped HRE discourse.

as a common statement of mutual aspirations – 'a shared vision of a more equitable and just world'. There were eight abstentions. See: www.un.org/rights/HRToday/declar.htm (accessed 12 January 2011). Referred to hereafter as the UDHR or the Declaration.

5 UDHR, 1948, Preamble.

6 Boutros Boutros-Ghali in his inaugural remarks at the International Conference on Human Rights, Vienna, 1993, in U. Baxi, *The Future of Human Rights*, Oxford University Press, New Delhi, 2008, p. 1.

7 UDHR, 1948, Preamble.

8 See F. Youngman, *Adult Education and Socialist Pedagogy*, Radical Forum on Adult Education Series, Croom Helm, Beckenham, 1983; and M. Mayo, *Imagining Tomorrow: Adult Education for Transformation*, NIACE, Leicester, 1997.

Evidence of HRE in UN conventions and associated instruments

The UDHR was the first formal international instrument that outlined teaching and education as a mode of dissemination. Education, it outlined, shall

> be directed to the full development of the human personality and to the strengthening of respect for human rights and fundamental freedoms. It shall promote understanding, tolerance and friendship among all nations, racial or religious groups, and shall further the activities of the United Nations for the maintenance of peace.[9]

However, little attention was directed to how this would be achieved, other than a statement by the UN General Assembly. This stipulated that the UDHR should be 'disseminated, displayed, read and expounded principally in schools and other educational institutions, without distinction based on the political status of countries or territories'.[10] There is evidence to show that commitment to human rights in the immediate aftermath of the Declaration was rather inconsistent. While the US and UK seemed committed to promoting human rights at home and imposing them on post-war Nazi Germany and its allies, they were less inclined to fly the flag of human rights for a new world order or vigorously promote the idea of human rights in their colonial territories.[11]

Over the next 20 years there were few formal UN Conventions or Declarations and no reference to human rights and education, until 1965 and the International Convention on the Elimination of all Forms of Racial Discrimination (ICERD). This Convention emerged in the wave of revolutionary struggles for independence that were sweeping their way across the Asian and African continents in particular between the mid-1940s until the early 1970s.[12] In the same period, inspired by the revolutionary struggles overseas and the non-violent resistance of Gandhi, the civil rights movement surged across the USA, spearheaded by non-violent grass-roots movements opposing the racist segregation laws and encouraging black voter registration, and the leadership of Dr Martin Luther King, who advocated peaceful resistance. By 1962 there were 70,000 people involved in the movement.[13] Article 7 of the ICERD ascribed a clear obligation on the member states to address and combat prejudice and racial discrimination through 'teaching,

9 Article 26(2) UDHR, 1948.

10 Comment of the General Assembly, 10 December 1948, www.un.org/en/documents/udhr/index.shtml (accessed 12 January 2011).

11 L. Henkin, 'Human Rights: Ideology and Aspiration, Reality and Prospect', in S. Power and G. Allison (eds), *Human Rights: Moving from Inspiration to Impact*, Palgrave Macmillan, New York, 2000, p. 10

12 Ibid., p. 22

13 J. Carter, 'The American Road to a Human Rights Policy', in Power and Allison (eds), *Human Rights*, p. 51

education, culture and information' and to promote 'understanding, tolerance and friendship among nations and racial or ethnical groups'.[14]

By the end of formal colonial rule many new states had joined the UN system, each claiming the right to participate in negotiation processes.[15] This meant that the UN General Assembly was transformed into a much more pluralistic body and compelled to take into account alternative and independent positions on human rights brought to the table by the representatives of these new member states. These representatives were not afraid to speak out against the abuses of Western states, and claimed the right to self-determination. While they stressed the importance of economic and social rights, the Western developed states continued to focus upon civil and political rights. The result was a bifurcation of human rights into two legally binding international covenants: the International Covenant on Civil and Political Rights (1966) (ICCPR), and the International Covenant on Economic, Social and Cultural Rights (1966) (ICESCR).

Article 13(1) of the International Covenant on Economic, Social and Cultural Rights (1966) (ICESCR) reaffirmed Article 26 of the UDHR and the right to education. State parties, it outlined, agree

> that education shall be directed to the full development of the human personality and the sense of its dignity, and shall strengthen the respect for human rights and fundamental freedoms. They further agree that education shall enable all persons to participate effectively in a free society, promote understanding, tolerance and friendship among all nations and all racial, ethnic or religious groups, and further the activities of the United Nations for the maintenance of peace.[16]

The ICCPR, however, did not make specific reference to education, although it did place an obligation upon Member States to respect the rights in the Covenant and take the necessary steps and 'other measures as may be necessary to give effect to the rights'.[17]

It appears, however, that the value of education as a tool to eliminate discrimination and promote equality was significantly acknowledged in the Convention on the Elimination of Discrimination against Women (CEDAW) in 1979. It highlighted the importance of education in promoting human rights which was something previously neglected, and outlined its object to eliminate

14 International Convention on the Elimination of All Forms of Racial Discrimination, 1965, Article 7.

15 The original number of 51 Member States (MS) of the UN increased to 154 MS by 1980. These included sharp rises in 1955 (16 MS) and in 1960 (17 MS). In 2011 there were 193 Member States of the UN.

16 Article 13(1) ICESCR (1966). This Article is also used as currency for the right to human rights education developed in later years is an essential part of the right to education.

17 Article 2(2) ICCPR (1966).

any stereotyped conceptions of the roles of men and women through educational processes and materials in school programmes.[18] According to Article 10: 'States Parties shall take all appropriate measures to eliminate discrimination against women in order to ensure to them equal rights with men in the field of education and in particular to ensure, on the basis of equality of men and women.'

Despite this, it was a further ten years before the Convention on the Rights of the Child (CRC) (1989) articulated a broad conceptual framework for HRE. The CRC is, to date, the most widely signed and ratified international instrument by Member States and it adopted a broad-brush approach to the education of the child.[19] It associated ideas of human rights and fundamental freedoms with those principles of cultural identity, language and values, understanding, peace, tolerance, equality and friendship, and the environment; while still acknowledging the principles enshrined in the UN Charter.[20]

The inclusion of clauses making reference to education in international human rights instruments is one argument that the development and formalisation of HRE has a legitimate basis. The idea of HRE was built on the assumption that people needed knowledge of international human rights norms and standards established in the various conventions, and both formal and informal education were increasingly seen as way in which international human rights could move between the global and the local. This was highlighted in a 1981 meeting of the Human Rights Committee considering the implementation of the ICCPR which stressed:

> it is very important that individuals should know what their rights under the Covenant [. . .] are and also that all administrative and judicial authorities should be aware of the obligations which the State party has assumed under the Covenant. To this end, the Covenant should be publicized in all official languages of the State and steps should be taken to familiarize the authorities concerned with its contents as part of their training.[21]

The strategy of mass publication and dissemination of international human rights instruments was affirmed in 1988 by the Committee on the Elimination of Discrimination against Women. This recommended that State parties should take appropriate steps to ensure the dissemination of the Convention and reports of

18 Article 10 (3) CEDAW (1979).

19 140 signatories and 193 ratifications: http://www2.ohchr.org/english/law/ (accessed 7 January 2011).

20 Article 29(1) CRC, 1989.

21 At its 13th session, the Human Rights Committee adopted General Comment Three in relation to the implementation at international level of Article 2, Human Rights Education and Human Rights Treaties. www.ohchr.org/Documents/Publications/HRTreaties2en.pdf (accessed 17 January 2011).

State parties, get translations and report on action taken.[22] The General Guidelines regarding the form and contents of reports to be submitted by States parties under the CRC also imposed a comprehensive and yet prescriptive obligation upon States when reporting to the Committee.[23] They outlined that States should describe the measures taken to make the principles and provisions of the Convention widely known, and also the extent to which the Convention was translated, publicised and made available; including how many within the education system and to the public at large. Indication, it stated, should be given of the number of meetings,[24] broadcasts and publications issued. Furthermore, States were required to provide evidence of:

> [t]he measures adopted to provide education on the Convention to public officials, as well as to train professional groups working with and for children, such as teachers, law enforcement officials, including police, immigration officers, judges, prosecutors, lawyers, defence forces, medical doctors, health workers and social workers;
>
> The extent to which the principles and provisions of the Convention have been incorporated in professional training curricula and codes of conduct or regulations;
>
> The steps taken to promote understanding of the principles and provisions of the Convention by the mass media and by information and publishing agencies;
>
> The involvement of non-governmental organizations in awareness and advocacy campaigns on the Convention, as well as any support provided to them. In this connection, an indication should be given of the number of non-governmental organizations who participated in such events during the reporting period.[25]

This prescriptive guidance highlighted the priority of mass education and training in the content of human rights instruments, rather than any significant effort to stress the importance of promoting understanding, tolerance and friendship in the maintenance of peace as originally stated in the CRC. The result, given the widespread ratification of the CRC by Member States, and the obligation to submit country reports to the Committee, was that these rigid guidelines in effect compelled states to initiate broad-scale state-funded education and training opportunities in international human rights to ensure they complied with UN criteria. Understood from this perspective, HRE was at this point arguably a question of state-centred rhetoric aimed at meeting UN guidance, rather than

22 General Comment No. 6 on effective national machinery and publicity adopted by the Committee on the Elimination Against Women in 1988, ibid.
23 Article 44, paragraph 1 (b) of the Convention (CRC/C/58).
24 Such as parliamentary or governmental conferences, workshops, seminars.
25 General comment under Article 44, paragraph 1 (b) of the Convention (CRC/C/58).

state-driven initiatives based upon a concern for the human rights of society or interest in HRE.

During this period, however, it appeared that it was UNESCO that took a leading role in the design and implementation of education programmes about human rights. The history of this engagement from 1948 to 1995 in the first instance is considered below.

UNESCO and the institutionalisation of HRE

In 1948, the General Conference of UNESCO adopted a resolution recognising the UDHR as the cornerstone for all of UNESCO's activities.[26] Two years later UNESCO was invited by the Economic and Social Council (ECOSOC) to encourage and facilitate teaching about the UDHR in schools and adult education and through the media. It was after this that UNESCO began laying the foundations upon which contemporary and global provisions are now based.

These activities started in 1953 when UNESCO established the Associated Schools Project (ASP). This supported *experiments* in schools around the world to promote the UDHR and the activities of the United Nations and, at a meeting in Paris, it set out to establish 'education for a world community'.[27] At this time there was still considerable mistrust both within and among member states. Communication was technically and logistically difficult and school exchanges were a challenge. Given this background 'the United Nations and UNESCO were treated with caution' and any curriculum units that touched on the ASP were regarded as 'suspect or subversive'.[28]

Nevertheless, the ASP grew and after ten years the network had increased to 191 schools in 42 member states.[29] At an international meeting held in Sèvres, France in 1963, which was attended by 53 member states, participants redefined

26 Resolution concerning the Universal Declaration of Human Rights, Records of the General Conference, 3rd Session, Resolution 8.1, 11 December 1948.

27 UNESCO, Resolution 1.341, 7th session of the UNESCO General Conference, 1952, in UNESCO, 'Celebration of the 60th Anniversary of the Universal Declaration of Human Rights', 2007, http://unesdoc.unesco.org/images/0015/001542/154277e.pdf (accessed 26 June 2012).

The ASP started out with 33 schools in 15 countries: Belgium, Costa Rica, Ecuador, Federal Republic of Germany, France, Japan, Netherlands, Norway, Pakistan, Sweden, Switzerland, United Kingdom of Great Britain, United States of America, Uruguay, Yugoslavia.

28 D. Suarez and F. Ramirez, 'Human Rights and Citizenship: The Emergence of Human Rights Education', CDDRL Working Papers, Stanford IIS, 2004, http://iis-db.stanford.edu/pubs/20682/ramirez_suarez_6.25.2004.pdf (accessed 19 January 2011).

29 Since its inception the ASP continued to grow in both its size and scope, and by 1993 the network consisted of 3,000 schools in 116 countries. By its fiftieth anniversary in 2003 this figure had more than doubled to 7,000 schools in 170 countries. UNESCO Associated School Project Network (ASPnet): Historical Review 1953–2003, 50th Anniversary International Congress, Quality Education for the 21st Century. 3–8 August 2003, http://unesdoc.unesco.org/images/0013/001305/130509e.pdf (accessed 18 January 2011).

the three themes of study: world problems and the role of the United Nations and its specialised agencies in solving them; foreign countries and cultures; and human rights.[30]

There were few other significant developments in this early period. Then in 1968 the First International Conference on Human Rights was held in Tehran, which largely focused upon overcoming racial discrimination and apartheid.[31] In the Final Act there was a substantial section entitled 'Education of Youth in the Respect for Human Rights and Fundamental Freedoms'.[32] This called upon states to engage with the media and promote the dissemination of ideas and knowledge to young people so they 'may learn of the aspirations of the world today and to understand other people' and engage in free discussion. This was viewed as an essential prerequisite for enhancing 'respect for the dignity of man and the variety of human culture'.[33] The International Conference on Human Rights invited UNESCO:

> To develop its programmes aimed at making children aware, from the time they start school, of respect for the dignity and the rights of man and at making the principles of the Universal Declaration prevail at all levels of education, particularly in institutions of higher learning where the future cadres are trained.[34]

In 1971, the United Nations Commission on Human Rights (UNCHR) also urged UNESCO to examine the desirability of having an independent scientific discipline of human rights. By 1973, it was encouraging UNESCO to develop education for human rights for all, at all levels.[35] Responding to these requests, in September 1974 UNESCO organised and convened the International Congress on Teaching of Human Rights in Vienna.[36] The outcome of the Congress was the 'Recommendation Concerning Education for International Understanding,

30 UNESCO Associated School Project Network (ASPnet): Historical Review 1953–2003, 50th Anniversary International Congress, Quality Education for the 21st Century, 3–8 August 2003. http://unesdoc.unesco.org/images/0013/001305/130509e.pdf (accessed 18 January 2011).

31 United Nations, 'International Conference on Human Rights', Tehran, Iran, 22 April to 13 May 1968, U.N. Doc. A/CONF. 32/41 at 3.

32 United Nations, 'Final Act of the International Conference on Human Rights', Tehran, 22 April to 13 May 1968, U.N. Doc. A/CONF. 32/41, Part XX, http://untreaty.un.org/cod/avl/pdf/ha/fatchr/Final_Act_of_TehranConf.pdf (accessed 8 February 2011).

33 Ibid., (3) and (4).

34 Ibid., (6).

35 J. Symonides, 'UNESCO's Contribution to the Progressive Development of Human Rights', in J.A. Frowein and R. Wolfrum (eds), *Max Planck Yearbook of United Nations Law*, Vol. 5, 2001, p. 311.

36 Resolution 3 (XXXIII) adopted by the Commission on Human Rights and Resolution 32/123 adopted by the United Nations General Assembly, in, OHCHR, Legislative History of the Convention of the Rights of the Child, Vol. 2, 2007, p. 161, www.ohchr.org/Documents/Publications/LegislativeHistorycrc2en.pdf (accessed 21 November 2012).

Co-operation and Peace and Education relating to Human Rights and Fundamental Freedoms (the Recommendation)'.[37] This was the most comprehensive and detailed document on HRE to date. It emphasised the need to respect human rights and promote knowledge of the international human rights instruments, and clearly linked ideas about human rights with development and peace.[38] While not having the power to regulate or mandate any specific activities, it was signed by 76 countries.[39] This symbolically demonstrated support for ideas about HRE generally as well as the curriculum design within.[40]

The Recommendation defined human rights as those outlined in the UN Charter, the UDHR and the International Covenants. Education, it stated, should be infused with the aims and purposes set forth in the UN Charter, the Constitution of UNESCO and the UDHR. It referred to the definition of education outlined in Article 26(2) of the UDHR that education should be directed to 'the entire process of social life by means of which individuals and social groups learn to develop consciously within, and for the benefit of, the national and international communities, the whole of their personal capacities, attitudes, aptitudes and knowledge'.[41] The Recommendation also outlined seven guiding principles of educational policy, including: an international and global perspective; understanding and respect for all peoples, cultures, values and ways of life; awareness of the global interdependence of peoples and nations; abilities to communicate; awareness of both rights and duties upon individuals, groups and nations; understanding of the necessity for international solidarity and cooperation; and the readiness of the individual to participate in solving the problems of his community, country and the world at large.[42]

Rather than referring to human rights specifically, it outlined ideas about international solidarity and cooperation and highlighted the need for a type of education which developed a sense of social responsibility and solidarity with less privileged groups; stressing the wrongs of war and violence, and the struggle against colonialism and racial hatred. In addition, it identified the significant relationship between economic growth, social development and social justice, the environment and natural resources.

The Recommendation did not focus solely upon the formal education system, but acknowledged a key part of solving the fundamental problems of mankind

37 UNESCO, 'Recommendation Concerning Education for International Understanding, Co-operation and Peace and Education Relating to Human Rights and Fundamental Freedoms', adopted by the General Conference at its eighteenth session, Paris, 19 November 1974, www.unesco.org/education/nfsunesco/pdf/Peace_e.pdf (accessed 20 January 2011).

38 The Recommendation has been a significant point of reference in other instruments on HRE.

39 D. Suarez and F. Ramirez, 'Human Rights and Citizenship: The Emergence of Human Rights Education', CDDRL Working Papers, Stanford IIS, 2004, p. 9.

40 UNESCO, 'Recommendation Concerning Education for International Understanding, Co-operation and Peace and Education Relating to Human Rights'.

41 Ibid., para. 1.

42 Ibid., para. 4.

was the participation of communities and families. Compared with what had gone before, the contents of the Recommendation were progressive and radical, taking ideas about human rights and education into new territory by suggesting that education should tackle questions of power and corruption. Education, it stated, should:

> include critical analysis of the historical and contemporary factors of an economic and political nature underlying the contradictions and tensions between countries, together with study of ways of overcoming these contradictions, which are the real impediments to understanding, true international co-operation and the development of world peace.[43]

The problems of mankind shaped the focus of education, which was directed towards the eradication of conditions which perpetuate human survival and well-being, including inequality, injustice and international relations based upon the use of force. Issues included:

(a) equality of rights of peoples, and the right of peoples to self-determination;
(b) the maintenance of peace; different types of war and their causes and effects; disarmament; the inadmissibility of using science and technology for warlike purposes and their use for the purposes of peace and progress; the nature and effect of economic, cultural and political relations between countries and the importance of international law for these relations, particularly for the maintenance of peace;
(c) action to ensure the exercise and observance of human rights, including those of refugees; racialism and its eradication; the fight against discrimination in its various forms;
(d) economic growth and social development and their relation to social justice; colonialism and decolonization; ways and means of assisting developing countries; the struggle against illiteracy; the campaign against disease and famine; the fight for a better quality of life and the highest attainable standard of health; population growth and related questions;
(e) the use, management and conservation of natural resources, pollution of the environment;
(f) preservation of the cultural heritage of mankind;
(g) the role and methods of action of the United Nations system in efforts to solve such problems and possibilities for strengthening and furthering its action.[44]

43 Ibid.
44 Ibid., para. 18.

Only five countries opposed the Recommendation; these were the United States, France, Germany, Australia and Canada.[45]

Over the next 20 years UNESCO organised a number of conferences. These included the International Congress on Teaching Human Rights in Vienna 1978, the International Congress on Human Rights Teaching, Information and Documentation in Malta 1987, the World Conference on Education for All in Thailand 1990 and the International Congress on Education for Human Rights and Democracy in 1993 in Montreal.

The 1978 Congress served to clarify the aims of the 1974 Recommendation and HRE. It reiterated that the teaching of human rights should be guided by the international human rights instruments, but that human rights education and teaching should aim at:

(i) Fostering the attitudes of tolerance, respect and solidarity inherent in human rights;
(ii) Providing knowledge about human rights, in both their national and international dimensions, and the institutions established for their implementation;
(iii) Developing the individual's awareness of the ways and means by which human rights can be translated into social and political reality and at both the national and international levels.[46]

Going further than the 1974 Recommendation the Congress stressed teaching and education in the 'spirit of respect for human rights' was not sufficient, and human rights 'should be taught as a subject integrated into the appropriate disciplines'. In particular it emphasised the importance of philosophy, political science, law and theology, where human rights should, it stated, 'be taught as a separate course'.[47] It also stressed the importance of family relationships as the source of self-esteem and respect for others, and the foundation of human rights, as well as supporting the idea of family life education in order to develop humane and equitable relationships.

The Congress pushed the boundaries of ideas on HRE in highlighting workers' education,[48] minority groups and women's rights, all conceived as particularly radical issues during the ideological battle of the Cold War. The development of curricula for the teaching of human rights, it stated, should be guided by two principles: knowledge of the law and legal means of action and the students' real-life conditions. UNESCO, it proposed, should organise seminars and workshops for the teaching of human rights to justice personnel, including policemen, lawyers

45 Suarez and Ramirez, 'Human Rights and Citizenship', p. 9.
46 UNESCO, 'International Congress on Teaching of Human Rights', Final Document, *Universal Human Rights*, Vol. 1, No. 3 (July–Sept. 1979), pp. 89–98.
47 Ibid., para. I (9).
48 An area of education pioneered by the International Labour Organization since 1919.

and judges, in addition to specialist courses for police forces and directors of prisons. The teaching of human rights should be included in the continuing education of professionals, including doctors and lawyers. Also, there should be established institutes for the teaching of human rights by associations of barristers and lawyers. In addition, the Congress also addressed training within the formal education sector.

It should be noted that at this time regional organisations also began to pass resolutions supporting the development of HRE. In 1978 the Council of Europe passed a resolution on Teaching Human Rights to Educators,[49] and then in 1985 passed a further recommendation on teaching rights education in schools.[50] In Africa, the Organisation of African Unity created the African Charter on Human and Peoples' Rights in Banjul 1981, which outlined the 'duty to promote and ensure through teaching, education and publication, the respect of the rights and freedoms contained in the present Charter'. In 1988 the Organization of American States declared an Additional Protocol to the American Convention on Human Rights (1960), which stated that 'education should be directed towards the full development of the human personality and human dignity and should strengthen respect for human rights, ideological pluralism, fundamental freedoms, justice and peace'.[51] In this sense, states all over the world were beginning to acknowledge a relationship between human rights and education, and a concept of HRE was being forged.

The end of the Cold War signalled a turning point in HRE, and was marked by the International Congress on Education for Human Rights and Democracy in Montreal 1993 which introduced the idea of HRE to the international political stage. The World Plan of Action on Education for Human Rights and Democracy (Montreal Declaration) emerged against a backdrop of various other developments within the UN system and the global political context.[52] These collectively changed the dynamic of human rights in the world. It was during this period that the UN began to intensify its peacekeeping operations, particularly on the African continent.[53] The UN had just emerged from an unsuccessful mission in Somalia

49 Suarez and Ramirez, 'Human Rights and Citizenship', p. 10, and A. Keet, *Human Rights Education: A Conceptual Analysis,* Lambert, Saarbrücken, 2010, p. 77.

50 Suarez and Ramirez, 'Human Rights and Citizenship', p. 10.

51 Protocol of San Salvador 1988, Article 13.

52 UNESCO, 'The World Plan of Action on Education for Human Rights and Democracy' (Montreal Declaration), Canada, 1993, www.unesco.org/webworld/peace_library/UNESCO/HRIGHTS/342-353.HTM#one (accessed 19 January 2011).

53 In 1992 the UN drafted 'An Agenda for Peace: Preventative Diplomacy, Peace-making and Peace-keeping' which directly linked ideas about democracy with respect for human rights (see www.un.org/Docs/SG/agpeace.html). This Agenda was the legitimate basis for UN intervention and peacekeeping then peace-building mandates during the 1990s and beyond. Human rights were central. Subsequently, in 1994 the UN General Assembly adopted the Agenda for Development, which was seen as providing an all-encompassing framework for international cooperation on development. The second of the two objectives was to enhance the role, capacity, effectiveness and efficiency of the UN in development.

with more fatalities than any other UN mission both before and after, at a cost of US$1.6 billion.[54] This was in the shadow of other UN missions.[55] Then in 1993 the UN began peacekeeping missions in five different countries within a seven-month period.[56] Despite South Africa emerging from decades of Apartheid in 1994, the period also witnessed atrocities and undeniable human rights failures in Bosnia, Cambodia and Rwanda.[57] After the apparent failure and expense of Somalia the UN clearly needed to find more sustainable and less costly alternatives to bring about security and peace. I suggest one of these alternatives was HRE. Taken together these occurrences perhaps contributed to a shift in UN strategy in the maintenance of peace and security, and the distinct change in tone from one of cooperation, solidarity and peace, to one of 'alarm' and 'urgency'.[58] Envisaged as a framework for action, the Montreal Declaration states that the last decade of the twentieth century is one

> experiencing the recurrence of the most serious human rights violations, caused by the rise of nationalism, racism, xenophobia, sexism and religious intolerance. These recurrences have led to the most abhorrent forms of ethnic cleansing including the systematic rape of women, exploitation, neglect and abuse of children and concerted violence against foreigners, refugees, displaced persons, minorities, indigenous peoples and other vulnerable groups.[59]

The situation called for 'special and anticipatory educational strategies aimed at preventing the outbreak of violent conflicts and the related human rights violations. Incremental changes can no longer be considered satisfactory.'[60] The Plan of Action explicitly linked the idea of democracy and societal transformation with human rights and education; it talked about human rights norms and universality previously absent in the other documents discussed.[61] Education seemed to be offered as a response to and preventative means of further outbreaks of violence.

> Education for human rights in a changing world is the thrust of this Plan of action. It should be participatory and operational, creative, innovative and empowering at all levels of civil society . . . Education should aim to nurture

54 The Somalia (UNOSOM II) mission ran from March 1993 until March 1995. There were 154 UN staff fatalities. www.un.org/en/peacekeeping/missions/past/unosom2facts.html (accessed 30 March 2012).
55 Angola, Mozambique, Central America, Afghanistan and Cambodia.
56 See United Nations Past Peacekeeping Operations, www.un.org/en/peacekeeping/operations/past.shtml (accessed 30 March 2012).
57 April 1994.
58 Montreal Declaration.
59 Ibid.
60 Ibid.
61 Ibid.

> democratic values, sustain impulses for democratization and promote societal transformation based upon human rights and democracy.[62]

The Montreal Declaration was the first official text to refer to the term ***human rights education*** which it called 'an exercise in democracy'.[63] HRE and training it stated should develop:

> participatory and inclusive learning contexts and curricula in response to the real needs of people. Educational processes and methodologies must be models for what the plan wishes to achieve in society as a whole. It is also imperative that learning programmes include approaches which assist people to understand and analyse their relations with power as well as with leadership styles and abuses.[64]

In addition, it also outlined for the first time that 'the education for human rights and democracy is itself a human right and is a prerequisite for the full realisation of social justice, peace and development'.[65] HRE thus began to take on a new guise, and it was from 1993 onwards that a clear framework for HRE itself began to take shape.

Three months later, the World Conference on Human Rights, the first of its kind since the Tehran meeting in 1968, adopted the Vienna Declaration and Plan of Action.[66] The Vienna Declaration highlighted HRE as a key feature and outlined that States were duty bound 'to ensure that education is aimed at strengthening the respect of human rights and fundamental freedoms'.[67] Education, it stated

> should promote understanding, tolerance, peace and friendly relations between the nations and all racial or religious groups and encourage the development of United Nations activities in pursuance of these objectives. Therefore, education on human rights and the dissemination of proper information, both theoretical and practical, play an important role in the promotion and respect of human rights with regard to all individuals without distinction of any kind such as race, sex, language or religion, and this should be integrated in the education policies at the national as well as international levels.[68]

62 Ibid.

63 Ibid., main lines of action, para. 4.

64 Ibid.

65 Symonides, 'UNESCO's Contribution to the Progressive Development of Human Rights', p. 313.

66 UNHCHR, 'Vienna Declaration and Plan of Action', adopted by the United Nations General Assembly on 23 July 1993, A/CONF./157/23, www.unhchr.ch/huridocda/huridoca.nsf/(symbol)/a.conf.157.23.en (accessed 1 February 1993).

67 Ibid.

68 Ibid., para. 33.

The protection and promotion of human rights was envisaged as a *global task* in which the burden was placed firmly upon States; human rights and democracy were stipulated as 'interdependent and mutually reinforcing', marking a significant change in language from what had gone before.[69] The Vienna Conference called on 'States and institutions to include human rights, humanitarian law, democracy and rule of law as subjects in the curricula of all learning institutions in formal and non-formal settings'.[70] HRE, it stated

> should include peace, democracy, development and social justice, as set forth in international and regional human rights instruments, in order to achieve common understanding and awareness with a view to strengthening universal commitment to human rights.[71]

It was a tone which continued in the 44th International Conference on Education in Geneva in 1994 when the Declaration and Integrated Framework of Action on Education for Peace Human Rights and Democracy was proposed.[72] This framework was later adopted by the UNESCO General Conference in 1995.[73] There was further sense of urgency in the language, which talked about global insecurity, ethnic hatred and massive violations of human rights:

> In a period of transition and accelerated change marked by the expression of intolerance, manifestations of racial and ethnic hatred, the upsurge of terrorism in all its forms and manifestations, discrimination, war and violence towards those regarded as 'other' and the growing disparities between rich and poor, at international and national levels alike, action strategies must aim both at ensuring fundamental freedoms, peace, human rights, and democracy and at promoting sustainable and equitable economic and social development all of which have an essential part to play in building a culture of peace. This calls for a transformation of the traditional styles of educational action.[74]

While the framework made reference to international human rights instruments, these were not given the same prominence as the Vienna Declaration and Plan of Action. Instead, the content of education was concerned with constructions of

69 Ibid., para. 8.

70 Ibid., paras 79 and 80.

71 The expressed relationship between human rights, democracy and peace building aligns with the wider UN agenda, providing both the basis and justification for prolonged intervention and nation-building functions all in the name of human rights and democracy and through peacekeeping and peace-building missions.

72 UNESCO, 'Declaration and Integrated Framework of Action on Peace, Human Rights and Democracy', 1995, www.unesco.org/education/nfsunesco/pdf/REV_74_E.PDF (accessed 2 February 2011).

73 Ibid.

74 Ibid.

peace, the ethical and philosophical basis of human rights and how they were translated into national and international standards, the basis of democracy and its various institutional models, problems of racism, sexism and discrimination. Particular attention, it stated, must be given to 'the problem of development and the history of every people, as well as to the role of the United Nations and international institutions'.[75] UNESCO also emphasised the importance of the 'socialisation' of human rights and 'agents of socialisation'.[76] What this provided was a glimpse of a vision for HRE which became quickly stifled over the next five years by the emergence of more definitive constructions of HRE considered in the next section.

1995 onwards

The 15 years following the Montreal and Vienna Declarations witnessed the mainstreaming of HRE via two avenues: first, the increasing activity, support and recognition of HRE by the UN General Assembly; and second, the shift in focus to states and the rising international pressure upon them to design and implement National Plans of Action for HRE.[77]

The proclamation of the Decade for HRE (1995–2004) (the Decade) was the result of plans and pressure instigated at the Montreal Congress and World Conference on Human Rights in 1994. The Resolution that proclaimed the Decade reaffirmed the recommendations of the Vienna Declaration and placed the responsibility for coordinating the accompanying Plan of Action in the hands of the newly constituted United Nations Office for the High Commissioner for Human Rights (OHCHR), an office that had been opposed by the Soviet Union for 30 years.[78] The Resolution suggested that:

> human rights education should involve more than the provision of information and should constitute a comprehensive life-long process by which people at all levels in development and in all strata of society learn respect for the dignity of others and the means and methods of ensuring that respect in all societies.[79]

This, and various subsequent resolutions, acclaimed HRE as a human right and a prerequisite for the realisation of human rights, democracy and social justice; furthermore, the same resolutions reaffirmed the relationship between human rights, democracy and nation building by specifically highlighting the experience

75 Ibid.

76 Ibid.

77 UNESCO and OHCHR, 'Plan of Action: World Programme for Human Rights Education (WPHRE), First Phase', UNESCO, New York and Geneva, 2006.

78 Resolution 49/184, in Henkin, 'Human Rights', p. 18.

79 UNESCO and OHCHR, 'Plan of Action'.

of HRE in United Nations peace-building missions.[80] This is significant when considered in light of the broader agenda of the United Nations in the early 1990s in which HRE became an operational part.

The Decade's Plan of Action[81] (POA) for HRE outlined five objectives: the assessment of needs and formulation of strategies; building and strengthening human rights education programmes at the international, regional, national and local levels; developing educational materials; strengthening the role of the mass media; and global dissemination of the UDHR.[82] The 'Introduction' appealed to all governments to contribute to the implementation of the POA and highlighted their international obligation to promote HRE. This was unlike previous relevant documents. The content of education, the POA now outlined, should include human rights, humanitarian law, democracy and the rule of law and be taught in the curricula of all formal and informal institutions and settings.[83] HRE, according to the POA, was unequivocally rooted in the provisions of the international human rights instruments, but attempted to progress earlier ideas about HRE by providing a definition as follows:

> training, dissemination and information efforts aimed at the building of a universal culture of human rights through the imparting of knowledge and skills and the moulding of attitudes, which are directed towards:
>
> (a) The strengthening of respect for human rights and fundamental freedoms;
> (b) The full development of the human personality and the sense of its dignity;
> (c) The promotion of understanding, tolerance, gender equality and friendship among all nations, indigenous peoples and racial, national, ethnic, religious and linguistic groups;
> (d) The enabling of all persons to participate effectively in a free society;
> (e) The furtherance of the activities of the United Nations for the maintenance of peace.[84]

While not necessarily asserting the will to further UN activities, these clauses brought together the wider aims of the UN global agenda, including peacekeeping

80 A/RES/48/127 of 20 December 1993; A/RES/49/184 of 23 December 1994; A/RES/50/177 of 22 December 1995.

81 UN General Assembly, 'Plan of Action for the United Nations Decade for Human Rights Education, 1995–2004: Human Rights Education – Lessons for Life', Appendix, in UNHCHR, 'Human Rights Questions: Human Rights Questions, Including Alternative Approaches for Improving the Effective Enjoyment of Human Rights and Fundamental Freedoms', A/51/506/add.1, 12 December 1996.

82 Ibid., Introduction.

83 Ibid.

84 Ibid., Appendix, para. 2.

and peace building, development, promoting good governance and the rule of law.

The development of an international model of HRE appears to have been a key aspect of the UN's global human rights agenda, and towards the end of the 2004 plans were already afoot for a second Decade.[85] This came in the guise of the World Programme of Human Rights Education (WPHRE) (2005–ongoing) where the tone was of a more pedagogical character and seemed increasingly concerned with the principles and process attached to HRE. Terms such as common, collective, partnership and cooperation were scattered throughout, alongside ideas to promote, ensure, provide and enhance, and the imposition of a framework of instruments, principles and methodologies. The WPHRE had six objectives:

(a) To promote the development of a culture of human rights;
(b) To promote a common understanding, based on international instruments, basic principles and methodologies for human rights education;
(c) To ensure a focus on human rights education at the national, regional and international levels;
(d) To provide a common collective framework for action by all relevant actors;
(e) To enhance partnership and cooperation at all levels;
(f) To take stock of and support existing human rights education programmes, to highlight successful practices, and to provide an incentive to continue and/or expand them and to develop new ones.[86]

The definition of HRE educational activities was lengthy and comprehensive, suggesting that HRE activities should:

(a) Promote the interdependence, indivisibility and universality of human rights, including civil, political, economic, social and cultural rights and the right to development;
(b) Foster respect for and appreciation of differences, and opposition to discrimination on the basis of race, sex, language, religion, political or other opinion, national, ethnic or social origin, physical or mental condition, and on other bases;
(c) Encourage analysis of chronic and emerging human rights problems (including poverty, violent conflicts and discrimination), which would lead to solutions consistent with human rights standards;

85 In Resolution 2003/5 the Sub-Commission recommended to the 60th session of the Commission to proclaim a second decade of HRE to begin on 1 January 2005. United Nations Decade for Human Rights Education (1995–2004): Report on achievements and shortcomings of the Decade and on future United Nations activities in this area. Para. 3, http://daccess-dds-ny.un.org/doc/UNDOC/GEN/G04/112/36/PDF/G0411236.pdf?OpenElement (accessed 14 February 2011).

86 UNESCO and OHCHR, 'Plan of Action', p. 13, para. 7.

(d) Empower communities and individuals to identify their human rights needs and to ensure that they are met;
(e) Build on the human rights principles embedded within the different cultural contexts and take into account historical and social developments in each country;
(f) Foster knowledge of and skills to use local, national, regional and international human rights instruments and mechanisms for the protection of human rights;
(g) Make use of participatory pedagogies that include knowledge, critical analysis and skills for action furthering human rights;
(h) Foster teaching and learning environments free from want and fear that encourage participation, enjoyment of human rights and the full development of the human personality;
(i) Be relevant to the daily life of the learners, engaging them in a dialogue about ways and means of transforming human rights from the expression of abstract norms to the reality of their social, economic, cultural and political conditions.[87]

Interestingly, the *furtherance of UN activity* was omitted in the WPHRE; instead, the last three clauses were revised to include:

(d) The enabling of all persons to participate effectively in a free and democratic society governed by the rule of law;
(e) The building and maintenance of peace;
(f) The promotion of people-centred sustainable development and social justice.[88]

In this apparently catch-all approach the language was less prescriptive and the tone arguably one more akin to the education and community development fields rather than those found in politics or law. The WPHRE does in this sense represent a further shift in HRE from one concerned with preventing the outbreak of violent conflict and violations of human rights in the Montreal Declaration in 1994, to a model of HRE interested in community development and social transformation.[89] The WPHRE arguably brought together the most important

87 UNESCO and OHCHR, 'Plan of Action', p. 14, para. 8.
88 General Assembly A/52/469/Add.1, in, UNHCHR, 'Human Rights Questions: Human Rights Questions, including alternative approaches for improving the effective enjoyment of human rights and fundamental freedoms', Guidelines for National Plans of Action for Human Rights Education, para. 10.
89 In the final evaluation of the first phase of the WPHRE, OHCHR outline that they had distributed questionnaires to 192 Member States of the UN, and as of 21 July 2010 they had received 76 replies all of which reported have policies which promoted HRE; 57 report having policies which explicitly refer to human rights, the right to education and rights-based approaches to the education system. The evaluation specifies that these commitments 'are

normative standards for HRE and articulated an integrative strategy unclear in previous representations of HRE. And yet, as Andre Keet argues, the 'conceptual incongruity of HRE has, at least in part, always resided in the entrenchment of a particular declarationist construction of HRE against the backdrop of efforts to provide it with a sharper and more critical pedagogical edge'.[90]

While phase one (2005–2009) focused upon the integration of human rights education into the primary and secondary school systems, phase two (2010–2014) was concerned with the inclusion of HRE in higher education and in training programmes for civil servants, law-enforcement officials and the military.[91] The draft Programme of Action for phase two introduced an additional principle for HRE activities to develop the 'capacity of duty-bearers' to meet their human rights obligations.[92] This seemed to accord with a general trend within international organisations to adopt a rights-based approach (RBA) targeting both rights-holders and duty-bearers as equally important in the realisation of human rights.

The increasing use of more programmatic language after 1995 is arguably indicative of efforts to embed HRE into institutional policymaking processes, and the draft POA for phase two actually used the term 'human rights education policies'.[93] It suggested that key features for HRE policymaking may include developing policies and legislation for ensuring the inclusion of human rights, in particular HRE in the (higher) education system; including HRE in education laws or adopting specific legislation on HRE; ensuring that all legislation is aligned with the principles of HRE and monitoring inconsistency in legislation; ensuring that policies are based on relevant research in human rights education; and, finally, developing policies and regulations with regard to university governance and management consistent with human rights principles.[94] This language then appears to illustrate that HRE is becoming more aligned with processes of governance, legislation and regulation.

Most recently in December 2011, the UN General Assembly approved the United Nations Declaration on Human Rights Education and Training

integrated in a range of legal and policy frameworks such as constitutions, education laws and legislation and policies related to specific topics such as child protection, disability, gender equality, domestic violence, sexual harassment and minority rights'. In UNHCHR, 'Final evaluation of the implementation of the first phase of the World Programme for Human Rights Education', A/65/322 at http://www2.ohchr.org/english/issues/education/training/evaluationWPHRE.htm (accessed 16 November 2012).

90 A. Keet, *Human Rights Education: A Conceptual Analysis,* Lambert, Saarbrücken, 2010, p. 84.

91 OHCHR, 'Draft plan of action for the second phase (2010–2014) of the World Programme for Human Rights Education', A/HRC/15/28, 2010, http://www2.ohchr.org/english/bodies/hrcouncil/docs/15session/A.HRC.15.28_en.pdf.

92 Ibid., para. 9(e).

93 Ibid., para. 24.

94 Ibid., para. 26.

(DHRET).[95] DHRET was motivated by a 'desire to send a strong signal to the international community to strengthen all efforts in human rights education and training through a collective commitment by all stakeholders', and reaffirmed the duty of states, outlined under the principles of international human rights instruments, to ensure that education was aimed at strengthening respect for human rights and fundamental freedoms.[96] It reiterated the necessity of HRE to promote, respect and observe all human rights and fundamental freedoms, highlighting the 'principles of universality, indivisibility and interdependence of human rights'.[97] Article 2 provided yet a further definition for human rights education and training:

> Human rights education and training comprises all educational, training, information, awareness-raising and learning activities aimed at promoting universal respect for and observance of all human rights and fundamental freedoms and thus contributing to, inter alia, the prevention of human rights violations and abuses by providing persons with knowledge, skills and understanding and developing their attitudes and behaviours, to empower them to contribute to the building and promotion of a universal culture of human rights.[98]

It stated that HRE encompasses education about human rights,[99] through human rights[100] and for human rights.[101] It would be fair to say, however, that the DHRET did very little to further extend the existing definitions of HRE, and tended to repeat much the content offered by the HRE texts of the 1990s.

Conclusion

This chapter's chronological mapping exercise demonstrates little evidence of attempts at institutional level to acknowledge the retrospective contribution of the various outcomes and detailed recommendations of meetings about human rights and education during the UNESCO leadership. Certainly, one could assume from the content and direction of the contemporary institutional

95 United Nations Declaration on Human Rights Education and Training, 19 December 2011, Resolution 66/137, http://www2.ohchr.org/english/issues/education/training/UNDHREducationTraining.htm (accessed 27 June 2012).
96 Ibid., Preamble.
97 Ibid., Article 1.
98 Ibid., Article 2.
99 Providing knowledge and understanding of human rights norms and principles, the values that underpin them, and the mechanisms for their protection; ibid., Article 2(2).
100 Learning and teaching in a way that respects the rights of both educators and learners; ibid.
101 Empowering persons to enjoy and exercise their rights and to respect and uphold the rights of others; ibid.

texts on HRE that it emerged as a result of the Vienna Declaration in 1994, rather than any earlier collaborative institutional, professional or community efforts.

What these developments do show is a gradual shift in the discourse of HRE over the last 60 years from an evidently plural and socio-political discussion and dialogue within education more generally into an institutionalised and technical discourse about the ways to distribute international human rights standards through HRE. Of course, the path of HRE has been ideologically driven in some respects and certainly seems to have responded to changing socio-political climate, but there appears to have been a clear shift in both the pace and tone of HRE discourse which coincided with end of the Cold War. This period was also marked by a shift in the leadership of HRE to the OHCHR and HRE appeared to become one aspect of the increasing peacekeeping missions and the UN human rights strategy.

After 1995 the tone of HRE discourse changed from one that had been concerned with discovering more about the meaning and purpose of educating for human rights, into an increasingly centralised and technical institutional discourse. Human rights were viewed as predetermined facts, and focused upon the language of process and methods through which international human rights standards would be imposed across Member States. HRE posited the production of human rights standards and norms firmly within the remit of the UN framework, and which effectively meant that if HRE actors chose to adopt the global HRE discourse, they would not only be constrained by the system, but also by the limitations of the discourse itself, that of universal human rights norms and standards.

This chapter, however, still leaves two questions unanswered in relation to the HRE discourse. First, how have HRE actors responded to the increasing institutionalisation of HRE discourse? And second, whose interests have been served by this institutionalisation?

4 Human rights education scholarship

While there is a wealth of both critical and practical scholarship on human rights, there appears to be very little scholarly work that fully explores the extent and implications of HRE. Nevertheless, this chapter considers the existing scholarship and how this has been influenced and shaped by the dominant global HRE discourse.

The HRE scholarship considered in this chapter is discussed in two sections. The first section discusses what might be called the critical scholarship of HRE, produced by academics with limited engagement in practice. The second considers the scholarship of practitioners, who have written about HRE using their personal experiences of practice and context. It will show that the latter is more generally focused upon methodological concerns rather than theoretical arguments. What becomes apparent is how little the two approaches actually engage with each other.

Critical HRE scholarship

In 1982, at a UNESCO Meeting of Experts on the Teaching of Human Rights, participants from all over the world discussed the need for HRE, the 'present achievements and constraints faced'.[1] As a result a collection of papers collated at the conference were published in a book, *Frontiers of Human Rights Education.*[2] This, as far as I am aware, is one of the first academic publications in English that refer specifically to HRE. In it, a few contributors acknowledge the potential problems with a global HRE model. For example, Asbjørn Eide highlights the dynamic relationship of human rights, the three generations of rights and the problem of international consensus.[3] Musa Ballah Conteh examines HRE from an African perspective, highlighting the two different approaches to HRE: the

1 A. Eide and M. Thee (eds), *Frontiers of Human Rights Education*, Universitetsforlaget, Oslo, 1983, Preface.

2 Ibid.

3 A. Eide, 'Dynamics of Human Rights and the Role of the Educator', in Eide and Thee, *Frontiers of Human Rights Education*, pp. 105–116.

historical and the legal.[4] A ***historical approach*** to HRE considers the evolution of human rights in the African context including themes such as slavery, communalism, resistance and resources. This is distinguished from a ***legal approach*** which is claimed to have an important role for human rights lawyers, but also the 'institutionalisation and better development of the legal protection of human rights'.[5]

This early work did not provoke any great academic interest. However, there have been a handful of scholars in the following decades who have written about HRE from a more critical perspective.[6] This literature is both reflective and prospective, in that the scholars are at the same time both theoretically critical of the current approaches to HRE, but also visionary in considering the ways HRE should and could, given the right foundations, instigate social change. There are four common themes among these scholars:

1 A technical orientation and transmission approach is limited and restrictive.
2 HRE is inherently political and part of an ideological struggle.
3 HRE is a tool for social change.
4 HRE consists of a range of diverse approaches.

The limitations of a technical orientation and transmission approach

The focus of some HRE processes upon the institutionalised and formal human rights language of norms and standards, as well as the associated framework and mechanisms, is not only viewed by certain scholars as restrictive but also 'potentially harmful'.[7] Alicia Ely Yamin suggests that one consequence of attempts to 'graffiti internationally enumerated rights onto indigenous societies' is that they now have no way of shaping 'concrete communities with highly developed ideologies of their own'.[8] In fact, she further argues, efforts being made in some developing countries to build HRE in non-formal settings through 'popular or grassroots education programmes [which] principally target marginalized,

4 M.B. Conteh, 'Human Rights Teaching in Africa: The Socio-Economic and Cultural Context', in Eide and Thee, *Frontiers of Human Rights Education*, p. 62.

5 Ibid.

6 Upendra Baxi, Sonia Cardenas, Alicia Ely Amin, Abraham Magdenzo, Obiora Chinedu Okafor and Sedrack C. Agbakwa are some examples of earlier HRE critique.

7 U. Baxi, 'Random Reflections on the [Im]possibility of Human Rights Education', 1996, www.pdhre.org/dialogue/reflections.html (accessed 20 May 2012); U. Baxi, 'Human Rights Education: The Promise of the Third Millennium?', in G. Andreopoulos and R.P. Claude (eds), *Human Rights Education for the Twenty-First Century*, University of Pennsylvania Press, Philadelphia, 1997; U. Baxi, 'Concepts of Human Rights: The Three Worlds of Human Rights' and 'Human Rights and Human Rights Education: Arriving at the Truth', in U. Baxi and K. Mann (eds), *Human Rights Learning: A People's Report, PDHRE*, New York, 2006, http://www.pdhre.org/report (accessed 11 January 2011).

8 A. Ely Yamin, 'Empowering Visions: Towards a Dialectical Pedagogy for Human Rights', *Human Rights Quarterly*, 15(4), 1993, p. 664.

disempowered or endangered groups and attempts to raise their awareness'[9] fail to address the theoretical underpinnings of human rights or the multiplicity of interpretations.[10]

International HRE is viewed by some as a way of creating and maintaining binary distinctions, sustaining the one-way transfer of human rights knowledge that disrespects and discounts other forms of knowing.[11] Obiora Chinedu Okafor and Sedrack C. Agbakwa[12] argue that international HRE has developed into a field of practice beset with mistruths, dogmatic and arrogant assumptions,[13] then mapping out and challenging three orthodoxies: the 'heaven–hell binary', the 'one-way traffic paradigm' and the 'abolitionist' paradigm examined in more detail below.

The *heaven–hell binary* is described as a dichotomy that splits the world into two conceptual communities, one hellish that violates human rights, and one heavenly that respects human rights. These distinctions are made primarily by distinguishing geographical locations,[14] for example the Western world and the Third World, but also through text. The way that HRE prioritises the construction of human rights through international treaties and related instruments, they argue, 'presents a particular picture of the good life that ought not be challenged at all, and is in any case, incontrovertible'.[15] They object to the way that other languages of human dignity, or other traditions and cultures that seek to project 'alternative visions of the good life',[16] are discounted.

The second orthodoxy is the *one-way traffic paradigm*. This is based upon an assumption that the 'student's ignorance is absolute' thereby justifying the educator's existence and the one-way flow of information from the teacher to the student.[17] They argue that HRE has therefore become a process of instruction rather than dialogue, and one which not only operates like this on an international level but also in the local context. Here the urban elites (including most human rights activists) believe that there is 'little, if anything at all, they [can] learn from the rural dwellers that live in the various countries'.[18]

The third orthodoxy is the *abolitionist paradigm*. This calls for the 'abolishment of local cultural practices that contravene the dictates of international human

9 These include programmes for prisoners, women and indigenous peoples that provide practical information about their rights and the procedures if they are violated. Ibid., pp. 652–653.
10 Ibid., p. 653.
11 O.C. Okafor and S.C. Agbakwa, 'Re-imagining International Human Rights Education in Our Time: Beyond Three Constitutive Orthodoxies', *Leiden Journal of International Law*, 14, 2001, p. 566.
12 Ibid.
13 Ibid.
14 Ibid., p. 566.
15 Ibid.
16 Ibid.
17 Ibid., p. 575.
18 Ibid., p. 580.

rights law'.[19] In this sense, rather than culture being viewed as a source of indigenous knowledge or resources, they argue that it is seen by the human rights movement as a 'pathological obstacle' to be overcome in the realisation of human rights.[20] The local population is viewed as incapable of transforming local cultures and practice themselves, which the HRE community view as static, 'ahistorical' and 'non-contextual', instead focusing upon the abolition of issues, while ignoring the historical, social or economic factors entwined in those practices.[21]

There is a scarcity of critique of HRE in current literature and, as Andre Keet points out, for most HRE actors 'the definitions framework of HRE is captured in declarations and conventions which at the same time provide an engraved standard for HRE'.[22] According to Keet, because HRE has been formalised and assimilated into the UN framework, it has become instrumental and so has rendered a critical pedagogical approach a 'logical impossibility'.[23]

The institutionalisation and bureaucratisation of the human rights language is seen to remove the idea of HRE from communities and experience,[24] as well as limiting and directing the scope and the practice of HRE.[25] According to Yamin this results in human rights being imposed on communities with complete disregard for their values or knowledge.[26] Also, as others claim, it is a type of HRE practice that is inherently discriminatory and exclusionary, in the way it focuses upon particular places and people, processes of instruction and the disregard of indigenous knowledges and cultures.[27]

HRE is political and part of an ideological struggle

The idea that HRE is political also implies that it is contentious. The invisible way that power operates to shape student consciousness or attitudes by 'creating a consensus' through faith and ideology has, argues Yamin, far-reaching implications for the teaching of human rights; especially if one considers the way that education can work to socialise citizens to accept this ideological level of power.[28]

19 Ibid., p. 585.

20 Ibid. Also see C. Name, 'How Should Human Rights and Development Respond to Cultural Legitimation of Gender Hierarchy in Developing Countries', *Harvard International Law Journal*, 41 2000, p. 381.

21 Okafor and Agbakwa, 'Re-imagining International Human Rights Education in Our Time', p. 585.

22 Keet, *Human Rights*, p. 192.

23 Ibid., p. 193.

24 Baxi, 'Concepts of Human Rights', p. 20.

25 See Keet, *Human Rights Education*.

26 Ely Yamin, 'Empowering Visions', p. 664

27 See Okafor and Agbakwa, 'Re-imagining International Human Rights Education in Our Time'.

28 Ely Yamin, 'Empowering Visions', p. 655; also see S. Lukes, *Power: A Radical View*, Macmillan, London, 1974.

The inherently political and value-laden nature of education is acknowledged by a number of HRE critics. Abraham Magdenzo claims that educators must be sensitive to the fact that '[i]deological struggles within education have occasionally led to intense social explosions, especially when such struggle is politically divisive'.[29] While HRE is potentially the most 'ground breaking form of human rights advocacy', Yamin suggests that it is also the most controversial.[30] This is not because HRE deals with cases or violations, but because it confronts people's 'outlooks'[31] and is a process where philosophical questions about what human rights mean, which have been buried, can come back 'to haunt the human rights advocate in the classroom'.[32]

Inserting norms into policy and national curricula, as well as developing formal and informal HRE strategies, may have the capacity to produce changes. However, Sonia Cardenas argues, that an apparent growing awareness of human rights or a state's involvement in HRE should not be taken at face value, or as evidence of a commitment to human rights.[33] Sometimes, she claims, state officials can learn the wrong lessons, despite human rights training and suggests some initiatives suffer from underfunding and inaccessibility. As a consequence 'promoters of HRE may inadvertently help replicate the patterns of abuse they claim to combat while failing to empower human rights victims'.[34] This means that while she asserts HRE can be 'inherently revolutionary' in the way 'it has the potential to generate social opposition, alongside rising demands for justice and accountability',[35] any acceptance of HRE by states should be approached with caution.[36]

And yet, it is these political and revolutionary tendencies that make HRE such a critical site of interpretative struggle, which can simultaneously be used as a site of regulation or resistance. This means that despite being critical of the institutional human rights framework, many of these critical scholars still believe that HRE is a tool of social change. This is the third common theme discussed below.

HRE as a tool for social change

While these scholars are critical of HRE, none of them appear to completely discount human rights as an idea or HRE as an approach. Instead, they all seem to share a common belief that HRE can be used as a means to instigate social change, but suggest that this should involve changes in conceptions and practice.

29 A. Magendzo, 'Problems in Planning Human Rights Education for Re-emerging Latin American Democracies', in Andreopoulos and Claude (eds), *Human Rights Education for the Twenty-First Century*, p. 472.
30 Yamin, 'Empowering Visions', p. 652.
31 Ibid.
32 Ibid., p. 643.
33 S. Cardenas, 'Constructing Rights? Human Rights Education and the State', *International Political Science Review*, 26(4), 2005, p. 375.
34 Ibid.
35 Ibid., p. 364.
36 Ibid.

There appears to be a common assertion among the scholars that the idea of human rights should be more connected to communities, local knowledge, and experience if it is to have any chance of 'restructuring political power in society'.[37] HRE communities should, claims Baxi, 'fully understand the contention that values and belief systems other than those crystallized in human rights norms and standards also define, and often more satisfactorily, ways of being, and remaining human'.[38]

Given this uniform appreciation of value for both human rights and HRE, attention then seems to shift to methodology. The multiple means by which HRE can be affected is acknowledged, which is the fourth common theme.

Diversity of HRE approaches

Increasingly apparent in more recent critical scholarship is the recognition by some scholars that HRE is multifaceted and, as such, can involve a number of different approaches. This is illustrated in the way that some scholars have started to map out the various different conceptions, models or approaches to HRE. While HRE still involves the pursuit of social change, it is viewed by these scholars as something which can be pursued by using HRE in a number of different ways. For example, Keet explores the 'alternative conceptual possibilities for HRE that can counter its anti-educational potential and unlock the potentialities that are inherent in its pedagogical promise'.[39] He does this by tracing the historical development of HRE and then mapping out the theoretical perspectives that enable him to show how different philosophical understandings might inform our understandings of HRE. While Keet describes the way that critical theory has informed critical pedagogy, he concludes that there appears to have been little effort made to link HRE with critical pedagogy. Keet demonstrates the fluidity and variety of meanings that could apply to HRE, as well as providing a conceptual map for 'constant and perpetual critical reflexivity that should inform the conceptual structure of HRE'.[40]

Ådne Valen-Sendstad also highlights the importance of the diversity dimension of human rights, but is focused upon schooling. He claims this can open HRE up to different approaches, backgrounds and experiences by making human rights more 'relevant and important to more people' in order that they reach out to various contexts and situations. There are three types of HRE, which he claims 'supplement each other and combine to address different important human rights and HRE issues'.[41] The first type focuses upon the foundation of and making sense

37 Ely Yamin, 'Empowering Visions', p. 664.
38 Baxi, 'Concepts of Human Rights', p. 23.
39 Keet, *Human Rights Education*, p. 20.
40 Ibid., p. 186.
41 Å. Valen-Sendstad, 'Theories of Human Rights in Relation to Understandings of Human Rights Education: The Relevance to Diversity', PhD thesis submitted to the School of Education, University of Birmingham, 14 April 2010, p. 258.

of human rights, which he calls ***normative dialogue/overlapping consensus***. Here, the important goal is to develop respect and understanding for human rights norms.[42] The second type, which he calls ***empowerment education***, either enables people to see their struggles and injustice as human rights violations, by developing the knowledge and skills to take up the struggle, or by informing people of human rights norms and standards, which he claims increases their awareness and the possibility of making claims.[43] The third type is ***double-responsibility***. This entails dealing with the moral dilemmas that are raised in the tension between the singular identity and the application of universal norms. It requires taking each dilemma as new and unique in order to take a fresh look at each case and not fall back upon old habits or routines; to make the decision when to apply human rights norms, when to change them, when to use them as a mean of protection or when to protect people from their misuse or misapplication.

Another approach, proposed by Monisha Bajaj, maps out HRE according to its purpose. She claims that most HRE initiatives are generally rooted in one of three categories: HRE for global citizenship, HRE for coexistence or HRE for transformative action.[44] Through three case studies of HRE in India, Bajaj shows how the content, pedagogy and action are approached in distinct ways according to each of the above categories of HRE. She claims that by better understanding the role of power, inequality and the ideological conditions that drive the content, pedagogy and outcome of HRE processes, 'scholars can develop a more nuanced picture of the vitality and promise of these social constructs and compacts'.[45] Keet, however, is more definitive in his claim that it is postmodernism that challenges the totalising nature of contemporary HRE discourse, and the way that this has helped to articulate an emergent critique of dominant forms of HRE.

Nevertheless, argues Keet, human rights universals and instruments should only be seen as one part of a range of discourses that are subject to critical analysis within HRE.[46] It must be rooted in an alternative pedagogical language and 'the notions of human suffering, compassion, needs, empathy and altruism'.[47] In addition, the way that human rights language displaces other moral languages should be problematised and HRE needs to transcend the dichotomy between the global and the local or universalism and particular.[48] It should open up an infinite number of spaces for enhanced human agency and further a commitment to solidarity within human suffering rather than an obsession with human rights

42 Ibid., pp. 247–248.
43 Ibid., p. 250.
44 M. Bajaj, 'Schooling for Social Change: The Rise and Impact of Human Rights Education in India', Continuum, New York, 2011, pp. 21–27.
45 M. Bajaj, 'Human Rights Education: Ideology, Location, and Approaches', *Human Rights Quarterly*, 33, 2011, p. 508.
46 Keet, *Human Rights Education*, p. 220.
47 Ibid., p. 222.
48 Ibid., pp. 223–224.

universalisms.[49] Keet suggests that by focusing upon the facilitation of human agency, HRE can highlight the possibilities of political action in relation to human rights, and so HRE processes should be anchored in a frame of 'critical postmodern pedagogy' which reconceptualises notions of social justice.[50]

Yamin, on the other hand, claims that if it is to be anything more than just a perpetuation of pre-existing power hierarchies, HRE should be developed by individuals themselves through the idea of human rights as critical consciousness. Rights should be viewed not as a singular ideology, but as 'a collection of individual concepts, a collection of separate rights traceable to basic notions of human nature'.[51] This approach is grounded in the idea of critical pedagogy where 'human rights serve as critical tools which permit students to unmask the power structures in their societies that inhibit the realization of their full potential as human beings'.[52] Yamin suggests that one should take a *dialectical* view of human rights as the basis of a transformative programme of education and that HRE is about empowering individuals to make choices for themselves in the fulfilment of their human dignity. The critical project, she claims, involves 'unmasking the power structures in society that impede empowerment [and] is inspired by an understanding of human integrity'.[53] Only when students and teachers are aware of the role of ideology and recognise themselves not only as subjects but as power holders, she claims, can they intervene to break the cycle.

Ultimately, there does appear to be agreement among some scholars about the plurality of theory and practice in HRE and that choices are available. The choice to navigate a particular path in HRE, Baxi argues, is essential because it offers a distinctive starting point for HRE in terms of its scope, objectives, principles, missions, pedagogies and strategies. It is a choice between pursuing HRE as a means to achieve social justice, equality and dignity for all, or the idea that we should pursue HRE to achieve vague political notions, such as good governance, post-conflict transformation, economic development or development.[54]

For Baxi, however, the way forward in HRE is through 'dialogical' means rather than any formal mechanism, and a self-reflexive learning process that should aim to understand the different ways that power is exercised through human rights structures and systems, and the ways in which the HRE endeavour can be a means of counter-action and resistance for human rights communities.[55] 'Quite simply', he states, 'HRE praxis is just another name for human rights struggles'.[56]

49 Ibid., p. 226.
50 Ibid., p. 228.
51 Ely Yamin, 'Empowering Visions', p. 661.
52 Ibid.
53 Ibid., p. 644.
54 Baxi, 'Human Rights Education', p. 147.
55 Baxi, 'Random Reflections on the [Im]possibility of Human Rights Education', p. 10.
56 Ibid., p. 1.

A further problem, identified by Cardenas, is that HRE has largely revolved around curricular activities in schools, whereas HRE for professional groups is relatively rare and most of it appears to have been conducted by NGOs, often affiliated with the Inter-African Union for Human Rights. Cardenas gestures towards an almost universal call for state–NGO cooperation and regional networking, which she suggests implies a greater role for international organisations that 'supply assistance and facilitate networking'.[57] Bajaj also touches upon the precarious role of NGOs in HRE and their positioning between the state and international community. The conflictive relationship between the NGOs and the state is rooted in the fact that HRE has predominantly grown out of human rights legal advocacy and activist work that often places members in direct confrontation with the state.[58] While the UN encourages HRE as a collaborative process, these tensions may not be easily rectified, especially when these same NGOs begin to introduce HRE into state schools.[59] The end product of HRE can often be very different from the original radical or activist-oriented approach, which goes through a process of 'de-coupling' where human rights become separated from the struggles from which they emerged.[60]

While these few scholars share some common concerns about HRE, this relatively small number of critical individuals ultimately demonstrates a general lack of critical engagement in HRE, hence the scarcity of literature. This highlights a critical problem in a lack of questioning and critique of the theory and practice of HRE resulting in it often being presented as self-evident and unproblematic. Also, while these critical scholars analyse some of the underlying theories and philosophies of HRE, many of these remain quite abstract. These critical scholars share some of the arguments offered in this book, which indicates support for the views and a growing concern about HRE among some scholars.

The next section in this chapter considers how the issues raised in the critical scholarship are replicated or remedied in the body of work that represents the practical scholarship on HRE. It provides some insight not only of the perception of the content, process and outcome of particular HRE activities, but also some insight into the ways that practitioners view human rights and HRE, through the nature of their texts, the language and terms, the style and genre adopted.

Practical HRE scholarship

The available scholarship on HRE in community-based settings to date has largely focused upon accounts of HRE practice in a variety of contexts and written by HRE practitioners. In this sense the written accounts of practice provide some insight, albeit from secondary sources, of the ways in which HRE is interpreted

57 Cardenas, 'Constructing Rights?', p. 371.
58 Bajaj, 'Human Rights Education', p. 488.
59 Ibid.
60 Ibid., p. 489.

and represented by those involved in practice and how they engage in the processes production, distribution and consumption of HRE discourse. This part if the discussion is different from above in that the scholarship focuses upon the authors' own experiences of practice, rather than any detached analysis or critique. The accounts show how these particular individuals express their understandings and interpretations of HRE through the focus of the texts on issues which the authors consider important. This means it is distinct from empirical research, which is determined by the observations and analysis of data that the researcher considers important.

Perhaps the most comprehensive collection of accounts of HRE to date is in the book *Human Rights Education for the Twenty-First Century*.[61] This is an edited collection of several chapters composed by a number of different HRE academics and practitioners. It is aimed at being both 'conceptually and practically useful' and the scope of the book is potentially broad, covering theory and practice in a range of formal and informal settings.[62] Nevertheless, despite a few attempts to engage with HRE critically, most chapters provide a more descriptive account of the ways in which HRE has been applied and practised in different contexts, including various political settings and for different types of people, such as post-war and development, or teachers, professionals and communities.[63] It also provides guidance on the resources and techniques for establishing an HRE programme, project or centre. What the content illustrates is the cross-contextual nature and sheer breadth of HRE practice, which covers a vast range of settings, people and issues. Perhaps, in this way it represents the appeal of HRE in that it can be interpreted broadly.

Nevertheless, this is not a text that engages critically with the complexities of HRE in terms of its philosophical and theoretical underpinnings, which means that there is an absence of discussion about what HRE actually means. Given this, the above common themes of the critical scholars provide a useful point from which to begin to examine some of the literature that exists on HRE in community-based settings. To see how these criticisms are addressed in practice requires considering the following questions: What appears to be the conception of human rights in this practical HRE scholarship? What processes and approaches are discussed in this practical HRE scholarship? What is the expressed or implied purpose of these accounts of HRE practice?

Therefore in order to show how the critiques above are replicated or remedied the analysis of practice will be under the following headings:

1 Conceptions of human rights
2 Processes and approaches to HRE
3 The purpose of HRE

61 Andreopoulos and Claude (eds), *Human Rights Education for the Twenty-First Century*.
62 Ibid., Preface, p. xxii.
63 Baxi, Dorsey, Magendzo.

Conceptions of human rights

Every chapter in *Human Rights Education for the Twenty-First Century* makes reference to human rights. However, there appears to be limited effort by the authors to question or interrogate what these mean. Betty Reardon defines human rights 'as enumerated in the Universal Declaration and the international standards' and acknowledges they are Western in origin. Despite this, she claims, they are generally accepted and 'the core principles are adaptable to most cultures'.[64] Some authors make reference to the international human rights instruments, while others make no effort to define human rights, and just say that people should be made aware of them, as if their presence should be obvious in any discussion about HRE.[65]

For example, Clarence Dias explains how in Nepal the obligation according to the Convention on the Rights of the Child (CRC) supplied the 'pretext for organizing workshops and programmes of education on the rights of the child'.[66] As well as the CRC,[67] there is also reference to the Convention on the Elimination of All Forms of Discrimination against Women (CEDAW),[68] but mainly UDHR, which is listed in the Index over 55 times.[69] While George Andreopoulos acknowledges that HRE has an 'instrumental role in creating a normative framework respectful of basic human rights and freedoms', he claims that HRE in post-conflict settings should be focused on issues related to human security in that particular context.[70] However he also points to the inclusion of the 'essential

64 B.A. Reardon, 'Human Rights as Education for Peace', in Andreopoulos and Claude (eds), *Human Rights Education for the Twenty-First Century*, p. 28.

65 D. Hicks, 'Conflict Resolution and Human Rights Education: Broadening the Agenda', in Andreopoulos and Claude (eds), *Human Rights Education for the Twenty-First Century*, p. 82.

66 C. Dias, 'Human Rights Education as a Strategy for Development', in Andreopoulos and Claude (eds), *Human Rights Education for the Twenty-First Century*, p. 56.

67 Also referred to in L. Neacsu-Hendry et al., 'Implementing Human Rights Education in Three Transitional Democracies: Romania, Slovakia, and Albania, in Andreopoulos and Claude (eds), *Human Rights Education for the Twenty-First Century*, pp. 499 and 510.

68 Hicks, 'Conflict Resolution and Human Rights Education', p. 82; D. Gierycz, 'Education on the Human Rights of Women as a Vehicle for Change', in Andreopoulos and Claude (eds), *Human Rights Education for the Twenty-First Century*, p. 100; U. Dow, S. Stumbras and S. Tatten, 'Women's Empowerment Initiatives from a Grassroots Level', in Andreopoulos and Claude (eds), *Human Rights Education for the Twenty-First Century*, p. 465.

69 Index, in Andreopoulos and Claude (eds), *Human Rights Education for the Twenty-First Century*, p. 635; examples include: S.P. Marks, 'Human Rights Education in UN Peace Building: From Theory to Practice', in Andreopoulos and Claude (eds), *Human Rights Education for the Twenty-First Century*, p. 48; G. Meintjes, 'Human Rights Education as Empowerment: Reflections on Pedagogy', ibid., p. 69; D. Gierycz, 'Education on the Human Rights of Women as a Vehicle for Change', ibid., p. 98; J. Paul Martin, C. Gitta and T. Ige, ' Promoting Human Rights Education in a Marginalized Africa', ibid., p. 447.

70 G.J. Andreopoulos, 'Human Rights Education in the Post-Cold War Context', in Andreopoulos and Claude (eds), *Human Rights Education for the Twenty-First Century*, pp. 15–16.

aspects of human dignity, and the multifaceted nature of the human being'.[71] Human rights are referred to as something with a practical value by Reardon, who states that they could be used as a 'vehicle for learning' about social relationships and interpretations of 'human identity and dignity'.[72]

As such, the accounts do seem to represent the multifaceted and plural nature of human rights outlined in Chapter 2, although most of these scholars share a common belief in human rights and do not present it as something which could be problematic. In saying this, the scholar's conceptions can be divided into two categories: those who refer to human rights in abstract terms, using such terms as dignity, justice and empowerment, and those who prefer to focus upon the more concrete expressions of human rights in international human rights instruments. Few scholars express human rights in terms of people's struggles or ideological social constructions.

What there appears to be a complete absence of in this scholarship is any recognition of the problems and challenges posed by the concept of human rights, especially if this is considered in relation to the energy and efforts that these practical HRE scholars have dedicated to describing and discussing the HRE processes and approaches.

Processes and approaches to HRE

There are a range of different processes described in the practical HRE scholarship. However, this book is focused upon those accounts concerned with HRE in community-based settings. Undoubtedly, the cultural and socio-political contexts vary dramatically, and there are accounts of practice in Cambodia, South Africa, the Philippines and Albania to name but a few. The HRE processes also involve the vast majority of any societies population: women, children, men, disabled, gay and lesbian, police enforcement officials, civil servants and state officials, NGOs, health professionals, teachers, and so on. The message, HRE is relevant and applicable to everyone.

In terms of informal community-based HRE, most of the accounts in the literature focus upon organised processes of education, such as mass information campaigns and workshops. There is also an account of the development of a countrywide HRE programme in Cambodia, which is described in three separate chapters, and covers the UNTAC programme, a women's rights workshop and a health workers' programme respectively.

Stephen Marks highlights the critical role that HRE played in the United Nations Transitional Administration in Cambodia (UNTAC), in which the UN mandate outlined that UNTAC had one year in which to *transform society* in Cambodia.[73] The Paris Peace Accords specifically stipulated that HRE was part

71 Ibid., p. 16.

72 Reardon, 'Human Rights as Education for Peace', p. 28.

73 Marks, 'Human Rights Education in UN Peace Building', pp. 35–50.

of the mandate of UNTAC,[74] and that the HRE task was to ensure that the Cambodian population understood both the content and significance of human rights when it came to constitution building and the integration of a bill of rights.[75] As the Head of the Programme on HRE, Marks describes how he embarked upon a strategic and intensive programme of HRE interventions, clearly supporting the use of the normative human rights framework for institutional modifications and constitutional reform.

What started out as an office of four staff in Cambodia rapidly expanded to include 21 provincial human rights officers: 'Khmer speaking educators, trained by the Component and assigned to each provincial human rights officer, working full time on training at the provincial level.'[76] Marks explains how a Trust Fund for Human Rights Education, established with money donated from Member States, provided $1.8 million of funds for HRE in Cambodia, which while arguably highlighting its importance also illustrates the way the format could be moulded and controlled using UN resources. These funds were to contract services among local and international NGOs having specialised staff and experience to target groups that the component staff were unable to train directly.[77] He describes how constitutionalism and human rights were 'popularised' throughout Cambodia, 'even in remote areas', because of 'marches, teaching, lobbying with governmental and parliamentary leaders, and spiritual guidance to the population'.[78] The active participation of monks is stated as having been crucial to the success of HRE, given that 90–95 per cent of the Cambodian population is Buddhist.[79] HRE, as Marks explains, adopted an organised structure, and in early 1993 UNTAC implemented a more 'systematic strategy' that 'trained "master trainers" who in turn prepared hundreds of monks to teach rights'.[80] Religion, according to Marks, 'is an important 'vehicle for reaching widely and deeply into society',[81] and should be an aspect of other HRE programmes.

The Cambodian HRE experience is also described by Donna Hicks, who explains how it included flying in two international HRE consultants, of which she was one.[82] Their challenge, she states, was to 'introduce to the Khmer women trainees their rights as women as articulated by CEDAW but to do so in a way that drew on their own life experiences of having their dignity violated'.[83] Over a

74 United Nations, 'Agreements on a Comprehensive Political Settlement of the Cambodia Conflict', United Nations, Paris, 23 October 1991.
75 Marks, 'Human Rights Education in UN Peace Building', pp. 36–37.
76 Ibid., p. 38.
77 Ibid.
78 Ibid., p. 41.
79 Ibid.
80 Ibid.
81 Ibid.
82 D. Hicks, 'Conflict Resolution and Human Rights Education', pp. 80–95.
83 Ibid., p. 82.

two-month period they trained 120 women as human rights trainers; these women would then in turn 'travel throughout the countryside to make as many women as possible aware of their legally protected human rights'.[84]

A third element of the HRE programme was developed for health professionals with the American Refugee Committee. This was instigated by project coordinators from the USA and Cambodia together with a national team, which also included the authors.[85] The account emphasises how health professionals were viewed as having a unique role in the promotion of human rights. The team produced a 24 curriculum and 100-page syllabi, providing 'an overview of human rights with special attention to health professional in protecting human rights'.[86] They highlight how 3,000 health professionals reportedly received the training and that the human rights material was provided and translated by UNTAC's Human Rights Component.[87]

While it seems that the programmes reached into all corners of society, the production and distribution of material and content was centralised and controlled by UNTAC. Marks describes how UNTAC estimated that approximately 120,000 people benefitted directly from human rights education and training, which he estimates would rise to several million, if they took into account the population of 9 million of benefitting from mass communication.[88] This involved the production and distribution by UNTAC of 400,000 training leaflets, and 100,000 copies of a 400-page book on official UN texts, as well as 500,000 basic leaflets, 200,000 stickers, 100,000 copies of the UDHR, 100,000 balloons and 82,000 posters. The specific message in these materials was that 'the peace in Cambodia must be built on human rights'.[89]

One of the key challenges often expressed in discussion about HRE is how 'to find relevance in cultures where these values are viewed as contradictory or, at least, inconsistent, with local beliefs'.[90] Many of the accounts of HRE practice describe how human rights were simplified and made relevant through the development of culturally appropriate materials in terms of the language, images and symbols. Again, Marks describes how in Cambodia Khmer artists were used to 'develop a logo representing a Cambodian landscape with the sunlight of human rights illuminating all aspects of Cambodian life in peace'. This was then

84 Ibid.

85 A. Keller, A.L. Horn, S.K. Sopheap and G. Otterman, 'A Cambodian Human Rights Education Programme for Health Professionals', in Andreopoulos and Claude (eds), *Human Rights Education for the Twenty-First Century*, pp. 345–358.

86 Ibid., p. 345.

87 Keller et al., 'A Cambodian Human Rights Education Programme for Health Professionals', p. 347.

88 Marks, 'Human Rights Education in UN Peace Building', p. 47.

89 Ibid., p. 46.

90 F. Tibbetts, Human Rights Education Associates, Listserv: June 2011, www.hrea.org/lists/hr-education (accessed 17 November 2012).

used on t-shirts, posters, book covers and 'the cover of a special Khmer edition of the Universal Declaration of Human Rights'.[91]

In South Africa, Ed O'Brien also describes how after visiting a rural Zulu community to assess their needs, the Community Legal Centre (CLC) wrote a Zulu book entitled *Human Rights* (*Amalungelo Oluntu*).[92] This used 'large cartoons to illustrate each article of the Universal Declaration of Human Rights' and on facing pages a simplified description of each article in Zulu and English.[93] O'Brien describes this as 'one of the best rural human rights educational resources [he] has seen to date'.[94]

Scholars describing a women's empowerment initiative in Botswana claim that a human rights framework was too 'academic and intellectual' for the village of Muchudi.[95] Therefore village members knowledgeable about human rights law conduct 'training courses on international mechanisms to widen the knowledge base of village women and to provide additional options for addressing women's rights issues'.[96] They explain that in this way the 'human rights framework is made applicable to the lives of rural women who can see beyond their village and country [and] view themselves as members of a wider world community of women faced with similar problems and striving for common goals'.[97]

These are a few examples of a number of accounts where attempts were made through the production of materials and resources, or process aimed at making the international human rights framework contextually and culturally appealing.

Another similar process described by these scholars is the integration of personal experiences into the HRE process and the local interpretations of human rights. Hicks explains that in Cambodia, as part of a process of what she calls interactive problem solving (IPS), women were asked to 'identify the main rights which have been denied, hidden, and disregarded in women's daily lives, and which have no expression in national and international legislation'.[98] Stories were shared of violence, torture, exclusion and slavery. The women were then asked to make a list of the rights they would like to see protected, which was then compared to the provisions of CEDAW. The result, states Hicks, was 'nearly complete overlap'

91 Marks, 'Human Rights Education in UN Peace Building', p. 46.

92 I have been unable to locate the literal translation.

93 E. O'Brien, 'Community Education for Law, Democracy and Human Rights', in Andreopoulos and Claude (eds), *Human Rights Education for the Twenty-First Century*, p. 427.

94 Ibid.

95 U. Dow, S. Stumbras and S. Tatten, 'Looking at Women's Empowerment Initiatives from a Grassroots Level', in Andreopoulos and Claude (eds), *Human Rights Education for the Twenty-First Century*, p. 456.

96 Ibid.

97 Ibid.

98 M. Suarez-Toro and R. Arrayo, quoted in Gierycz, 'Education on the Human Rights of Women as a Vehicle for Change', p. 107.

between the two.[99] Using women's experiences to make them 'aware of their human rights needs', in her view, is both 'powerful' and 'empowering'.[100]

A further HRE process with women focused not only on those rights that had been denied, hidden or disregarded, but also those rights which had been 'gained by women through their struggles, strengths and support from others'.[101] It is these ideas, claim Maria Suarez-Torro and Roxana Arrayo, which contribute to the construction of a 'new pedagogy of human rights education, where women appropriate and reconceptualise human rights legislation as "instruments" of the people to fulfil their needs'.[102] At the same time they also 'develop strategies that rebuild a body of women's rights of prevention, protection, and promotion of dignity and the qualitative transformation of society'.[103]

These descriptions show how the nature of the process is crucial to determining how and when to introduce the idea of human rights. Rarely is it actually introduced at the outset, but instead, as the above examples show, any introduction of international standards or laws is usually preceded by discussions of experience and the mapping out of commonalities or ideas. Often, however, these discussions appear to be a methodological strategy used to introduce the human rights idea.

Garth Meintjes provides an example of how this can happen in the case of an NGO working in fishing villages in the Philippines. He explains how the process involves community organising activities, and planning takes place on-site, rather than in an office. People in the community are 'encouraged to meet and define their local needs and problems',[104] and at the point 'when the maximum consensus is achieved' the group introduces what they call their 'barefoot lawyers who help reinterpret needs in terms of rights'.[105] The group then begins to talk about and construct 'remedial strategies'. These include the 'formulation of petitions, the drafting of new legislation as well as litigation and presentations by lawyers to administrative boards'.[106]

Earlier in the chapter, Meintjes claims that any notion of HRE as empowerment must locate any target group in terms of 'time-space', and question the 'oppressive patterns of social, political, and economic organisation'.[107] However, it is not clear in this example how this community-based process analysed or questioned the hidden or broader agendas, especially those of the law, legal standards and systems upon which the strategies appear to be ultimately focused.

99 Hicks, 'Conflict Resolution and Human Rights Education', p. 83.
100 Ibid.
101 Suarez-Toro and Arrayo, quoted in Gierycz, 'Education on the Human Rights of Women as a Vehicle for Change', p. 107.
102 Ibid
103 Ibid.
104 Meintjes, 'Human Rights Education as Empowerment', p. 74.
105 This is generally another term that is used for paralegals who are usually not formally qualified lawyers, but individuals who have received some legal or human rights training, and tend to work in more rural communities.
106 Meintjes, 'Human Rights Education as Empowerment', p. 74.
107 Ibid., p. 66.

The idea that HRE processes can *help* individuals and groups reframe their experiences, needs and problems by introducing the idea of human rights is also apparent in other accounts. In Tracy Holland's description of HRE with street and working children in Latin America, she claims that the articles in the UDHR and the CRC that deal with education 'must be used to help children reconstruct their conception of education, and then through this new conception to reframe their personal experience'.[108] HRE is only successful, she argues, 'once ways can be found to make children internalise these rights and assimilate them into their own body of knowledge'.[109]

Holland describes how this can be done through a rights-related narrative process involving fictional or non-fictional stories and experiences. For example the story of a 13-year-old boy who works and is not paid is discussed by a group of children in terms of child labour and the exploitation of children, and their rights and freedoms as a child.[110] In another way children are thrown into chaotic fictional situations which they are required to act out and engage in. She gives the example of a group of Chinese students being 'thrust into the drama of Tiananmen Square', in which they can consider abstract meanings of human rights in terms of real situations.[111]

The apparent challenge of communicating the meaning of rights in the local context is reinforced by Ed O'Brien. It is an account of how, together with a local organisation, he visited a rural Zulu community to conduct 'a human rights education session on a hillside outside a tribal courthouse'.[112] He describes the facilitator's discovery that in fact no equivalent word actually exists for human rights as 'unfortunate' rather than problematic.[113] O'Brien then explains how the HRE process involved community role plays in order to help the team 'learn the current human rights problems the community faced', and explains how the beating of women by their husbands for failing to perform 'wifely duties' generated a 'major debate'.[114] It was a 'good result of the discussion', he claims, when 'the chief stepped in and said "our country's laws now forbid such actions, and we have to begin to change some of our traditional ways of doing things"'.[115] The importance of creating awareness and understanding is clearly important for O'Brien, who draws direct linkages between particular concepts and ideas of success. As he states, 'the interconnection between law, human rights and democracy came up in this very successful workshop'.[116]

108 T. Holland, 'Human Rights Education for Street and Working Children: Principles and Practice', *Human Rights Quarterly*, 20(1), 1998, p. 181.
109 Ibid.
110 Ibid., p. 183.
111 Ibid., p. 184.
112 E O'Brien, 'Community Education for Law, Democracy and Human Rights', p. 426.
113 Ibid. There is no equivalent word in many African languages.
114 Ibid., p. 426: alongside the theft of cows, corrupt officials and gender-based violence.
115 Ibid., p. 427.
116 Ibid.

However, an alternative approach to HRE in South Africa is evident in the process of charter making, which is a channel for rights claims to be incorporated into the larger political process of transition. Ellen Dorsey explains how the charter-making movement in South Africa grew out of the liberation movement as a way of giving 'voice to the rights of communities of people traditionally excluded from the political process'.[117] A charter serves as a 'channel for rights claims to be incorporated into the larger political process', produced from a dialogue that serves as a 'legitimate representation of the demands of that community'.[118] It is 'a process of the *articulation of claims* that arise from discrimination and oppression, the process of *developing consensus* about what those claims mean in terms of the structure of the political regime and institutions for protection in the future'.[119] In general, these accounts show how criticisms voiced by scholars in the previous section are in fact generally being replicated rather than remedied. What this analysis demonstrates is an apparent preoccupation with designing and implementing methodologies that prioritise participation and knowledge transfer.

Despite being unable to identify any common trend in the way these scholars conceptualise human rights, they undoubtedly all believe in the idea of human rights, and see it as a useful tool that can *help* people define, articulate and express their problems, needs and experiences. How, then, do these same individuals understand and express the purpose of HRE?

The purpose of HRE

The focus of HRE practice in encouraging people to articulate and express their problems in terms of human rights appears to be the predominant and most immediate aim of HRE. In Holland's discussion of HRE for street and working children, she claims that the objective 'is simply to have human rights become a new metaphor reshaping these children's lives'.[120] Reardon, however, believes that HRE has a dual purpose: as a cross-cultural study of human rights, where they can be used as 'vehicle for learning' about social relationships and 'interpretations of human identity and dignity' and also in order to 'learn and assess levels of tolerance both across contexts and cultures, where human rights standards can be used to measure how various cultures live up to the standards'.[121]

In a similar kind of 'benchmarking' exercise in development, Dias claims that HRE helps to 'monitor existing development activities in terms of human rights impact', as well as 'promote understanding of the rationale for development', and

117 E. Dorsey, 'Charter Making and Participatory Research', in Andreopoulos and Claude (eds), *Human Rights Education for the Twenty-First Century*, p. 123.

118 Ibid., p. 119

119 Ibid., pp. 123–124 (emphasis in original).

120 Holland, 'Human Rights Education for Street and Working Children', p. 181.

121 Reardon, 'Human Rights as Education for Peace', p. 28.

secure effective participation and accountability in development processes. HRE, he states, is 'vital to the struggle for justice'.[122]

Not only does it seem to be a way of assessing performance and accountability at state level, but on a more personal level it appears to be linked with ideas of empowerment. As Garth Meintjes points out, there are two versions of empowerment. The first is *static empowerment* which, he claims, is a 'fixed rigid and ahistorical conception' and focuses upon the present structural or institutional disparities of power and directed at those who are presently viewed as 'alienated, marginalized, silenced, or oppressed'.[123] Individuals with this conception, he claims, tend to focus their efforts upon 'making existing hierarchical structures more accessible', and have a tendency to ignore those who are presently empowered and the ways they contribute to the oppression.[124]

Instead, *dynamic empowerment* recognises the importance of time and space when determining the needs of any particular group, and their position in terms of historical, social, political and economic circumstances, which are changing all the time, and requires understanding and questioning 'oppressive patterns of social, political, and economic organisation'.[125] If any HRE process is to be empowering, he argues, it should adopt the latter.

However, according to Andreopoulos in the case of post-conflict, HRE pedagogical strategies need objectives that are at the same time cognitive, attitudinal and empowering,[126] and refers to increasing awareness and understanding, developing sensitivity and enabling communities to define their own needs and how to meet them.[127]

The idea that HRE puts the individuals with knowledge of human rights in a better position than they were in before is supported by nearly all the scholars. However, Dorsey's charter-making approach has a distinct starting point in that people are viewed as already having knowledge of their rights. The primary goal as she states '*is not to instruct* society about the nature of democratic institutions or even global human rights norms, but to generate society wide discourse about rights'.[128] It is, as Dorsey suggests, a 'process of creating human rights'.[129]

In a more recent work Dorsey continues this explanation of 'rights creation' together with Paul Nelson.[130] Here they discuss the right to water and to essential

122 Dias, 'Human Rights Education as a Strategy for Development', pp. 52–53.
123 Meintjes, 'Human Rights Education as Empowerment', p. 67.
124 Ibid.
125 Ibid., pp. 66–67.
126 G.J. Andreopoulos, 'Human Rights Education in the Post-Cold War Context', in Andreopoulos and Claude, *Human Rights Education for the Twenty-First Century*, p. 15.
127 Ibid.
128 Dorsey, 'Charter Making and Participatory Research', p. 120.
129 Ibid., p. 124.
130 P.J. Nelson and E. Dorsey, *New Rights Advocacy: Changing Strategies of Development and Human Rights NGOs*, Georgetown University Press, Washington, DC, 2008.

medicines, and argue that while the political power comes in part from these rights social origins and power to mobilise social movements, it is

> the political and legal leverage they have afforded in shaping international policy or action has depended profoundly on their status as internationally recognized legal standards in human rights covenants and treaties and on the skilled interpretation and application of those standards in particular situations.[131]

Does this offer, as Baxi suggests, a broader way of conceptualising human rights through HRE? Dorsey's view is that while new rights, such as the right to water, do sometimes emerge from these processes, it is more often 'the popular assertion of the right and the new forms of action for the right's defense and promotion' that is new.[132]

It becomes clear through practical accounts that these scholars do not necessarily interpret or articulate human rights as international standards. However, it is evident they believe in human rights, and the way that knowledge of them can empower people in pursuing social change. In this way, then, most of these accounts of HRE have tended to involve processes that aim to raise awareness of the existence of those rights, either as inherent or as international standards; to give them meaning and relevance using the learner's knowledge, experiences and symbols of the local context.

Conclusion

The apparent tendency of the small body of available scholarship on HRE has been to describe the methods and processes of HRE, rather than any significant effort to interrogate the theoretical or challenging foundations of HRE. In the past, HRE has largely been confined to practical analysis by those working in the international institutional, state or community context. It is only more recently that HRE has started to emerge as a unique field worthy of academic attention, rather than a marginal aspect within the discipline of education.

Despite evidence of sporadic engagement there is a continued paucity of analysis based upon theoretical or philosophical critique, and very few writers start with the notion that HRE could in fact be problematic. One reason for the lack of critical analysis could be that both human rights and education are theoretically complex, multifaceted and pluralistic in nature; this makes them difficult to classify or prescribe within an institutional framework, and even more difficult to navigate and implement in practice. Far simpler, perhaps, for an institutional model of HRE, which claims to be globally viable, to adopt an approach based on clarity

131 Ibid., pp. 170–171.
132 Ibid., p. 172.

and universality of content together with a clear action plan and guidelines. The UN model of HRE takes this course. However, a lack of interrogation, whether deliberate or careless, risks the uninformed application of an institutionally produced form of HRE, and disregard of the implicit challenges wrapped up in its very construction.

5 Case study

Human rights education in Tanzania

This chapter is a case study of 12 months empirical research conducted in Tanzania between 209–10. It outlines the historical and contemporary socio-political context and how historical visions from the leadership of Julius K. Nyerere influenced how HRE discourse has developed in Tanzania. Its purpose, then, is to describe some of the ways in which HRE is conceptualised and practiced in Tanzania. These observations provide an insight into the way HRE discourse impacts upon local practice and also shapes the relationship between institutional structures and society. As an empirical study the findings are contextually grounded, based upon what individuals said about HRE and the practice observed in Tanzania.

What this chapter will show is that despite Tanzania's history, the findings from the fieldwork reveal a predominantly technical HRE discourse from NGOs in community-based settings, where human rights are often expressed as predetermined facts and HRE practice becomes transmission of those facts.[1]

The chapter is divided into three parts. The first part highlights the different conceptions of human rights expressed by participants in the research. The second part outlines how they also appeared to conceptualise the idea of HRE. In so doing, connections between these two are considered. The third part describes the structure and practice of HRE that was observed, and the processes that were adopted, all formative of the evident HRE discourse. This shows that on a local level HRE practice principally involved the cascading-down of information through an international, regional and national network of intermediaries, and informal, but organised, modes of communication that include mass education campaigns, workshops and community training organised and delivered by NGOs.

Situating the case study and its limitations

The objective of the empirical fieldwork was to test the thesis and examine how HRE was conceptualised by NGOs in community-based settings in Tanzania. Not

1 Discursive orientations outlined in Chapter 2 included: technical, interpretative, critical and counter-hegemonic.

only did this involve looking at text, speech and language, but also sites of HRE discourse and social interactions. Of particular concern was how power was exercised through the organisation of the HRE space within Tanzania, as well as localised sites of HRE discourse. I decided therefore to examine discourses identified as HRE by the interviewees and NGOs, rather than my own views, so took guidance from the organisations and staff working on the ground in Tanzania. This means that, despite being potentially significant, the theoretical and logistical construct of this macro and micro critique of HRE discourse does not include the broader community-based action or struggles in Tanzania. While these may be considered, both by other actors and myself, to be within the broader remit of HRE discourse (especially given the four orientations outlined in Chapter 2), they are not considered here. Instead, I suggest they should be a significant aspect of any future research into HRE discourse.

By using a range of different qualitative methods, as well as different sources of information, I was able to evaluate HRE discourse from a variety of standpoints and corroborate the findings. Each of the methods employed during the fieldwork is outlined in the table in Appendix 1.

Participant NGOs

The four NGOs that participated in the study were the Legal and Human Rights Centre (LHRC), the Women's Legal Aid Centre (WLAC), the Global Network for Religions of All Children (GNRC) and Kiota for Women's Health and Development (KIWOHEDE). Both the LHRC and WLAC feature substantially in the observations. GNRC and KIWOHEDE offer a background insight into HRE discourse.

Staff from each of these organisations stated that they conducted HRE activities and that they were willing to participate in the research.[2] While the LHRC and WLAC conducted similar types of HRE, using mass education, community workshops and a train-the-trainer model, GNRC offered an alternative perspective of HRE through its Peace Club networks in schools and weekly student debates. KIWOHEDE, on the other hand, worked on a service delivery basis where their main role was to pull children and young people out of domestic work and provide them with a basic education and skills.

While the LHRC and WLAC operated through national networks of paralegals, GNRC and KIWOHEDE engaged with groups of young people. I felt, together with the interviews and planned focus group discussions, these sites of HRE discourse would provide micro-data on HRE discourse which could then be placed and analysed within the broader historical, social and political HRE framework in order to identify the crucial actors, interests, resources, discourse

2 This was either stated by interviewees, described on their websites or expressed by others. In the case of the LHRC and WLAC all these applied.

and struggles involved. The place of HRE discourse within the context of the NGOs structure and activities in discussed briefly below.

Legal and Human Rights Centre (LHRC)

The LHRC has been in existence since 1995 and is one of a few prominent legal activist organisations in Tanzania, employing 48 staff.[3] It originally emerged from the legal aid work of the Law School at the University of Dar es Salaam and the Tanzania Legal Education Trust (TANLET), which formed the LHRC as an independent and autonomous organisation in 1994. It is therefore clearly an NGO with firm Tanzanian foundations and history. However, it has become increasingly reliant upon international funders to finance its work. The LHRC in the Tanzania Human Rights Report 2011 outlines as partners as the Embassy of Sweden, Norwegian People's Aid, Foundation for Civil Society, Accountability in Tanzania and the Embassy of Finland.[4]

Today, the LHRC staff are frequently featured in national newspapers as a result of their press conferences and lobbying activities, and are often referred to as experts in the field of human rights in Tanzania. They describe their activities as focusing upon the provision of legal advice and counselling, advocacy and lobbying, strategic litigation, campaigning and policy work. The LHRC describes its mission and vision for a just and equitable society by creating 'legal and human rights awareness and empowerment among the general public and, in particular, the underprivileged sections of the society through legal and civic education, advocacy, research, follow up of human rights abuses and provision of legal aid'.[5] One of the objectives outlined in the LHRC Operational Plan 2010–2012 was to increase the capacity of civil society, parliament and the media to address rights violations and monitor decision-makers. They aim to achieve this using a number of different interventions. These are focused on increasing the capacity of communities to participate in democratic processes and to address human rights violations; grooming future leaders and human rights activists in a human rights culture; and, enhancing the voice of civil society organisations, media and parliament to hold decision-makers accountable.[6]

The LHRC website outlines that the 'Mass Education and Paralegals Unit' coordinates 'training through seminars, workshops, media, and advocate programs'.[7] This includes the facilitation of several workshops and trainings at grassroots level, including training for paralegals who were community volunteers trained on legal and human rights issues. Once trained, according to the LHRC

3 See LHRC website at www.humanrights.or.tz/?page_id=86 (accessed 14 January 2012).

4 LHRC, Tanzania Human Rights Report 2011, www.humanrights.or.tz/wp-content/uploads/2010/09/TANZANIA-HUMAN-RIGHTS-REPORT-2011.pdf (accessed 2 April 2013).

5 See LHRC website at www.humanrights.or.tz/?page_id=75 (accessed 14 January 2012).

6 See LHRC website at www.humanrights.or.tz/?page_id=485 (accessed 14 January 2012).

7 See LHRC website at www.humanrights.or.tz/?page_id=491 (accessed 14 January 2012).

website, the 'paralegals become competent grassroots trainers and have the responsibility to empower their community on legal and human rights issues and assist their community to solve simple legal problems'.[8] This Unit also focused on the sensitisation and awareness of the public and some specific groups in society, in addition to the production of weekly radio and TV programmes and publications such as books, manuals, booklets, leaflets, posters and fliers.

The website descriptions describe a sophisticated and organised structure of work. In reality, though, the LHRC activities and approach was complex and multifaceted, in that it appeared to engage in community-based struggles at different levels of interaction and in various forms. Not only do they have offices in Dar es Salaam and Arusha, they also work with nationwide networks of paralegals and human rights monitors throughout Tanzania. They operate busy legal aid clinics, which includes a mobile service, where the lawyers will travel to more remote areas to liaise with the paralegals and advise the community. On the two days I visited the legal aid clinic in Dar es Salaam there were lines of people waiting outside for advice and staff had little time for a break. Nevertheless, human rights 'awareness' remains a key part of its work, especially through the media (radios, television, newspapers), as stated in the LHRC Annual Report 2011, this is 'because most of paralegals and the public have been learning different aspects of legal and human rights through different programmes'.[9]

They seem to have a precarious relationship with the government, and historically staff, in particular Executive Director Dr Helen Kijo-Bisimba, have voiced clear opposition to certain government policies and action. The LHRC has been actively involved in the struggle over forced evictions both in the Loliondo District[10] and Dar es Salaam,[11] supported strikes by public sector workers and investigated reports of chemical waste spillage by a multinational gold-mining company. On the whole, it appears to be an organisation that will speak out against injustice and violations. This has occasionally resulted in individual staff members being beaten and arrested.

That being said, the LHRC is a Tanzanian NGO whose activities are largely reliant upon funding from overseas donors. This means that they are in a somewhat

8 Ibid.

9 LHRC, Annual Report 2011, July 2012, p. 69.

10 In 2010 the LHRC visited Loliondo following reports from the media indicated that police officers under the order of district authorities had torched Maasai Bomas rendering them homeless. 'About 1,000 families were uprooted from their ancestral homes, while 54,000 head of cattle were also removed on allegations of invading a privately-owned game sanctuary run by a private hunting investor, Ortello Business Corporation. Most people, including old women and children, were rendered homeless after their houses were torched during eviction. The LHRC issued a press statement with other organisations to air its discontent.' See LHRC website www.humanrights.or.tz/?page_id=123 (accessed 23 March 2013).

11 On 5 February 2010 residents of Kipawa in Dar es Salaam were evicted from their residential areas to pave the way for the expansion of Julius Nyerere Airport and been relocated to areas with inadequate facilities. The LHRC made efforts to publicise and support their plight through the media. See ibid.

precarious position when defining the organisational strategy and how they work with communities. Their work is intrinsically tied up with those priorities of the international funders.[12]

I spent the majority of my time in the field with the LHRC. Not only did they facilitate my research but they also provided logistical support and resources, and my base was at the LHRC office in Dar es Salaam. This provided an opportunity to get to know some of the staff members, many who would meet in the morning for breakfast and an informal chat about work. This appeared to be an important aspect of the work ethos and an opportunity for the managers, administrative and support staff to meet and talk. It was by spending time within the organisation and through these informal gatherings and conversations that I gained most insight. It is these insights that underpin the research findings and data from the more formal methods. My description of the other organisations is limited to what I learned during intermittent visits to the offices, interviews and through information online.

Women's Legal Aid Centre (WLAC)

The Women's Legal Aid Centre (WLAC) was established in 1994 and emerged out of the SUWATA Legal Aid Scheme for Women. The mission was 'to promote access to justice and advocate for gender responsive policies for women and children'.[13] Figures from a 2006 Annual Report stated that WLAC employed 17 staff members, six volunteers and three volunteer media officers.[14] They are also a well-known activist organisation both nationally and globally and, in 2009, an advocate at the centre featured in the *Guardian* newspaper after being invited to speak at the International Conference on CEDAW.[15]

A major part of WLAC's work is the provision of legal aid through three legal aid clinics[16] as well as the establishment and mentoring of paralegal units around the country. WLAC has to date managed and mentored 23 paralegal units around the country,[17] and, according to an interview conducted as part of a research project in 2009, had 6,350 members.[18]

12 The Statement of Financial Performance for the Year Ended 31 December 2011 stated that grant income accounted for US$2,075,133 of a total income of US$2,333,153. LHRC, *Annual Report 2011*, July 2012.

13 See WLAC website at www.wlac.or.tz/history.php (accessed 17 January 2012).

14 WLAC Annual Report, 2006.

15 R. Faulkner, 'My Fight for Women's Rights', *Guardian*, 13 November 2009, www.guardian.co.uk/world/2009/nov/13/tanzania-women (accessed 17 January 2012).

16 According to the WLAC website, since 1989 the legal aid clinics have served **52,412** clients; see www.wlac.or.tz/what.php (accessed 17 January 2012).

17 See www.wlac.or.tz/wparalegals.php (accessed 17 January 2012).

18 F.P. Myamba, 'Domestic Violence Rights Movement in Tanzania: An Exploration', PhD thesis, Western Michigan University, 2009, p. 116.

On its website WLAC stated it had two ongoing campaigns. The first focused on the 1999 land laws,[19] 'which do away with customs and traditions discriminating women on issues of land ownership. Men and women under the land laws have same rights to acquire, use and dispose land.'[20] Its aim is to promote and strengthen the implementation of the laws, raise community awareness, increase the capacity of village councils and ward tribunals and enable access to justice for women. This campaign focused upon two regions that had high reported incidences of land disputes.[21]

The second campaign, called Tunaweza ('We Can'), was part of a global movement to end violence against women. The campaign, started by Oxfam GB, was 'grounded on the understanding that people change when they recognize something as their own problem, acknowledge they can change and have the ability to change'.[22] This campaign, initiated in Tanzania in 2007, employed a number of strategies, among them the Gender and Development Training Series, which included raising public awareness using radio programmes and the use of newspapers, comic strips and comedy, community mobilisation events, youth dialogues and debates, school mobilisation and outreach events, campaigning around the international days.[23]

A significant aspect of WLAC's work was legal and human rights trainings, which mainly focused on community awareness of women's rights. These were claimed to contribute to an increased public understanding and knowledge on women's human rights, enabled individuals to access, promote and protect their rights. This was so WLAC could implement result-oriented, community-focused and meaningful advocacy campaigns.[24]

Global Network of Religions for Children (GNRC)

The GNRC is an interfaith network of individuals and organisations dedicated to securing the rights and well-being of children everywhere. GNRC members come from all the world's major religions and many other spiritual traditions. While it had a large network around Tanzania, the headquarters of GNRC in Dar es Salaam employed three staff and worked mainly through the student members of Peace Clubs and other volunteer members.

19 The Land Act (Cap 113), the Parliament of Tanzania, 1999, http://rita.go.tz/laws/History%20Laws/Land%20(law%20of%20Prorerty%20and%20Conveyancing)%20Ordinance,%201923%20(cap. %20114).pdf (accessed 21 November 2012); and the Village Land Act (Cap 114), the Parliament of Tanzania, 1999, http://polis.parliament.go.tz/PAMS/docs/5-1999.pdf (accessed 21 November 2012).

20 See www.wlac.or.tz/what.php (accessed 17 January 2012).

21 Muleba district, Kagera region and Kyela district, Mbeya region.

22 See WLAC website at www.wlac.or.tz/what.php

23 Ibid.

24 Ibid.

The website of GNRC explains that its aim is to 'awaken the peace traditions residing in the threads of the African cultures to weave together a cloth of peace particularly focusing on the younger generation',[25] so that children will grow up in an environment where their rights are protected and their voices heard and considered in all forums of society. GNRC Africa describes its core values as 'working for peaceful societies, communities and neighbourhoods',[26] which will, they claim, 'ensure that social justice, equality, respect and opportunity for all'[27] are realised.

The GNRC Coordinator for Africa in 2009, Zameer Noorali, explained how the organisation conducted many activities but that part of their work involved making sure that children were aware of their rights. Activities including the establishment of student-led Peace Clubs in schools and weekly student discussions about issues of their choice. One of the regional priorities identified for Africa was ethics education, which 'facilitate and empower children and young persons to become global citizens mindful of who they are in relation to others, environment and their roles in enhancing a respectful society and community'.[28]

Weekly student debates were held on a Wednesday afternoon either at the office or at the Alliance Française in Dar es Salaam. Students attended from a range of different schools from around Dar es Salaam to discuss topics they had chosen. This was a forum where secondary school pupils could come and discuss various issues they normally selected, and included topics such as the mining industry, political corruption, violence against children and child labour. Students were given a space to air their views freely and attempt to build common consensus on recommendations. The plan was to put these views into a report and forward to the relevant government ministry. In each forum there were between 30 and 50 pupils mostly in their teens.

I have used my observations of the student debates only as background information given that the occasional absence of an interpreter had prevented me from keeping comprehensive records.

Kiota Women's Health and Development (KIWOHEDE)

KIWOHEDE's focus and concern is the vulnerability of children, youth and women, as well as, the different forms of abuse, sexual violence and exploitations that jeopardise their health and dignity.[29] Based in Buguruni, one of the low-income areas in Dar es Salaam, KIWOHEDE explained that it was 'committed to work with poor communities in Tanzania to promote, children, youth, women's

25 See GNRC, Africa website at http://africa.gnrc.net/en (accessed 17 January 2012).

26 Ibid.

27 Ibid.

28 See GNRC, Africa website at http://africa.gnrc.net/en/priorities/ethicseducation.html (accessed 17 January 2012).

29 KIWOHEDE was founded in 1998 by health workers.

dignity and respect of their rights to lead healthful and non-traumatised life'.[30] It states that it worked in seven regions in Tanzania, which are Dar es Salaam, Dodoma, Arusha, Singida, Iringa, Mbeya and Ruvuma. The website states that KIWOHEDE has 22 Rehabilitation Centres 'operating for children affected by worst forms of abuse; of these ten centres have residential facilities'.[31]

I visited KIWOHEDE on three occasions, interviewed staff and observed a morning discussion that was held among the young people attending the centre. I also had a chance to talk with some of them and conducted very conversational open interviews. The information gathered does inform the research and has been taken into account in the analysis. However, because of my lack of time with the organisation and because much of the material was taken in note form they have not been used as part of a detailed analysis.

Background and history

A history of education and social transformation in Tanzania

Julius Nyerere was concerned with equality and introduced a political system based on the idea of *Ujamaa*, which drew on a body of thought from all over Africa, and embraced the Swahili concept of *utu* or common humanity.[32] *Ujamaa* is grounded in the belief that a person only becomes a person in their relations with and through other people, through the willingness to share, as well as forgiveness and reconciliation.

Nyerere 'valued the general and not the particular' and the 'individual could be sacrificed but not the community'.[33] For Nyerere, freedom of the individual came second to the interests of society which were pursued regardless of individual wishes.[34] As such, the good of the individual and the group were not always determining factors in society's decisions, but both had 'constantly to be served'.[35]

30 www.kiwohede.org, homepage

31 Ibid.

32 The similar concept of *Ubuntu* exists in South Africa.

33 H. Kijo-Bisimba and C.P. Maina, 'Mwalimu Nyerere and the Challenge of Human Rights', in C. Chachage and A. Cassam (eds), *Africa's Liberation: The Legacy of Nyerere*, Pambazuka Press, Kampala, 2010, p. 149. Despite an overwhelming recognition of his political and ideological significance, criticisms continue to be levelled at some of his decisions, policies and laws that clearly violated the rights and freedoms of the individual. Nyerere refused to integrate a Bill of Rights into the Tanzanian Constitution for over 20 years and it was only incorporated in 1984 as a result of pressure. Nyerere continued to use and extend certain oppressive colonial laws that curtailed the freedom of individuals, including the Penal Code 1945, the Collective Punishment Ordinance 1921, the Townships (Removal of Undesirable Persons) Ordinance 1944 and the Deportation Ordinance 1938, which allowed the Head of State to deport citizens from one part of a country to another. Ibid., p. 152.

34 Kijo-Bisimba and Maina, 'Mwalimu Nyerere and the Challenge of Human Rights', p. 149.

35 T. Huddleston, 'The Person Nyerere', in C. Legum and G. Mmari (eds), *Mwalimu: The Influence of Nyerere*, Africa World Press, London, 1995, p. 2.

Nyerere explained that 'underlying everything must be a consciousness that the very purpose of society – the reason for existence – is and must be the individual man, his growth, his health, his security, his dignity and, therefore, his happiness'.[36] For him the ideal society was based upon the idea of human equality, on the freedom and unity of society's members.

Given Nyerere's training and profession as a teacher, he saw the role of education in achieving an independent Tanzania as crucial; it was not only about learning the skills to take Tanzania forward but about reclaiming the values of Tanzanian culture and traditions.[37] For Nyerere education was a means to break free from the colonial past and to forge a liberated and progressive Tanzania.[38] He outlined his vision through two important political ideas, education for self-reliance and education for liberation.[39]

Education for self-reliance and liberation

Nyerere's thoughts on liberating education cannot be separated from his conception of a more participatory political and development process. The overriding principle for Nyerere was that education is political. The struggle for education is a particular kind of political struggle in which every individual has a stake.

His 1967 paper 'Education for Self-Reliance' (ESR) was seen by some as 'a treatise that bore the philosophical stamp of a national leader intent on making a country's education system part of the larger socio-economic machine aimed at benefitting everyone'.[40] In this document Nyerere launched a scathing attack on the segregated and racist educational system imposed by the British colonialists claiming that it 'induced attitudes of human inequality, and in practice underpinned the domination of the weak by the strong'.[41] It was therefore entirely inappropriate for a Tanzanian society that was used to transmitting values and knowledge from one generation to the next, and a 'deliberate attempt to affect revolution in the society',[42] one that accepted its status and submitted to the colonial power.[43]

36 J.K. Nyerere, *Freedom and Unity*, Oxford University Press, Dar es Salaam, 1966.

37 J.K. Nyerere, 'Musoma Resolution: Directive on the Implementation of "Education for Self-Reliance"' (November 1974), in E. Lema, I. Omari and R. Rajani (eds), *Nyerere on Education/ Nyerere Kuhusu Elimu: Selected Essays and Speeches, 1954–1998*, HakiElimu and E. & D. Ltd, Dar es Salaam, 2005, p. 100.

38 J.K. Nyerere, 'Education for Self-Reliance' (March 1967), ibid., p. 69.

39 Ibid.; and J.K. Nyerere, 'Education for Liberation' (20 May 1974), ibid., p. 124.

40 Ibid.

41 Nyerere, 'Education for Self-Reliance', p. 69.

42 Ibid.

43 The first four years of independence (1961–1964) witnessed a massive investment of resources and energy by the government in education. The government abolished racial and religious segregation in schools, increased the number of schools around the country and pupil enrolment in secondary schools, made African history and the national language of Swahili an integral part of the curriculum, and pupils also had lessons on civics.

Education should 'foster the social goals of living together, and working together, for the common good'.[44] It must, he argued, 'inculcate a sense of commitment to the total community, and help the pupils to accept the values appropriate to our kind of future, not those appropriate to our colonial past'.[45]

In 'Education for Self-Reliance', Nyerere made reference to the pre-colonial informal 'learning through living and doing',[46] where people were taught skills, knowledge and values relevant to that society, together with tribal history and tribal relations with others and with the spirits, through the stories of the elders. The lack of formality did not make this form of education any less important or meaningful; in fact, argued Nyerere, 'it may have made the education more directly relevant to the society in which the child was growing up'.[47] The purpose of ESR, as stated, was to 'transmit from one generation to the next the accumulated wisdom and knowledge of the society, and to prepare the young people for their future membership of the society and their active participation in its maintenance or development'.[48] In 1974 Nyerere reaffirmed ESR, but highlighted that 'the main purpose of education is to enable man to liberate himself'[49] and overcome the obstacles of the environment and oppression. Nyerere claimed that while a man may be physically free, he may still be 'unfree if his mind is restricted by attitudes and habits which limit his humanity'.[50]

Education was expressed as something more than activities in the classroom, but learning from experience and sharing and discussions about matters that affect people's lives. It was not seen as something that was part of life, but continuous throughout life. Tanzanians had to break free from their entrenched modes of thinking and embrace new ideas and ways of doing in order to keep up with the rest of the world.

While Nyerere rarely made reference to human rights specifically, justice and equity were a constant theme. Education was viewed as a means of overcoming the subjectification and segregation imposed through colonialism in terms of race, class and nationality, and later through the globalisation of institutional power structures. The inculcation of moral values was an implicit rather than explicit element in the political transformation, and something people engaged with throughout their life to further the common good.

The priority for Tanzanians was to strengthen and use their knowledge in order to remain free from the exploitation and control of other nations. Education was therefore both a moral and technical imperative, and a political and social tool, driven by the larger social struggle for Tanzania's freedom from oppression. In

44 Nyerere, 'Education for Self-Reliance', p. 72.
45 Ibid.
46 Ibid., p. 68.
47 Ibid.
48 Nyerere, 'Musoma Resolution', p. 100.
49 Ibid., p. 101
50 Nyerere, 'Education for Liberation', p. 124.

'Adult Education and Development',[51] the liberation of man is placed at the centre of development rather than the production of goods and wealth. Nyerere argued that man can only liberate himself through 'the expansion of his power over himself, his environment, and his society'.[52] More than just training and workshops, education included 'what is generally called "agitation"' and included *purposeful* 'organisation and mobilisation'.[53] The first function of adult education, he claimed, was to 'inspire both a desire for change, and an understanding that change is possible'.[54]

Dialogue and discussion about human rights were often sidelined by the emphasis on broader social transformation, and individual rights were regarded as sacrificial for the greater good of society.[55] The development of the consciousness of the individual in terms of their transformative possibility was acknowledged as an important part of the struggle for global economic and social justice.[56] This meant that development may not necessarily promote or respect human rights. Nyerere's pursuit of the common good stifled any active and participatory civil society that was often viewed as a challenge to political power. Between 1961 and the 1970s, there were only seven NGOs formed in Tanzania; this rose to 18 towards the end of the 1980s.[57]

Nyerere and the nationalist party Chama Cha Mapinduzi (CCM) opposed the inclusion of a Bill of Rights in the Tanzanian Constitution[58] and together with the Preventative Detention Act 1962, which gave the President unchallengeable powers to detain individuals for long periods of time without trial, the government of Tanzania had a free hand to do what it wanted. However, the 1980s witnessed global changes (which have been referred to in Chapter 3), especially the collapse of communism, which had major implications for Tanzania.

NGOs and education for human rights in Tanzania

The 1983 constitutional debate, spearheaded by the Tanganyika Law Society (TLS), advocated for a Bill of Rights to be included in the Constitution and opened the way for its incorporation in 1984 and the eventual transition to multipartism.[59] However, opposing the government was not an easy task and a

51 J.K. Nyerere, 'Adult Education and Development', Opening Speech to the International Adult Education Conference, Dar es Salaam (21 June 1976), in Lema et al. (eds), *Nyerere on Education,* p. 133.

52 Ibid., p. 135.

53 Ibid., p. 138.

54 Ibid., p. 137.

55 Nyerere, *Freedom and Unity*; Huddleston, 'The Person Nyerere', p. 2.

56 Ibid.

57 A.S. Kiondo and C. Mogella, 'Historical Development of the Civil Society in Tanzania', in A.S. Kiondo and J.E. Nyang'oro (eds), *Civil Society and Democratic Development in Tanzania*, MWENGO, Harare, 2006, p. 24.

58 Constitution of the United Republic of Tanzania 1977.

59 Fifth Constitutional Amendment, Act No. 15 of 1984.

number of individuals were deported or taken into custody as a result.[60] Nyerere's record in relation to human rights is therefore not straightforward.

The Legal Aid Committee established by the Faculty of Law at the University of Dar es Salaam in 1967 to provide legal aid to the poor was 'radically transformed' in the 1980s and intimately tied up with the socio-economic differentiation that divided civil society between the haves and have-nots.[61] It was increasingly viewed by the government as a political body and some progressive academics thought it would be unsafe to continue to use it as a vehicle for democracy and social justice. This group of lawyers ostensibly shared the 'same ideological persuasion [and] all were socialist striving to serve the masses'.[62]

It was this group that established the Tanzanian Legal Education Trust (TANLET) in 1988. TANLET's activities included organising human rights seminars, legal literacy projects, publications, and annual lectures; it also functioned as a base for 'young activists undertaking politically sensitive assignments like organising the fledgling democratic movement for multiparty politics'.[63] They became deeply involved in this movement 'agitating for and giving civic education on multiparty politics'. As a result it was threatened with deregistration in 1991 and in 1994 launched a project focusing upon the legal and human rights aspects of the struggle, establishing the Legal and Human Rights Centre (LHRC).

At the national level, the 1990s in Tanzania witnessed a mushrooming of both civil society organisations (CSOs) and NGOs; between 1990 and 2000 the number of registered NGOs on the Tanzanian mainland increased by 1205 per cent, from 163 to more than 2700. In the same period in Zanzibar they increased from 10 to 189.[64] One reason suggested for this growth is that it was part of a general trend and a change in the nature of political organisation that was spreading across the continent.[65] The structural adjustment policies of the World Bank and the International Monetary Fund (IMF) increasingly required that NGOs fill the gap left behind by the withdrawal of social and welfare services by the state. Tanzania signed up for the standard version of structural adjustment in 1986.[66]

60 James Mapalala who supported the Movement for Revocation was arrested, detained without trial and deported to Mafia Island. His arrest was immediately followed by that of two academics and an advocate who he had consulted.

61 Legal and Human Rights Centre, *Through a Crucible of Human Rights Struggles in Tanzania*, LHRC, Dar es Salaam, 2006, p. 10.

62 Ibid., p. 17.

63 Ibid., p. 19.

64 J.E. Nyang'oro, 'Civil Society, Democratic Governance and Political Development in Tanzania: An Introduction', in Kiondo and Nyang'oro (eds), *Civil Society and Democratic Development in Tanzania*, p. 11.

65 Ibid.

66 This entailed the evaluation of the Tanzanian shilling, demand management, liberalisation of prices, reduction in the budget deficits, the raising of interest rates to market levels, elimination of government subsidies, reduction of state investment in the economy and the

It is claimed that the government has shown little support or interest in funding NGOs and in the past has warned them not to become involved in politics. The state regulated the activities of NGOs through the enactment of the NGO Act[67] in 2002 aimed at weakening control of the organisations of the activities they carried out.[68] Other organisations, which became viewed as too contentious or politically threatening, also faced the threat of deregistration. Examples of this include BAWATA, a women's empowerment organisation and Hakielimu.[69] However, for decades NGOs and civil society have found ways of getting around the authoritarian administration, but the challenges mean that things can take time, and it took TANLET nearly ten years to establish the LHRC. The LHRC has today established a non-partisan policy under which the management can belong to a political party of their choice, as long as it doesn't interfere with the work of the LHRC.[70]

The civic education work undertaken TANLET was taken over by the initial outreach agenda of the LHRC. This included working with communities, the public and specific groups such as the 'police, magistrates, prison warders and parliamentarians'.[71] It included not only mass outreach through the media but also workshops and training. The one-year plan of the LHRC was to train four communities on their rights. Training was done for selected pastoralists representatives, hunters and gatherers, followed by a needs assessment, with the objective of not only defining the legal and human rights issues but also potential paralegals.[72] It encompassed

> human rights generally, the Universal Declaration of Human Rights, the Tanzania Bill of Rights, women's rights, children's rights, land laws, laws of marriage, laws of inheritance, police and citizens' rights, corruption as a human rights issue, sexual offences, rights to bail and local government laws.[73]

It therefore appears that the original human rights struggle emerged from and was tied up with the struggle against colonialism, oppression and authoritaria-nism, where the human rights discourse was based upon the idea of constitutional rights and democracy. At the same time, there were parallel developments that opened up Tanzania to the international human rights discourse. There was a

encouragement of the private sector. See H. Campbell and H. Stein (eds) *The IMF and Tanzania*, SAPES, Harare, 1991.

67 NGO Act no. 24 of 2002.

68 Legal and Human Rights Centre, *Through a Crucible of Human Rights Struggles in Tanzania*, p. 24.

69 Ibid.

70 Ibid., p. 23.

71 Ibid, p. 41.

72 Ibid.

73 Ibid, p. 42.

growing international movement, linked to the establishment of NGOs and CSOs, that encouraged people all over the world to demand their rights, especially in the international women's movement. It was the call made in 1985 at the Third World Conference on Women in Nairobi that encouraged the establishment of a number of women's organisations in Tanzania.[74] A number of women's organisations in Tanzania were formed as an indirect result, including the Tanzania Gender Networking Programme (TGNP), the Women's Legal Aid Centre (WLAC), the Tanzanian Women's Lawyers Association (TAWLA) and the Tanzania Media Women's Association (TAMWA).

The development of human rights discourse in Tanzania is therefore the result of two socio-political changes. The first was very much situated in the call for people's power and the anti-colonial struggle, while the second accompanied the opening up of Tanzania to increasing international influence, not only in terms of finances but also in terms of ideas and discourses. A key objective of the fieldwork was to understand the dominant HRE discourse of NGOs in community-based settings and how this has been shaped through the exercise of power. So what is the current terrain of HRE discourse in light of these historical developments?

The context of transformation in Tanzania

According to official statistics Tanzania is one of the poorest countries in the world and heavily reliant upon state aid and donor funding from international agencies.[75] It also faces a number of obstacles in the realisation of some basic human rights. For example, while it has a diverse cultural and ethnic population, it has been reported that a number of contemporary challenges threaten the lifestyle and culture of many communities.[76] Further reports about harmful practices relate to certain cultural belief systems.[77] The country's precarious financial state means that it is open to exploitation from foreign multinational corporations as well as from internal government officials through corrupt practices.[78] In addition,

74 WLAC, TGNP, TAMWA and TAWLA.

75 According to UNDP's 2011 Human Development Index (HDI) Tanzania is rated 0.466, which ranks the country 152 out of 187 countries with comparable data. HDI arguably represents a push for a broader definition of well-being and provides a composite measure of three basic dimensions: health, education and income. http://hdrstats.undp. org/en/countries/profiles/TZA.html (accessed 20 May 2012).

76 It is home to approximately 120 different ethnic groups, and for some of these groups like the pastoralists, their lifestyles and culture are being threatened by increasing pressure on land from commercial development.

77 These included the human rights violations and killings associated with harmful traditional practices, including the killing of individuals suspected of witchcraft (especially older women), the killing of albinos for their body parts, female genital mutilation (FGM) and widow cleansing.

78 The Tanzania Human Rights Report 2009 described the forced eviction of the Maasai in 2009 where police 'forcefully and unlawfully invaded the Maasai indigenous land' in the

HIV/AIDS continues to be a huge problem for the population and has a number of consequences in terms of social structures and poverty.[79]

While Tanzania faces many challenges, it is similar to many other African countries. It has a rich and diverse cultural and traditional heritage, and a history of popular struggle and resistance that often becomes lost in the narrative of poverty or human rights. An important question to consider was whether Tanzania had submitted to dominant conceptions of human rights, or if there was evidence of a continuing struggle to reject Western conceptions evident in the orientation of HRE discourse. My assumption was that if there was evidence of resistance to dominant conceptions of HRE here, I could reasonably conclude that there would be similar patterns, or even less questioning of the global orientation of HRE, in other countries.

The 2009 NGO Sustainability Index for Sub-Saharan Africa stated that according to data from the Ministry of Community Development, Gender, and Children, there were 3755 registered NGOs operating in Tanzania.[80] Despite rapid growth, the Tanzanian NGO network seemed dominated by relatively few centralised national organisations. These included the Legal and Human Rights Centre (LHRC), the Women's Legal Aid Centre (WLAC), the National Organisation for Legal Assistance (NOLA), HAKIELIMU which coordinates the Friends of Education Network and the Tanzania Gender Networking Programme (TGNP). These are well-established NGOs which have stood the test of time and most have been in operation since the early 1990s.[81] It is these organisations that have helped to coordinate, train and advocate for numerous community-based organisations (CBOs). Connected to the national organisations, the role of a CBO is often to implement the national strategy at local level.

Loliondo game reserve in the Arusha region. About 200 *boma* (Maasai homes) were burned and women were sexually harassed. Clashes between communities and the government over land use are increasingly common and this is a problem that has become exacerbated by multinational corporations. The governmental promise of a commercial agricultural policy has threatened food security and the sustainably livelihood many communities rely upon; in addition there was continued toxic waste pollution from the Mara gold mine owned by a multinational mining company which has affected the health of local people, some of whom died. The Legal and Human Rights Centre, 'Tanzania Human Rights Report', 2009, p. 134.

79 In 2007 there were about 1.8 million people who were HIV positive, and it was estimated that about 8000 to 10,000 people died every month due to HIV-related diseases. The prevalence of HIV/AIDS has resulted in both social and economic problems in Tanzania, including the increasing numbers of orphans and escalating poverty, which the 2009 Human Rights Report claimed is due to the fact that HIV/AIDS kills mainly the youth population, the main contributor to the national workforce. TACAIDS and World Bank, 'Effective Reporting on HIV and Aids', 2007, p. 6.

80 USAID, 'The 2009 NGO Sustainability Index for Sub-Saharan Africa', 2009, p. 124, www.usaid.gov/our_work/democracy_and_governance/technical_areas/civil_society/angosi/ANGOSI_Reports/2009/2009_African_NGO_Sustainability_Index_TZ.pdf (accessed 20 May 2012).

81 Except NOLA which was formed in 2002

Andrew Kiondo and Cosmas Mogella claim that an attempt to survey CBOs alone has revealed numbers totalling more than 13,000.[82] In addition, there are long-standing and active professional organisations and associations such as the Tanzanian Women's Lawyers Association (TAWLA) and the Tanzania Media Women's Association (TAMWA). In Dar es Salaam you also find all the major UN agencies, country-specific development agencies such as the Department for International Development (DFID),[83] USAID and many more; then there are the head offices for international organisations such as Oxfam, Save the Children and World Vision, which only represent a handful of organisations in a vast development field.

The importance of NGOs is often justified on the premise that they contribute to increased democratisation, good governance and the strengthening of civil society. This allegedly emerges from their ability to empower the disadvantaged in society, protect citizens from the arbitrary use of state power, and enhance participation in political and policy decision-making.[84] Kiondo, however, has recognised that the question of empowerment is complex and raises the important question of 'who is empowered and how?'.[85] He argues that while many NGOs push for the interests of some disadvantaged sections of society, they fail to involve them directly in the struggle that seeks to promote their interests.[86]

The lack of resonance among some NGOs staff with communities and civil society issues is evident in the data of the 2009 Sustainability Index, which identified that while access to legal aid was available, most lawyers were not conversant with civil society issues.[87] There was low capacity in public agencies to implement NGO-related laws, competing interests among NGO actors at various levels, and government misconceptions about NGO roles and responsibilities.[88] The Index highlighted the lack of connection between NGO work and the local communities, where local issues were not usually among the priorities of programming. The fact that most donors funded the implementation and operationalisation of global agendas, such as the Millennium Development Goals (MDGs), resulted in NGOs 'being more accountable to the donors than to their own members, much less to the people they serve'.[89]

Issa Shivji, probably one of the most prominent and critical academics in Tanzania, argues that 'the sudden rise of NGOs and their apparently prominent role in Africa is part of the neo-liberal organisational, and particularly ideological

82 Kiondo and Mogella, 'Historical Development of the Civil Society in Tanzania', p. 28.
83 This has recently been changed to UK Aid.
84 Kiondo and Mogella, 'Historical Development of the Civil Society in Tanzania', p. 31.
85 Ibid.
86 Ibid., p. 32
87 USAID, 'The 2009 NGO Sustainability Index for Sub-Saharan Africa', p. 125.
88 Ibid.
89 Ibid., p. 126.

offensive'.[90] Banished to the discourse of human rights and not development, the issues of equality and equity become embraced by the advocacy of NGOs as rights, rather than a terrain of people's struggle.[91]

According to Shivji, 'human rights activity cannot be separated from the general struggle of the people against oppression . . . human rights struggles are an integral part of general social movements and that is where human rights activity should be located'. He argues that in order to relocate themselves at the grassroots and in community struggle NGOs must do three things. First, create distance between themselves and 'imperialist' funded organisations; second, distance themselves from authoritarian state structures; and, third, move away from any elitist orientations if they want to work with the people and in communities.[92]

Conceptions

Conceptions of human rights

Already discussed in Chapter 2 is the way that conceptions of human rights as facts, interpretations, struggles or social constructions could impact upon understandings and approaches to HRE. The theoretical literature on human rights shows a plural and complex field of competing and contrasting interpretations. Given this, one would expect to find some evidence of an interpretative struggle on the ground and in practice in any given locality. However, what the findings from the interviews show is a predominantly technical orientation to HRE. This is illustrated below.

NGO staff and international organisations

The interviews I conducted with NGO staff appear to show a prevailing conception of human rights as facts; in essence they are 'rights that you have by the fact of being a human being',[93] said one interviewee. Another went further in explaining:

> I mean the actual entitlements which are natural and inherent because he is a human being. These are basic entitlements, whether they are provided by the law or not, they are basic entitlements a human being needs for his humanity.[94]

90 I. Shivji, *Silences in NGO Discourse: The Role and Future of NGOs in Africa*, Fahamu, Oxford, 2006 p. 12.

91 Ibid., p. 10.

92 I. Shivji, *The Concept of Human Rights in Africa*, Codesria: London, 1989, pp. 88–89.

93 Interview 1, 4 April 2010.

94 Interview 2, 24 November 2009.

Supporting a *natural* conception, a third interviewee claimed that 'people have rights which make them human because when people don't have rights their humanity is affected somehow'.[95] Another said that when referring to human rights he meant 'it is something which is inherent and no one can take it away from you, you have it and it is inborn, so if it is inherent, you can claim'.[96] Human rights were viewed as important because they were viewed as 'the basis of life itself'.[97]

While these interviewees commonly expressed the idea that we are all born with human rights, these same individuals would primarily refer to the defined principles embedded in the UDHR. Asked where they thought human rights came from, some made reference to both national and global formal sources. For example, one interviewee said:

> If you say maybe I have a right to live, you look at the Constitution, you have to look at the Criminal Procedure Act and what it says about the right to life, you have to look at the regional instruments, the international instruments, you have to look at the number of cases decided at the national courts, what do the community think about their rights, it entails all those things.

In spite of the above, a couple of interviewees did acknowledge that defining rights was not easy and instead linked it with the idea of struggle:

> You know to define this is not so easy but there are a lot of poor people in Tanzania and there is a lot of wealth unevenly distributed and there are a lot of possibilities for a few people and very few possibilities for a lot of people. And these are sort of differences that have to do with your rights as a human being.[98]

One person interviewed expressed an alternative type of understanding. She had started work as a teacher and retrained as a lawyer later in life, but had been involved in HRE work for about 20 years. This interviewee said that as part of her earlier work she spent time working in the rural areas with Maasai communities who she used to stay with for days and weeks at a time, ensuring she returned year after year. Consistency and integration was necessary, she claimed, in order to understand more about their way of life and build a firm and trusting relationship between the NGO and the community. This way the Maasai women would feel safe and comfortable sharing their personal histories. She explained how HRE was also often built into her everyday life and gave the

95 Interview 3, 29 October 2009.
96 Interview 4, 23 April 2010.
97 Interview 5, 18 September 2009.
98 Interview 6, 21 April 2010.

example of the way in which she integrated discussion of human rights into kitchen parties. Kitchen parties are organised for a Tanzanian woman just before she gets married, traditionally the aim is to ensure that the woman is equipped with all the utensils and knowledge that she will need for married life. '[T]he name itself', she said, 'just puts you in the kitchen'.[99] Her goal was to bring in another perspective to the traditional view that a woman must not question her husband, as she explained:

> I was in a party three days ago and I decided to talk about wife battery, because sometimes they say it is a private thing and you should just keep it private, and I said it was wrong and they should not remain quiet, it is a criminal offence.[100]

While human rights were generally regarded as unproblematic, a few interviewees were more critical. These individuals were either academics or had studied overseas for some time and returned to work in an activist capacity. One claimed that 'the human rights discourse is trapped in this larger conundrum of the development enterprise being a false game'.[101] Another stated that the human rights discourse was too abstract to offer any solution, and while not outright rejecting it, he stated:

> You want this conception of abstracted human rights discourse and re-utilising it is part of that transition and paradigm shift because previously that is not how discourse was constructed, previously the discourse is emphasised or underlined by the historical, political or social framework you cannot abstract.[102]

Only one person claimed that human rights were defined by the people themselves:

> Human rights are not defined in New York . . . rights are not defined outside our communities because rights evolve, how rights are practised in Sudan or Somalia today is different for example from other areas but then they evolve.[103]

Despite the common reference to international norms and standards, the focus group discussion with NGO staff in June 2010 appeared to reveal a much more considered, reflective and deeper interrogation by some of the same individuals who had previously been interviewed. One said that the African perspective of

99 Interview 3, 29 October 2009.
100 Interview 3, 29 October 2009.
101 Interview 7, 22 January 2010.
102 Interview 8, 8 December 2009.
103 Interview 9, 24 April 2010.

human rights is highly affected by the African concept of justice. Unlike the West, African justice merges with human rights, and the word *haki* in Kiswahili means both 'rights' and' justice'. This lack of separation, he claimed, caused confusion for people, who expect that the law will deliver justice and deliver human rights when they go to court. He claimed that a possible reason why when people referred to *rights* they used examples of legal claims as points of reference was because there was no perceived separation between what the law says and what human rights instruments state.[104]

The African Charter on Human and People's Rights was acknowledged by other focus group participants as carrying a different and more African perspective of human rights, which meant many African states borrowed human rights principles from international instruments and tried to make them fit into their societies, so they tended to miss the patriarchal structure of African societies which is the key issue.

There was an apparent strong sense of affinity among the participants to this African sense of identity in terms of the way that human rights were conceived and used. Some went further in saying that HRE was viewed as adapted and had a foreign meaning, so was not suited to the African context. There was agreement that HRE should be changed and made more relevant in order for communities to embrace it. Further discussion questioned whether NGOs could in fact achieve synergy in the discourse on HRE in Tanzania because of the different ways that people can and do understand their human rights. 'Should everyone understand or value the same things? Will there not always differences?' one participant asked, going on to explain that a man could understand human rights by learning through his own experiences and, while he may not articulate them as a lawyer or UN expert, it did not mean he did not understand or have knowledge of his rights. After decades of debate, Tanzanians will never agree, claimed one participant; 'even the UN cannot define human rights, and nobody knows exactly what it is', he concluded.[105]

This demonstrated that when given the opportunity and space to reflect and discuss their work, some NGO staff did have greater insight and opinions about the complexities and challenges associated with a universal idea of human rights. This was a deeper perspective missing from their interviews. Nevertheless, what became apparent through observations was that much of this reflection and knowledge did not appear to feed into either HRE policy or practice. Instead, questions and complexities were replaced by the certainty and validity of definitive human rights principles embedded in international, regional or national instruments.

The questionnaires revealed a wider range of responses and conceptions of human rights and these are discussed in the next section.

104 Focus Group, LHRC, 2 June 2010.
105 Ibid.

Responses to questionnaires by workshop participants

There was a diverse range of conceptions about human rights in the responses of participants to the 116 questionnaires. The first question asked participants how they understood the term human rights. The responses show how human rights were predominantly expressed as something that related to 'being human', and 32 participants (28 per cent) made reference to this in their answer. Other high responses included 25 (22 per cent) references to specific rights, and also 19 (16 per cent) references to equality or non-discrimination. The references to specific human rights included: the right to education, right to be heard, freedom of expression, right to life and to be respected, right to vote, right to identity, right to participate in decision-making, right to be valued, right to shelter, right to marriage, right to love and affection. One participant wrote: 'Human rights is the sustainable programme dealing with the rights of women, children, elders, youths and orphans. These rights are put by the institution to supervise equality in the community.' Fewer participants explained their understanding of rights in terms of the law, although there were still 13 (11 per cent) responses describing human rights in terms of the law or legal entitlements:

> Human rights is about understanding your country legal rights and international and national conventions.
>
> Every human being should be respected, identified and protected by the law.
>
> Human rights are the regulations and rule which protect the human and his environment in the struggle for livelihood, so that they can combat all forms of violence and discrimination in order to have peace and life.

In seven responses (6 per cent) human rights was stipulated as the LHRC or a similar NGO or institution, and five responses (4 per cent) associated human rights with the idea of freedom and democracy. In one example:

> Human rights is the situation of the people to be free which will enable him/her to have his or her own decision on basic things without breaking the law of the country, also to have freedom of expression.

The common reference to 'being human' as part of human rights was supported by an equally common reference to equality. Despite this, there were diverse conceptions of human rights and while participants had clearly considered how they understood human rights, their answers demonstrated a diversity of understanding and conceptions.

This personal and plural interpretation of human rights was further emphasised by the responses to the second question, which asked participants to consider when they had first encountered human rights. The three predominant conceptions of human rights – being human, the naming of specific rights and equality – are then broken down and compared in terms of how each of these groups considered they were first confronted by human rights. What becomes immediately apparent is that over half (52 per cent) of the respondents, who explained human rights by making reference to specific rights (22 per cent), gave examples of their experiences to explain how they had first encountered human rights.

Each response began, 'I encountered human rights . . .':

> . . . especially the right to health, when my father was suffering from *gauglii* [Kiswahili word]. He was referred to the KCMC Hospital for further treatment. However the regional hospital had no ambulance to transfer him to the hospital in Kilimanjaro. We further transferred him to KCNC but it was too late to save his life. He passed away due to the bureaucracy to see a specialist doctor.

> . . . due to discrimination I faced in my family as I am a girl, so I was deprived of my right to education compared to the boys who went to school to get education. I was also discriminated in decision-making in my family because I am a woman and they regard me as knowing nothing, and all issues concerning my future were decided by men.

> . . . when my land was repossessed without the due process of the law and due to corruption.

> . . . when I was sacked from leadership without the consent of other leaders and my voters who put me in that position.

> . . . when I did domestic violence to my wife and when I discriminated against another woman. Therefore rights are for all regardless of religion, tribe or sex.

> . . . when I was deprived of my education rights due to poverty.

The only other high response came under the heading of 'other' from the participants who had expressed human rights as related to 'being human'. A number of these respondents wrote that they had encountered human rights many years before, while others still had quite personal responses.

There were very few respondents who replied that they had first encountered human rights in a workshop (12 per cent) and even fewer through school, although a few more respondents made reference to hearing about human rights through the radio, TV or newspapers (13 per cent). These responses show that contrary to assumptions made about a lack of knowledge, individuals in the community do reflect upon and have their own conceptions of human rights that are often informed by personal experiences and factors.

Conceptions of HRE

While interviewees had commonly referred to human rights as inherent and universal, they gave more definitive responses to questions about HRE and referred to the concrete international principles or national laws. My observations of localised sites of HRE practice often reflected this orientation of content in workshops focused upon international human rights instruments, local laws or stories of experience, and a preoccupation with raising awareness of expressions of human rights. This was arguably disconnected to the various expressions of human rights from interviewees initially.

Interviewees were asked the question, 'What do you understand by the term HRE?' The responses predominantly associated it with *raising awareness* of human rights. HRE is 'about making people realize they are rights they are entitled to',[106] said one interviewee, repeating an idea proposed by other interviewees about 'making people' do something. HRE is 'to make people know their rights',[107] or 'about making people understand about human rights'.[108] Another said that HRE was about 'getting people to understand what is in the documents, what are their rights'.[109]

Another interpretation was that HRE was viewed as something *given* to people. HRE is the 'knowledge which is given to people in their rights',[110] said one interviewee, or HRE is when 'people have been given an awareness on what rights are',[111] said another. One thought that HRE was education 'provided to the community pertaining to human rights in general',[112] saying that even talking about human rights in general was a process of education.[113]

There was a recurrent classification and distinction expressed between the *target* of HRE as 'people', 'their' or 'them' and NGO staff, who never said that HRE should include their *own* learning. HRE processes were claimed to be about *making people* know their human rights through awareness-raising provisions. Their own choice of language implied a conception of HRE as an act imposed upon or influencing an individual, as something external, provided or given, rather than the surfacing of an internal knowledge that was gained through experience.

Taken together, the interviewees expressed an overarching assumption that the masses of people in Tanzania did not know their human rights. This assumption was reinforced by specific comments by some that people in Tanzania did not know about human rights and that a lack of knowledge was seen to lead to human

106 Interview 10, 5 October 2009.
107 Interview 11, 23 September 2009.
108 Interview 12, 13 November 2009.
109 Interview 13, 30 November 2009.
110 Interview 3, 29 October 2009.
111 Interview 14, 25 September 2009.
112 Interview 1, 4 April 2010.
113 Interview 15, 30 November 2009.

rights abuse. As one interviewee put it, the 'rights are there but they are not known and that's why people are being abused'.[114] During the course of the interviews other individuals also made unprompted references to rural areas, indigenous people, culture and traditions when they were talking about HRE and the need for awareness:

> We have paralegals, for example, in an area occupied by indigenous people in East Africa and they are still hunting and gathering. We think that they are entitled to the lifestyle they have chosen and should be left to do what they think is right according to their culture and traditions. We thought we should train them on their rights.[115]

In fact, the assertion that there is lack of knowledge about human rights becomes a very real possibility if the international human rights instruments and legal texts are interpreted and used as the concrete expression of human rights. Considered from this perspective human rights does then become a set of technical facts learned through a didactic process of transmission rather than a process of learning through experience.

In the interviews HRE was expressed as 'the type of education focusing more on human rights', 'training about rights' or making 'people know their rights'. These views were qualified by reference to international instruments. It is 'the education related to the realisation of the Declaration of Human Rights',[116] stated one interviewee; others also made reference to the UDHR and other UN conventions, including the CRC and CEDAW. Another explained that the focus of that NGO 'starts with UDHR because that's where we started with human rights coming into existence'.[117]

There were, however, some alternative expressions of HRE.[118] One person distinguished between the formal education provided to university students and informal trainings in the community through workshops and trainings, but also through media programmes and newspapers. HRE, he concluded, 'is a kind of knowledge on human rights that is being shared amongst the people, to raise their awareness on how they can define their human rights, protect their human rights and protect those of the people around them'.[119] Expressing human rights as integral to our humanness, another referred to the concept of humanity rather than any concrete definitions. In HRE, she normally began by talking about human beings, distinguishing between human rights as natural and 'for every human' that she called moral rights, and the legal expression of human

114 Interview 3, 29 October 2009.
115 Interview 2, 24 November 2009.
116 Interview 16, 27 May 2010.
117 Interview 5, 18 September 2009.
118 These were outlined in Chapter 2 as technical, interpretative, critical and counter-hegemonic.
119 Interview 2, 24 November 2009.

rights that helped to organise society. 'That is why we have laws', she said; 'those laws should not infringe our humanity but they should enhance our humanity'.[120] A third person made no reference to the instruments, instead emphasising the indivisibility and universality of human rights; in the end 'we are all the same', she said.[121]

While there were different conceptions, human rights were predominantly viewed as facts and the task of HRE was to raise awareness of these facts. This was emphasised in the response of an NGO staff member:

> There are different provisions of human rights, UDHR, CRC and different declarations both international and regional which Tanzania has signed and ratified. It is one thing to have these documents sitting on paper but really getting people to understand what is in the documents, what are their rights, entitlements, responsibilities what are their obligations. That is my understanding of HRE.[122]

HRE, then, tended to be viewed as a process of translating the international norms or national laws into the local context. As one NGO lawyer explained:

> HRE means to educate people, to make people know their rights which they are born with, but that they are also documented under international instruments like the UDHR. So you have a wider thing, but you need to reduce it to fit the local community so that they can understand they have rights. So HRE as I understand it is making people aware of their rights and how to enforce it.[123]

From this perspective, the methods used to translate human rights standards from global standards into the local context were particularly important and tended to be a key feature of HRE workshops and training. Many of these HRE processes also involved the translation of international instruments and national laws into local languages, in this case Kiswahili. The production of leaflets and handbooks about various aspects of human rights was used to communicate information about human rights to the community. Materials included training manuals on human rights issues for NGO staff and communities. One Tanzanian NGO had

> translated CEDAW into the local language into Swahili so that it may be of help in training and so forth. But we also have several books, like 'Women's Human Rights Step by Step' that was also translated from English into Swahili that is also being used in different training.[124]

120 Ibid.
121 Interview 9, 24 April 2010.
122 Interview 13, 30 November 2009.
123 Interview 11, 23 September 2009.
124 Interview 5, 18 September 2009.

HRE was viewed as specialist and there was a common view that in order for human rights to be accessible in communities, the international human rights texts and principles needed to be simplified 'according to the level of understanding of the people'.[125] This was, claimed one interviewee, because 'most of the community members are not educated like you and me; they have a minimum standard seven education'.[126] Communities had to be approached in a certain way, said one Tanzanian NGO interviewee, and asked to interrogate cultural or traditional behaviours and consider why they came up with particular rules. 'It is more of an art', this interviewee said, 'and a bit technical'. The terms are sometimes quite technical 'but you put it in a more accessible language', and trainings have to be 'repeated several times for people to articulate it. It is not like a onetime event that you go there one day and present something and the next day expected them to understand.'[127]

Many NGOs tend to engage in processes of translating the international human rights standards or national laws and processes into understandable and contextually relevant terms. One Tanzanian NGO staff member explained that when people mentioned ideas about human rights in their own context, you can 'guide them' to translate these rights into the human rights framework or the Constitution. Sometimes, she said, 'I think people know what they want but maybe being able to articulate that as a right and how she can enforce that as a right is a challenge.'[128]

Linked to this conception was an apparent assumption that *training* in human rights increased the individual's capacity to demand and claim their human rights. 'What we are trying to do', said one staff member, is 'train the children so they can demand their rights, because when they know it they can demand and we are training the duty bearers as well to understand children's rights'.[129] The conception that knowledge of international human rights standards and the formal mechanisms of enforcement can help individuals make demands and claims against the state is the idea that in fact these government and legal structures were accessible, cooperative and capable of supporting these claims.

Reality, however, does not appear to meet these expectations, and Tanzania NGO staff highlight the challenging and problematic nature of the ineffective systems. One describes the process of pursuing a legal claim or lobbying the government on human rights as 'boring' and the way that an individual can fight for several years and get nothing. This interviewee went on to explain how this particular NGO attempted to connect the government and elite with the grassroots. They had become an 'intermediary', in an effort 'to get the government to open the door'. However, this was followed by the question asking, 'how long

125 Interview 11, 23 September 2009.
126 Ibid.
127 Interview 17, 23 September 2009.
128 Ibid.
129 Interview 18, 3 November 2009.

can you be the voice for the voiceless? You should give them their own voice', she said.[130]

This sense of frustration is echoed by others who talk about the 'global trend' of governments redirecting their efforts to the private sector, and deprioritising women's issues.[131] While some NGO interviewees thought that HRE was having an impact on the way people mobilised and wanted to see change, the slow response of the government and lack of change was in the end 'frustrating' and brought a level of 'fatigue'. This was the word expressed by one NGO staff member who described working for ten years on an issue and still being unable to see any indicator that the government wanted to do something.[132]

Nevertheless, more than one interviewee stated that people in Tanzania were demanding accountability and taking the issue of rights seriously, indicating that from the NGO perspective at least HRE appeared to be having some impact. However, others expressed the ongoing problem with the legal systems and government responding to this increased demand. People's voices often were not heard and the government and state structures did not respond to their demands. As one interviewee explained, Tanzanian people did not trust the courts, and that it was evident in the way they increasingly protested and threw stones at presidential vehicle escorts, which he took as an indicator of people's anger at not being heard. HRE, the interviewee claimed, arguably contributed to that kind of reaction, because while people now knew their rights, they did not know how to enforce them.[133] Another stated that while human rights in the form of legal demands against the state and state officials were rising, the courts were ill equipped to deal with them and the government turned a blind eye.

Practice

The structure and practice of HRE in community-based settings

So far the chapter has focused upon those conceptions of human rights and HRE articulated mainly by interviewees but also the responses of workshop participants to questionnaires. This section now considers the structure and practice of HRE observed in the fieldwork, which revealed that HRE in Tanzania was organised at three levels. The first level was a programme of mass education and usually involved large-scale media campaigns using the TV and radio and sometimes posters. The second level involved training national organisations, national networks of volunteer paralegals and other community members in aspects of international, regional and national human rights laws and instruments.

130 Ibid.
131 Interview 2, 24 November 2009.
132 Ibid.
133 Ibid.

The third level entailed these networks of volunteers communicating this knowledge to people living in the community.

Given that the previous section has shown how the prevalent conception of HRE was awareness-raising, an objective of organisations was logically to *reach* as many people as possible. Many national organisations therefore appeared to use a combination of methods to access the community, often combining mass education with more focused workshops. An interviewee from one paralegal organisation explained how they used seminars in communities, based upon a timetable. These would involve discussions about the UDHR and then an evaluation of what had been covered and whether participants had really understood. They also formulated and conducted theatre performances in market places, to 'show the problems of GBV and show the problems that women have when they cannot discuss family issues and are beaten by men'.[134]

The awareness-raising and training approach mentioned by interviewees in the previous section tended to be programmatic, and while certain NGOs identified human rights issues with and for communities, HRE strategies remained separate and were generally designed exclusively by the NGO staff. One process described involved an initial needs assessment, which included reading newspapers, reports and letters from monitors and speaking to people. This was followed by a field visit where staff conducted interviews with the population about the issues identified. It included all levels of society in order to get a range of opinion. Finally, and back at the office, the NGO staff would discuss the issues raised in order to devise an organisational strategy, which usually included the training of trainers.[135]

A number of NGOs tended to use a training-of-trainers approach to HRE as a key part of their work. This involved providing information to 'paralegals and human rights monitors so they can train others in the community', and it was common practice for NGOs in Tanzania to run community education workshops or training.[136] In the case of those NGOs explicitly associated with HRE work, they operated through networks of community volunteers who often lived in rural communities outside the main cities of Dar es Salaam and Arusha. These volunteers were not paid, although they tended to receive an allowance in addition to transport and accommodation costs for attending a workshop. Volunteers were *trained* through workshops usually on topics that organisers had identified as necessary and important. There were many groups of paralegal workers and similar volunteer groups within Tanzania who were associated with different organisations.[137] Each organisation seemed to have its own network but many appeared to be working on overlapping issues.

134 Interview 12, 13 November 2009.
135 Interview 20, October 2009.
136 Interview 14, 25 September 2009.
137 For example, paralegals and Village Legal Workers, LHRC; Community Justice Facilitators, UNICEF; paralegals, WLAC, paralegals, NOLA plus other networks.

In some cases paralegal organisations had established themselves as NGOs with their own funding. One example was the Morogoro Paralegal Centre (MPLC), which was established in 1993 by the Executive Director who had originally trained as a teacher. It was established after the Women's Legal Aid Centre (WLAC) had visited Morogoro to conduct a workshop with about 20 people on human rights, the Land Act, the Marriage Act and child rights. It prompted the participants to conduct further trainings of this nature with the community but also to resolve legal problems. They then established an office and convening once a week on a Friday to meet with clients and resolve legal problems through mediation. There are 20 of these paralegal organisations all around Tanzania which appear mainly to rely upon the contributions of volunteers in communities.[138] In 2005 these paralegal entities formed the Tanzania Paralegal Network (TAPANET) which aims to promote information exchange, capacity building and a legally uniform system.[139]

It was the difficulties associated with access to justice, together with logistical and financial challenges, that seem to be addressed to some extent by working through a network of locally based volunteers. Tanzania is vast and the rural areas can be difficult to access, particularly during the rainy seasons, when certain roads become impossible to pass and meetings are difficult to coordinate. In this sense working through volunteers therefore was one of the only effective modes of delivery in processes that rely upon information transfer, unless staff were willing to move to the rural areas on a more permanent basis, which I gathered from interviews and discussions was rarely the case. However, this type of structure can inadvertently support the cascading-down of information from the NGOs to the community and lead by a select group of professionals.

Many of the organisations who viewed themselves, and were viewed by others, as conducting HRE work, did have a legal underpinning and, for the most part, employed lawyers who took responsibility for this aspect of the work. These included the LHRC, WLAC, NOLA, Women in Law and Development in Africa (WILDAF) and TAWLA. While some of these organisations did have a few non-lawyers on the staff, they were predominantly staffed by qualified lawyers or law graduates. A number of staff interviewed had explained that studying human rights law was part of their degree.

A lack of time and resources were two key challenges raised by NGO staff in interviews. Some said they were unhappy about the insufficient time, stressing the pressure that was levelled at staff to keep up to date with the workload, and a wish for more time to reflect. I observed how many NGO staff were consistently busy and some came in and worked at weekends to catch up or

138 Arusha, Ukonga, Tanga, KIWAKIJA, Kiteto, Songea, Shinyanga, Kibaha, Mbeya, Lindi, Muungano wa Wanawake Mufindi, Kigoma, Moshi, Mwanza, Mtwara, Kyela, Iringa, Dodoma and Morogoro.

139 TAPANET is organised under the remit of WLAC and was officially registered as a legal entity on 12 October 2010, www.wlac.or.tz/tapanet.php

conduct trainings. Because of these challenges some staff saw the task itself as overwhelming:

> First off is that our capacity versus people who need our service do not correlate. Many people need our services, because we have to operate the whole country but due to limitation of funds and maybe man power we cannot advise the whole country, so many people need our services but we cannot do all. The second challenge is the capacity is that there are many things to do at a very short time so we are rushing things to accomplish things the time is not enough.[140]

This person also explained there were financial constraints that limited how they worked, and that a lack of time for reflection resulted in her 'like a stranger to certain things' in relation to her work when she went overseas, whereas in Tanzania there was no time to think as they were 'always busy with [their] activities'.[141] The pressurised nature of the job and lack of time to reflect about practice were expressed as real concerns. Staff at the LHRC would have a formal meeting once a week to discuss schedules, and also had the opportunity to meet informally over breakfast or tea to chat about work. However, the nature of the work entailed days and weeks away from the office, and many staff were often away from the office and travelling around Tanzania.

One reason given for these constraints was that the apparent boom in NGOs, together with limited donor finance, had created a sector organised around the struggle for funds and resources. This also meant that collaboration was sometimes 'influenced by resources or lack of it', so that most organisations wanted to 'work individually, identifying their own comfort zone, and making sure that the small undefined power struggles stayed among themselves'.[142]

Donor-driven finance arguably has consequences for the strategic direction of an NGO, imposing limitations on time and outcomes. A key feature of donor finance is that every three to five years an NGO has to write up strategies and funding proposals using a range of standardised processes. NGO programmes must often fit with the criteria of the donors, which means they will often be shaped around these; they must also be able to provide short-term measurables mapped out in a log frame matrix, which many international institutions use. This means that NGOs have little time to reflect upon their work, and once objectives are set and funding approved these must then be implemented and achieved by the next funding cycle. This in itself imposes external limitations on the way that NGOs can organise their activities.

Despite an apparent commitment of NGO staff, HRE processes were therefore often constrained by funders and funding, resources and time, factors that

140 Interview 14, 25 September 2009.
141 Ibid.
142 Interview 19, 27 November 2009.

determine the way that HRE is planned and implemented from the outset. However, there still appeared to be a common conception of human rights as facts and HRE as awareness-raising which also has an impact on the way people understand the task and their role.

The practice of HRE in Tanzania

These examples are from fieldwork conducted in Tanzania (2009–2010) and findings from the observation of three sets of workshops. The discussion focuses both on the structure and organisation of the processes but also the delivery of content.[143] These HRE spaces highlight the interactions between the institutions and society on a localised level, which in turn point to some of the broader problematic issues with HRE and how these impact on grassroots interventions. This provides only a snapshot of HRE practice, rather than the full extent of potential HRE activity in Tanzania, which means that its scope is limited. However, what it does show are the HRE discourses of those NGOs delivering what they call HRE in community-based settings. These findings can then be compared against the broader HRE discourse evident at the global institutional level and the scholarly accounts of practice.

A series of four LHRC workshops on the Maputo Protocol[144]

The first set of observations are in relation to a series of workshops organised by LHRC in March 2010 and conducted in Dodoma, Manyoni, Mpwapwa and Morogoro. The aim of the workshops was to raise awareness and discuss the provisions of the Maputo Protocol (Protocol). The Maputo Protocol is the Protocol to the African Charter for Human and People's Rights (ACHPR) (1981) on the rights of women in Africa; it was adopted by the African Commission on Human and People's Rights on 11 July 2003, but only entered into force over two years later on the 25 November 2005 when it was ratified by 15 states.

While the ACHPR recognises women's rights, the provisions were commonly acknowledged as inadequate for the lives of African women.[145] This is because the ACHPR is seen as emphasising the importance of African customs and values

143 A series of four LHRC workshops on the Maputo Protocol, February–March 2010; three LHRC workshops on land rights, May 2010, and a three-day WLAC workshop for journalists on GBV, March 2010.

144 Workshops conducted in Dodoma on 9 February 2010, Manyoni on 10 February 2010, Mpwapwa on 11 February 2010, Morogoro on 2 March 2010.

145 Article 18(3) covers the protection of the family, promises to ensure the elimination of all discrimination against women and also ensure protection of the rights of women. Article 2, the non-discrimination clause, provides that the rights and freedoms enshrined in the charter shall be enjoyed by all irrespective of race, ethnic group, colour, sex, language, religion, political or any other opinion, national and social origin, fortune, birth or other status. Article 3, the equal protection clause, states that every individual shall be equal before the law and shall be entitled to the equal protection of the law.

without addressing the concern about many customary practices, such as female genital mutilation (FGM), forced marriage and wife inheritance, which 'can be harmful or life threatening to women'.[146] Women's organisations have been campaigning since the mid-1990s for the adoption of the Maputo Protocol that is seen to fill this gap. In addition, it is claimed that the existing international instruments on women's rights[147] 'have not involved a conceptual shift or effected structural changes needed to implement their resolutions'.[148] The Protocol is claimed to go 'beyond the abstract of laws protecting women's rights' and focuses more upon concrete actions and goals needed to ensure implementation and ensure women's rights in Africa.[149]

The Protocol is seen by many to be specifically tailored to the rights of women in Africa, and the Articles include protection from traditional practices that are harmful to health, including FGM,[150] the protection of women from exploitation and degradation,[151] reproductive rights including the right to abortion,[152] the right to food security[153] and consideration of women in the enactment of legislation relating to marriage, in particular polygamy, forced marriage, early marriage and the rights of widows.[154] As one proponent claims:

> The Protocol is worded to take account of the African experience. The right to food security, the encouragement of the creation of a system of social protection in favour of women working in the informal sector makes real sense to African women. The protocol takes women's rights from a universal setting to one where all are able to access them.[155]

Nevertheless, the challenge moves from one of ratification to domestication, implementation and the realisation of these rights for women in many African countries. Tanzania is no different, and while they ratified the Protocol in 2007, it has not been domesticated into Tanzanian law. There is still much opposition in African countries and beyond to the Protocol. There are two contentious factors that drive the opposition. The first is Article 14 on health and reproductive

146 M. Wandia, 'Rights of Women in Africa: Launch of a Petition to the African Union', Pambazuka News 162, 24 June 2004, in F. Manji and P. Burnett (eds), *African Voices on Development and Social Justice: Editorials from Pambazuka News*, Pambazuka, London, p. 95.
147 CEDAW, 1979, and the Beijing Declaration and Platform for Action, September 1995.
148 UNDP, HDI 2011, p. 98.
149 Z. Kamil Ali, 'A Plea for Ratification', *Pambazuka News*, 162, 24 June 2004, in Manji and Burnett (eds), *African Voices*, p. 105.
150 Maputo Protocol 1981, Article 5.
151 Ibid., Articles 2, 3 and 4.
152 Ibid., Article 14.
153 Ibid., Article 15.
154 Ibid., Articles 6, 7, 20 and 21.
155 Kamil Ali, 'A Plea for Ratification', p. 105.

rights,[156] which includes abortion and contraception, and is opposed mainly by Catholics and some Christian groups. The second are the articles on FGM, polygamous marriages and other traditional practices,[157] to which some Muslims object.

The LHRC was the primary organisation coordinating the efforts to pressurise the government to domesticate and implement the Protocol into Tanzanian law. As part of these efforts the LHRC organized a series of community-based workshops in 2010 not only to raise awareness of the Maputo Protocol and the provisions, but also to provide an opportunity to discuss and get feedback on the controversial articles. This project was part of the Oxfam GB 'Raising Her Voice' programme which 'aims to promote the rights and capacity of poor women to engage effectively in governance at all levels'.[158] Oxfam GB's partners in seven African countries[159] had decided to ensure that the provisions of the Maputo Protocol were reflected in the national legal frameworks and implemented effectively to ensure concrete improvements. In 2010 the LHRC received US$65,837 in funding from Oxfam GB for this programme. Raising Her Voice was funded by the Department for International Development (DFID) Governance and Transparency Programme.[160]

In organising these workshops the LHRC had tasked a local facilitator, who was a paralegal volunteer to invite community members from the surrounding villages, which included other paralegals as well as community representatives, including pastors, teachers, representatives of local CSOs and village leaders. In each workshop there were between 45 and 55 participants.[161] Meals and allowances were provided for the participating individuals. The workshops were all led by the same LHRC staff members, who always dressed very smartly or in a manner you

156 This article includes the right to choose any method of contraception and also stipulates that State parties shall take appropriate measures to 'protect the reproductive rights of women by authorising medical abortion in cases of sexual assault, rape, incest, and where the continued pregnancy endangers the mental and physical health of the mother or the life of the mother or the foetus'.

157 Article 5 calls for the elimination through legislation of FGM, Article 6 states that the minimum age for marriage should be 18 and that monogamous marriage is preferable and Article 20, which is less contentious, and makes provisions for widows' rights.

158 See Oxfam GB website http://policy-practice.oxfam.org.uk/our-work/citizen-states/raising-her-voice (accessed 6 April 2013).

159 Gambia, Liberia, Mozambique, Nigeria, South Africa, Tanzania and Uganda.

160 'The DFID Governance and Transparency Fund (GTF) was established to **empower citizens** through strengthening the capacity of civil society to represent their interests **and hold governments to account**. The GTF is tackling a broad range of governance issues including among others: access to improved public services in the areas of health, education, and water and sanitation; access to justice and human rights; increasing security; public expenditure monitoring; conflict prevention; natural resource management; and, controlling corruption.' See KPMG, DFID Governance and Transparency Fund 2010/2011 Report, 1 December 2011, prepared by KPMG for the Department for International Development.

161 Mpwapwa, 30 women and 23 men; Manyoni, 25 women and 21 men; Dodoma, 33 women and 23 men.

would expect in an office environment, the women in skirt suits and the men in smart trousers and a shirt. Workshop participants also appeared to have dressed-up for the workshop, and while some wore formal attire, others dressed in LHRC t-shirts. Workshops lasted between four and six hours, and while many participants had come from the immediate area, some had travelled for many hours on buses from the villages in order to attend. LHRC staff sat at the front of the room behind a table facing the participants and in three out of four of these workshops they were elevated on a stage. Participants sat either in lines or in a semi-circle facing the LHRC staff, and generally raised their hands if they wanted to say something, before being invited to speak; however, in discussions some individuals would intervene spontaneously.

Each workshop tended to follow the same structure: the LHRC was introduced by the facilitator,[162] who explained the reasons for the workshops and then asked the participants to decide on the agenda for the day. Once the agenda was complete the participants also volunteered some ground rules for the day.[163] In Mpwapwa, the local facilitator did ask the participants for their expectations of the workshops. Their answers included gaining an awareness of rights and their meaning, especially of women's and children's rights, being empowered, school-girl pregnancies, the protection of rights, the right to be heard, to change attitudes and eliminate the spirit of dominant superiority of men.[164] The same format and techniques were repeated in each workshop.[165] While the local facilitator introduced and concluded the sessions, it was the LHRC officer who led the workshops, standing at the front or walking around the room, with the Maputo Protocol in hand, while talking.

I had been told previously in an interview that the goal of the LHRC was for participants to leave these workshops with an awareness of the Maputo Protocol and its provisions. This way the participants could support the LHRC's call to the government for ratification, but also it was so the staff had awareness of the most contentious issues and opposition to the Protocol. 'What we aim to see', said the LHRC officer, 'is that the Protocol is domesticated and implemented in Tanzania, so we are educating and lobbying and awareness creation so that the public know that the Protocol is important and we have to domesticate it'.[166] If people are aware of it, she explained, they can ask their leaders to pressure the

162 These are locally based volunteers who for this particular event had been given the responsibility of organising the workshops and inviting participants.

163 Timekeeping, switching off your phone and respecting others' point of view were mentioned in all the workshops, others included total participation, many discussions, silence when others are talking and asking permission to leave the room.

164 When asked about this initial exercise at each workshop, the GPO mentioned that they felt this activity was important in order to ensure participation.

165 Staff at the LHRC had stated they provided internal training for the paralegals and village legal workers on facilitation techniques in order to equip them to conduct further training in the community.

166 Interview 14, 25 September 2009.

'government to domesticate this Protocol, because it is very good Protocol'.[167] In each of the five workshops, she would explain the functions of the LHRC, and emphasise how one was to ensure the implementation of the Maputo Protocol by the Tanzanian government. The purpose of the workshop, she said to participants, was to explain the Protocol and collect their views on any proposed amendments; 'Tanzania must sign all international laws', she stated in one workshop.

She would then explain the ratification and domestication process of regional human rights instruments, and the differences between a monist and dualist system, emphasising that Tanzania had to domesticate the Protocol in order for it to be binding in law. A synopsis of the Swahili translations of some terms was also provided.[168] When a couple of participants in one workshop raised concerns over the use of the word 'Protocol', they were told by the LHRC officer that as a matter of international policy those drafting the Protocol ('they') had agreed what to call it, and therefore it is a Protocol.

Each article of the Protocol was read out, either by the LHRC officer or by a volunteer participant, and while it seemed participants could raise questions and issues that were relevant to their own lives, the discussion was repeatedly bought back to the Protocol. Issues raised by participants often related to social, traditional or cultural practices. In one workshop a participant stated that 'there are certain traditions and cultures where if the wife bears a child the husband must move from the house for two years and does not provide any support'.[169] This is 'discrimination to women', the LHRC officer stated, and 'a challenge . . . if Article Seven comes into force it may be a problem'.[170]

On a number of other occasions participants raised issues. For example, one person asked, 'Why do people employ house girls, usually very young, and how are they protected in the house?' After a short discussion they were told it would be discussed later.[171] It never was. Another person asked how the LHRC could help the tribes that think when the husband does not beat his wife, they see him as not loving his wife, and how will they help the women who see beating as love. In response, the LHRC officer paused, looked at another staff member, and then stated 'by providing education through paralegals'.[172] Nothing further was said.

Two contentious issues were raised in the workshops. In the first,[173] a man asked about gay and lesbian rights, something that I had learned was illegal and socially taboo in Tanzania.[174] According to the Penal Code Act 1945 (revised 1998)

167 Ibid.
168 Mkataba (Convention), Agano (Covenant), Tamko (Declaration), Nyongoza (Protocol).
169 LHRC Workshop on the Maputo Protocol, Manyoni, 11 February 2010.
170 Ibid.
171 LHRC Workshop on the Maputo Protocol, Morogoro, 2 March 2010.
172 LHRC Workshop on the Maputo Protocol, Dodoma, 9 February 2010.
173 Ibid.
174 According to the 2007 Pew Global Attitudes Project, 95 per cent of Tanzanian residents said that homosexuality should be rejected by society, making it the highest rate of the

carnal homosexual acts are punishable with imprisonment of 30 years to life. He was briefly told it was illegal and there was no further discussion. The second was about the practice of polygamy in a workshop attended by both Muslim and Christian participants.[175] Article Six of the Maputo Protocol states that 'monogamy is encouraged as the preferred form of marriage and that the rights of women in marriage and family, including in polygamous marital relationships, are promoted and protected'.[176] According to the law, polygamous marriages were legally valid and recognised in so far as traditions, customs or religious rites accommodate them.[177] It was an issue raised by participants in all the workshops, but on this occasion the LHRC officer did acknowledge that while according to the Protocol monogamy should be preferred, it did cause 'a lot of confusion with Islamic law'. The subsequent discussion revealed some of the diverging opinions and disagreement. One man stated:

> Man 1: They are capable to keep four wives so why should they keep only one. It is defended according to the Koran, self-certification if someone having more than one wife. According to the Koran, a man can have as many wives as he wants. There is no limit.

Other participant responses followed:

> Man 2: monogamous marriage still preferable but this law would lead to a lot of confusion and discussions as a man is not bound to one wife.
>
> Man 3: Article Five is only an advice and not compulsory, the law says one thing but when it comes to society it doesn't work as there are different views and practices. It cannot work.
>
> Woman 1: Previous times when the man was very rich it may be OK, but now when they have five wives and thirty children, how are they going to maintain them? It is no longer OK. Women do not get sexual satisfaction when men have many wives and they may end up going outside for sex, such as happens in Zanzibar. [There is applause from the women participants]

44 countries surveyed. The Pew Global Attitudes Project, 4 October 2007, http://pewglobal.org/files/pdf/258.pdf.

175 LHRC Workshop on the Maputo Protocol, 9 February 2010.

176 Maputo Protocol, Article 6.

177 Section 10(2) of the Law of Marriage Act (1971) states that 'a marriage contracted in Tanganyika whether contracted before or after the commencement of this Act, shall':

(a) If contracted in Islamic form or according to rite recognised by customary law in Tanganyika, be presumed, unless the contrary is proved, to be polygamous or potentially polygamous: and

(b) In any other case, be presumed to be monogamous, unless the contrary is proved.

> Man 4: The vision of this article due to the presence of HIV/AIDS, at this time monogamy is more preferable to polygamy as it makes it easier to fight HIV/AIDS.

> Woman 2: Interpretation of the Koran to make sure that when there is a problem with the first wife a man cannot marry another, but often men marry without consent.

These comments provoked a further response from the first man:

> Man 1: It is not spreading HIV/AIDS in districts such as Mtwara and Zanzibar, but also other places like Makete have high HIV/AIDS rates and these areas are mainly Christian.

The LHRC officer stated that 'in coastal regions there is a lot of probate problems compared to other areas and this is caused by polygamous marriage'. The exchange, the longest witnessed in the workshops, was then brought to an end by a participating pastor, who said:

> Every religion has its rituals, the Bible says one thing and the Koran another. Interpretation of the Bible is that a man cannot give equal love to two or more wives. There must be variations of love. If we invite discussions from Muslims and Christians we will not reach a consensus.

Everyone remained quiet and there was no further discussion, then after a few seconds the LHRC officer reverted to reading out the Protocol.

A series of three LHRC meetings on land rights

The second set of observations was of a series of three meetings in May 2010, also organised by the LHRC, to follow up on training conducted on land rights six months previously for villages in the SULEDO Forest Land Reserve. The name SULEDO originates from the three wards that the forest crosses: Sunya, Laiseri and Olgira. The SULEDO Forest in Kiteto District is *miombo* woodland that has been under community management since the mid-1990s and is an officially gazetted Village Land Forest Reserve since 2007.[178] The village area is 268 000 ha out of which 167 000 ha is a Village Land Forest Reserve (VLFR). The population in the area is, according to the 2002 census, 24,189 consisting of the four ethnic groups Maasai, Wanguu, Wakamba and Wakaguru.[179]

178 Miombo woodland is 'a dry wooded area with sparse deciduous growth', www.thefreedictionary.com/Miombo+Woodland%2FSavanna.

179 ORGUT, 'Technical Assistance to the SULEDO Forest', 01/02/2008–30/06/2009, www.orgut.se/referenceinfo.aspx?rid=890; also see 'SULEDO Village Forest Land Reserve:

In 2001, The Land Act and The Village Land Act came into force.[180] These two new land laws call for rural land in Tanzania to be governed through a community-based land-tenure management system. Administration and management of land and resolution of conflicts are now the responsibility of the villages. These land laws require the establishment of a Village Land Adjudication Committee (VLAC) and a Village Land Council (VLC). The Land Management Programme (LAMP) has been running in the district since 1991 with the financial support of the Swedish International Development Cooperation Agency (SIDA), and working with other international organisations, namely ORGUT and the LHRC. Literature on LAMP specifically states that it:

> supports the district councils in their efforts to empower village communities to control and sustainably manage the land they use and to know their rights and obligations. It is often lack of knowledge of rights and obligations among local politicians and villagers that is the stumbling block in securing land rights. Lack of knowledge, coupled with the pressures of a growing population, migration, and different cultures vying for use of scarce land, create conflicts – sometimes violent conflicts.[181]

Part of this programme has involved 'training' over the years of Village Legal Workers (VLWs), volunteers from villages who 'travel around the villages to educate others in their community about the land laws, create greater awareness of land rights and help minimise land-related conflicts'.[182] VLWs are regarded as an essential aspect that contributes to the success of the programme by raising awareness in communities of the new land-management procedures and mechanisms for conflict resolution who over the years have been recruited, trained and monitored by the LHRC.

The three meetings on land rights were also arranged by the LHRC.[183] I had been told that the staff wanted to gather specific information about the interim six months since they last visited. This included the training that had been conducted by VLWs, who were like paralegals and volunteered in the community, the distribution of information about the new land laws and processes, and also how specific land issues had been handled by the VLCs. The meetings were organised directly with community members and seemed less formal in style than the Maputo Protocol workshops. Often community members had to be

Access to Land and Other Natural Resources for Improving People's Livelihoods', Third European Development Forum on Rural Development, presentation, 30 March 2011.

180 The Land Act (Cap 113), the Parliament of Tanzania, 1999 and the Village Land Act (Cap 114), the Parliament of Tanzania, 1999.

181 SIDA, 'Land Rights and Villagers: Experiences of Securing Access to Land', Lamp Booklet Series, www.orgut.se/files/lamp/lands.pdf (accessed 1 November 2012).

182 Ibid.

183 Workshops were conducted in the Kiteto District in the SULEDO forest in Olgira, Laiseri and Sunya villages on 4 and 5 May 2010.

gathered when we arrived and the meetings were held in the local village office. The meetings lasted between one and two hours, there were no allowances and no meals provided for participants. In all the meetings the LHRC officer repeated the same questions, asking for details about the nature and frequency of trainings, the number of people who had attended, and if the VLC had received complaints about land matters.

In most of the meetings it was apparent that there had been very little training conducted and participants wanted to explain the possible reasons this. For example, in Laiseri, the villagers had been preoccupied with cultivating the land between December and January, and then planting crops for the next year. In Sunya, the Chairman of the VLC explained that the community found it hard to organise training during periods of cultivation, and because they were faced with hunger, people had to work hard in order to find food when the rains did eventually arrive. Only after this time was it acceptable to conduct training, but even then people would often not attend meetings. In each case the LHRC officer stressed the importance of training the community and focused upon the process rather than the problems.

In another meeting in Olgira, a man explained how the VLW had conducted training on the new system of leadership and channels through which to solve disputes. He explained these were done twice with about 25 to 30 people for two hours in the afternoon. Another said that he had done training on land laws (*utarudu*), and after this meeting there was a Village Assembly where other people were trained, and then another meeting to ensure people had understood the meaning of the land laws and environmental conservation. After some discussion about the issues covered, the LHRC officer stated that while VLWs can make some contributions at a Village Assembly, it did 'not count towards training'. He then went on to clarify that in order to constitute training the VLWs must arrange with the Village Assembly to set aside two hours to teach people specifically on land issues. 'Meetings where land issues are raised are not trainings', he concluded.[184]

Following this comment, another man stated that while they knew the laws, they could not be expected to have training once and then become a teacher of laws. It was difficult, he continued, when VLWs received such short training and then were expected to deliver further training in the community. While the LHRC had previously given a one-day training course to VLWs that provided them with information on the new land laws and processes, the need for more training was consistently repeated.

It took time to reach these villages, although there was a constant sense of rushing both on the journeys between the workshops but sometimes also during the workshops, where the opportunity and space for prolonged discussion appeared to be limited.

184 Workshop in Laiseri village, 4 May 2010.

A three-day workshop for journalists on gender-based violence

The last set of observations related to a three-day workshop organised by the Women's Legal Aid Centre (WLAC) in March 2010 for a group of journalists on GBV. GBV continues to be a grave reality for many women in Tanzania. The findings of a report conducted by USAID Health Policy initiative in 2008 indicate that 'many forms of GBV, including intimate partner violence and rape, are seen as normal and accepted by both men and women'.[185] Women and girls are also frequently blamed for causing or provoking GBV. In part, due to blame and shame, women and girls rarely report GBV to authorities or seek other kinds of treatment and support. The report quotes a study conducted by the World Health Organization (WHO) in 2002 found that 41 per cent of ever-partnered women in Dar es Salaam, and 87 per cent in Mbeya District, had experienced physical or sexual violence at the hands of a partner at some point; 29 per cent of those had received injuries, and over a third of them had been injured in the last year. In both locations 15 per cent of the women reported that their first sexual experience had been forced.[186]

While the law imposes punishment for sexual violence in the Sexual Offence Special Provisions Act (1998), there are gaps that remain in the legal system. In particular, domestic violence is only minimally addressed in The Law of Marriage Act (1971).[187] Recent research carried out in Tanzania in 2009 found that most women are vulnerable to domestic violence due to lack of access to education and employment, in addition to their economic dependence on spouses.[188]

This workshop followed a similar training organised for the same group of journalists on the property rights of women and children in 2009. In the previous workshop the journalists made a resolution that they should play a role to educate society through newspapers and media in general, but outlined their need for further capacity building and training. This workshop was a response to this request and aimed at educating the journalists about GBV so that they had the knowledge and skills to enable them to educate society on the issues through media with the aim of bringing changes in society.

In addition to classroom-style teaching and discussions WLAC incorporated field visits into the workshop, which they claimed was to ensure 'the full participation of the journalists' in order to 'learn more about GBV'.[189] The workshop focus was upon the stories of individuals who had experienced and survived GBV. Its aim was to paint a broader interpretation of GBV than that

185 M. Betron, 'Gender-Based Violence in Tanzania: An Assessment of Policies, Services, and Promising Interventions', USAID Health Policy Initiative, 2008, www.mcdgc.go.tz/data/PNADN851.pdf.

186 E.G. Krug, L.L. Dahlberg et al. (eds), *World Report on Violence and Health*, WHO, Geneva, 2002.

187 Law of Marriage Act, No. 5 of 1971, the Parliament of Tanzania, 1971, http://polis.parliament.go.tz/PAMS/docs/5-1971.pdf (accessed 21 November 2012).

188 LHRC, Tanzania Human Rights Report 2009, Dar es Salaam, p. 82.

189 A three-day workshop for journalists on gender-based violence, WLAC, March 2010.

represented in the international or regional human rights instruments, and in particular CEDAW and the Maputo Protocol.

The final workshop for journalists on GBV was planned by WLAC but focused upon the stories of those individuals who had experienced and survived different forms of GBV.[190] In this workshop it was all women or young girls. There were 13 journalists participating in the workshops who had all been given leave from their newspapers or workplaces to attend. I understood that most were reporters for newspapers and the television.

The workshop had been organised over three days. The first two days of the workshop started as a plenary session at the WLAC offices in Dar es Salaam. These serve as both the office and a legal aid centre where the public can come and ask for legal advice. After the plenary the journalists were provided with breakfast. The group then broke into three and left in pre-ordered taxis for various field visits in the city. The choice of field visits included the head office of KIWOHEDE, an NGO which works with domestic workers and sex workers, a special centre for domestic workers, and one of the few crisis centres in Tanzania for victims of domestic violence. The third day was organised as a full-day workshop and was an opportunity to discuss the lessons learned from the visits.

At the beginning of the first day the 13 journalists sat around a large table in the WLAC conference room with the staff, while the Head of Department for Lobbying, Advocacy, Networking and Monitoring explained the nature of GBV, stressing that 'gender-based violence is the chaos that comes from unequal power relations between a man and a woman'.[191] The objective of the field visits was explained as a way of exposing the journalists to personal accounts of GBV, in order that they could gain a better insight of the suffering and experience, with a view to influencing and improving their future reporting on GBV. The joint session lasted no more than an hour.

I accompanied and observed the visits of six journalists to the centre for domestic workers and the crisis centre. In the first location, at the centre for the domestic workers, young girls had either escaped domestic slavery or were still working in homes. They had come to the centre either for safety and/or some basic education skills. In the room were approximately 25 girls, with an estimated wide age range of between ten and 20 years. The room was organised so that the girls were facing a line of the seated journalists, who had been accompanied by a staff member from WLAC, my interpreter and myself. The manager of the centre was present.

The girls were asked to share their stories with the journalists about their experiences, but I was not sure if this had been agreed in advance. Some told their experiences of being sent from the rural areas after their parents had died, and how some had been enticed into sex work or subjected to sexual abuse and

190 A three-day workshop for journalists on gender-based violence, 29–31 March 2010.
191 Ibid.

rape. None of these girls attended school, those that had attended were been forced to stop when they started domestic work. In the meeting the journalists sat opposite the girls, who recounted their experiences. While there was an opportunity to ask questions at the end, only one journalist took up this opportunity.

During the course of the visit many of the girls became upset and did not wish to share their experiences. In one instance when the room fell silent, the sole male journalist leaned forward on his chair, pointed to two girls directly in front of him, and told them to tell their stories; one reluctantly began to speak quietly while staring at her hands. 'Speak up', he told her twice, 'we can't hear you'. The girl did try to speak a bit louder but continued to look at her hands and was clearly upset. Only the other girls offered comfort. The journalists all left after an hour – it was lunchtime – and this brought the first day to a close. On the following day's visit to the crisis centre we arrived to find only the manager and no women in attendance, so the manager gave a short explanation to the journalists about the centre, towards the end, but before he had finished speaking, the journalists stood up to leave. They had not even introduced themselves. The WLAC staff member asked the journalists to sit down and introduce themselves, which they did, then left.

The third day was a group session to discuss the lessons learned from the field visits. It was held at a meeting room in the city library, and journalists and WLAC staff sat together around a large table. The staff explained to journalists that the purpose of the session was to discuss three things: first, the experience (*uzoefu*); second, what was learned (*tumejifunza*); and third, what the journalists would tell society (*tunaiambia nini jamii*). The journalists were then split into three groups according to the various field visits and engaged in group discussions which were reported to the other journalists and WLAC staff.

During this workshop some of the journalists had seemed overly concerned about the financial allowance that they were receiving for attending the workshop, complaining that it was not enough. It became clearer on the final day that some felt they were in fact doing *work* that was the responsibility of WLAC. Maybe I misconceived the interactions but a number of the journalists had appeared in a rush to leave the field visits as soon as possible, and appeared reluctant to engage in dialogue on any of the field visits. I am unsure whether any further preventative efforts could have been made by WLAC to limit any possible opportunities for abuse or disrespect in the field visits or guard against unequal relations of power. A lack of commitment to learning and hierarchies of power are arguably some of the challenges NGOs have when planning these types of HRE processes.

A common element linking all the workshops was their focus upon the transfer of information within the site of HRE practice. Each HRE process appeared to have been organised in order to either give or gather information, rather than a dialogic or research process based on the sharing and exchange of knowledge. This reinforces the idea that human rights are claims and demands which require the knowledge and skills of both the principles and processes attached. Only the

WLAC workshop seemed to start out with an alternative perception, which was challenged by a lack of engagement by participants. These workshops focused upon the local dissemination and communication of information and were often part of a broader HRE outreach strategy consisting of mass media campaigns for the broader dissemination of information through TV, radio or the print media. These raise clear questions about the exercise of power in the organisation of spaces and through discourse.

Evidence of alternative orientations

These individual workshops need to be analysed as part of the historical and socio-political context of HRE discourse in Tanzania, as well as, the interviewees' conceptions about human rights and HRE. Taken together they illustrate that the NGOs explicitly associated with HRE practice have tended to adopt a predominantly technical orientation towards HRE discourse which aligns itself to the international and regional human rights norms and standards and the transmission of those through workshops, rather than a critical or counter-hegemonic orientation that questions the institutional form of human rights and aim to rupture the dominant knowledge and structures that maintain inequality and injustice. Despite this, findings from the interviews do highlight a greater consciousness among NGO staff of this struggle than was evident in practice and it would appear that the conflict between ideas and interests embodied in the HRE discourse is quite complex. Nevertheless, there are certain structural forces embodied in the relationships between the global and the local, discussed in Chapter 7, that appear to drive a predominantly technical HRE discourse.

Because of its complex and contradictory nature of course there was evidence of discourses of resistance both in academic rhetoric and localised civil society action in Tanzania. I will briefly outline a few of these that are relevant to the research and that I came across during the fieldwork period.

Tanzania Gender Networking Programme (TGNP) and the Gender Festival 2009

TGNP was registered in 1993. It emerged from a series of workshops with women's organisations focusing upon gender relations and the place of women in Tanzania. Donor agencies had introduced Women-in-Development (WID) projects in response to the WID agenda, in conjunction with the UN Declaration of 1975–1985 as a Decade for Women, Peace, Equality and Development. However, there was concern that these were attempting to neutralise issues, moving women away from liberationist and emancipatory tendencies and the concerns of ordinary men and women. TGNP's mission was commitment to 'contributing to social transformation leading to the creation of a vibrant Tanzanian society . . . promote gender equality and social equity and through empowerment of women and other marginalised sections of the community'.[192] It describes its main approach and methodology as being grounded in participatory methods where 'women and men assessed oppressive and exploitative situations, analysed their causes and acted to overcome them'.[193] One of the original founding members and a leader of the TNGP is Majorie Mbilinyi. Born in the USA, she moved to Tanzania in 1967 and became actively involved in the struggle for socialism and self-reliance and challenged patriarchy in society. Mbilinyi's ideas and approach are still firmly rooted in the original struggle and she continues to argue that the major issues are 'the exploitative and oppressive structures and relations of production and reproduction, which are overdetermined by the further strengthening of imperialist relations'.[194] Mbilinyi advocates group-centred and people-centred leadership, which are defined by the collective and where decisions are made as a collective through participatory dialogue and debate. IT should also encompass ongoing learning where the dynamics 'allow for continual reflection, criticism, self-criticism and counter-criticism'. She argues that people-centred leadership can be promoted through transformative pedagogy 'whereby each student feels compelled to do their best for the common good as well as for their own individual achievement. This, Mbilinyi claims, takes place through animation, which TNGP and a number of organisations in Tanzania, she states, have adopted. Animation is where the role of the facilitator is to 'creatively listen and learn from the oppressed, exploited groups with whom they work and to create an interactive process of experiential learning whereby people assess their situation, analyse the basic causes and act to change it'.[195] In 1996 TGNP organised the first Gender Festival (GF) which was aimed at facilitating the networking of individuals and focused upon Gender, Education, Health and Land. It was preceded by workshops on Gender Education which were attended by 91 individuals from the media and workers from other fields. TGNP became part of various coalitions and networks (Gender Land Taskforce, National Land Forum) in Tanzania, which opposed government efforts to push through liberal land reform. They took on the task of raising awareness and 'imparting analytical gender skills to women and men parliamentarians in understanding the gender impact of land reform and to articulate the issues of concern to the majority of women and the poor'.[196] The TGNP has continued to organise bi-annual Gender Festivals, each of which deal with an issue that affects marginalised men and

192 Chachage S.L. & Mbilinyi M, Introduction, in Chachage S.L. & Mbilinyi M (eds), *Against Neo-Liberalism: Gender, Democracy and Development*, Tanzania Gender Networking Programme & E&D Publishers: Dar es Salaam, 2003, p. 9.

193 Ibid.

194 Mbilinyi M, 'Reflecting with Nyerere on People-Centred Leadership', in, Chachage C & Cassam A, *Africa's Liberation: The Legacy of Nyerere*, Pambazuka Press: Kampala, 2010, pp. 77–92, p. 78.

195 Ibid., p. 88.

196 Ibid., p. 10.

women. Another activity is their weekly Gender and Development Seminar series which involve presentation about particular issue and concerns.

During September 2009 I attended the Gender Festival held at the TGNP headquarters in Dar es Salaam. The theme was 'Making Resources Work for Marginalized Women: Economic Justice and Livelihoods of Marginalized Women in the Context of the Global Economic Crisis and the Scramble for African Resources'. This was at the initial stages of my research when I was still trying to gather information about organisations and had no interpreter; therefore I have not analysed the GF in detail but discuss it in light of the history and preceding discussion about TGNP. What it shows is an alternative possibly critical or counter-hegemonic orientation in HRE – despite not being called this. This Gender Festival was organised jointly between the TGNP and Tanzanian and the Feminist Activist Coalition (FemAct). It was described on the website as:

> an open forum for likeminded individuals and organisations to come together to share experiences and knowledge, to celebrate achievements and assess challenges ahead, to strengthen networking and coalition-building, to build capacity and to contribute to public debate and plan collectively for social change from a feminist perspective.[197]

This Gender Festival provided the opportunity for more than two thousand activists to come together in one space for 'analysis, research, activism, capacity, development, strategic planning and art'.[198] The plenary paper opens with a quote from Nyerere:

> Our people's demand for independence, however, derived its major strength from their demand for human dignity and freedom. They wanted to govern themselves, in their own interests . . . on balance, it cannot be said that we have fulfilled our people's hopes for democracy and Human Rights.[199]

The paper then begins with a clear tone of resistance:

> Who are we? Who am I? How do we position ourselves in this moment of his/her story, when Africa is undergoing another 'scramble for Africa,

197 Tanzania Gender Networking Programme Gender Festival 2011, Gender, Democracy and Development: Land, Labour & Livelihoods! Guidelines and Concept Note for Performances and Presentations, Http://www.tgnp. org/images/stories/2011/Gender%20Festival%202011%20presentation%20guidelines%20%20concept%20note.pdf (accessed 20 May 2011).

198 Ibid.

199 Mwalimu Julius K. Nyerere, Nigerian Institute of International Affairs, 1986, in Mbilinyi M, 'Tanzania Gender Networking Programme: Economic Justice and Livelihoods of Marginalized Women in the Context of the Global Economic Crisis and the Scramble for African Resources', Plenary Paper for Gender Festival 2009, 9 September 2009.

heightened by the global fiscal/economic crisis of 2008/9? The big powers competing among themselves for natural resources and military/political hegemony. With unheard violence against women and children. There is no neutrality here, no middle ground.'

What I observed at the Gender Festival was that it was clearly an opportunity of interaction and spaces were made available for discussion, dialogue and for ordinary people to have a voice. At this meeting I observed one particular staff member from WLAC. She was giving a presentation on gender-based violence in a similar format to the WLAC workshop I later observed for journalists. It focused upon the stories from the people who had experienced GBV, and individuals were either telling their stories themselves or having them recounted by WLAC. At one point the WLAC officer was telling observers the story of a woman who was sitting next to her, how she had been beaten on several occasions by her husband, which had nearly killed her. After explaining the woman's experience, she asked her to stand up. The lawyer moved towards the woman and lifted her headscarf to expose to the *audience* a very large scar on her head from injuries she had sustained as a result of the beatings. While this was an open venue for the general public the format remained the same and appeared to focus upon the experiences of the women who had experienced GBV first and the contents of the law second.

There were a number of other opportunities for people to share their stories and individuals were given the chance to speak in front of the hundreds of participants, who included international representatives, as well as Tanzanian NGOs and communities. I observed a number of these including an occasion when a man stood up with a microphone and explained that he was homosexual and that he worked as a sex worker. This was a subject I had not heard raised or discussed in public.

The TGNP and their activities clearly demonstrate an alternative critical and, at times, radical approach to awareness and *education* that is grounded in notions of praxis, critique and common sense. Another possible example of a critical or counter-hegemonic orientation to HRE was a protest by a group of pastoral women in April 2010 and discussed in the next section.

A public protest for livelihood rights by Maasai women in Tanzania, April 2010

This book was introduced with a story of the mass protest on 6 April 2010 of Maasai women from all over the region who had gathered together in order to protest against the forced eviction.[200] In 1992, the government of Tanzania is alleged to have secretly leased over 4,000 square kilometres of the Loliondo Game Controlled Area in the Ngorogoro District to a businessman from the United Arab Emirates for hunting purposes. It has been reported that the boundaries of

200 See Chapter 1: Introduction.

this land have constantly been expanded and, as a result, the Maasai people of the region have constantly suffered displacement.[201] It has led to ongoing conflict and violence.

On 29 May 2010 I attended a breakfast meeting of NGOs and stakeholders at the Policy Forum in Dar es Salaam. I had been invited by a previously interviewed Tanzanian consultant. At this meeting a representative of Oxfam Ireland explained the situation and how civil society space in Tanzania appeared to be shrinking, asking participants how civil society should respond. The representative argued that civil society should have the space to challenge, disagree and defend their rights, and argued that NGOs had a responsibility to protect. The talk left participants with a question: what are the opportunities to push out civil society space and how do we do this?[202]

So while spaces in Tanzania do open up alternative discourses of HRE that may not necessarily be labelled as such. On the periphery of the predominant human rights and HRE discourses there are alternatives. For example, there has been a call more recently, led by some of the more critical intellectuals at the University of Dar es Salaam, for a return to the values that were embedded in the Arusha Declaration of 1967, which set out the political vision for Tanzania based upon ideas of socialism.[203] Others, in addition to Issa Shivji and Marjorie Mbilinyi, are engaging in critique using creative and alternative modes of organisation, such as Helen Kijo-Bisimba, Rakash Ranjani and Chambi Chachage, to name only a few who have a more public profile in Tanzania. The above discussion shows, however, that ordinary people who know their rights are being violated organise themselves and engage in HRE in spontaneous and creative ways as acts of resistance.

In spite of this broader context, in Tanzania I was consistently advised to approach legal organisations in order to examine HRE work, the LHRC and WLAC in particular. Two staff from a national well-established NGO that advocates the right to education stated their organisation did not conduct HRE specifically, so suggested I contact the LHRC. Others indicated that it was these NGOs which conducted HRE with communities and explained how they worked with community-based paralegals. One consequence of this association between legal organisations and HRE was that it was viewed as something technical and specialised for an 'educated elite', and thus created a hierarchical structure on the basis of expertise that ran from the lawyers through paralegals and into communities. Another consequence was that the HRE actors inadvertently adopted the role of translators, where the task was to make the various forms of international, regional and national texts on human rights understandable for the majority of the Tanzanian population.

201 Global Non-Violent Action Database, 'Maasai Women Protest Land Seizure in Tanzania, 2009', see http://nvdatabase.swarthmore.edu/content/maasai-women-protest-land-seizure-tanzania-2009 (accessed 23 March 2012).

202 Notes taken at the Policy Forum Breakfast Meeting, 29 May 2010.

203 At the Julius Nyerere International Festival Week at the University of Dar es Salaam (2009) that called for the re-appropriation of the values in the Arusha Declaration 1967, see, http://udadisi.blogspot.co.uk/2009/03/julius-nyerere-intellectual-festival.html

Conclusion

Chapter 2 demonstrated that human rights are both plural and complex concepts. This case study does indicate that the same complexity among different discourses does exist to some extent in the local context of Tanzania. However, in terms of NGOs specifically identified and engaged in HRE practice in community-based settings, there does seem to be a prevailing conception of human rights as predetermined facts, which are entrenched into the international and regional human rights instruments. Because these NGOs predominantly set off with this assumption their task implicitly becomes twofold. First, the task is to raise awareness of the content and principles of human rights as predetermined facts, and second, they aim to make human rights relevant and acceptable in the local context. The dichotomy of human rights discourse that is evident in the historical context has been shaped by external and internal power relations where the HRE discourse is controlled, not only though global institutions and processes of distribution, but also because the NGOs identified themselves with the global human rights discourse, rather than the Tanzanian one. What this chapter has shown is how NGOs as intermediaries can support and perpetuate the operation of the global HRE framework.

Given that knowledge of human rights often relies upon either international texts or national legislation, the implementation of new laws will often depend not only upon the support and activism of the NGOs but also the volunteers, who are the direct means through which the national NGOs often reach the communities. One advantage of working with volunteers is that they are constantly engaged and have an understanding of the issues that the communities face. However, this then means that the national organisations, which spend time developing the strategies, can risk becoming more detached from these issues and the people concerned with and affected by them. It is arguable that unless the volunteers are directly involved at the planning stage of the strategy there is the danger there being of a gap between the community issues and the organisational strategy.

Evidence of this gap between the human rights reality and human rights rhetoric did emerge in the course of the workshops. The language of the Maputo Protocol did not seem to adequately address the challenges that were raised in the workshops by the participants. In the land rights meetings, there seemed to be a lack of understanding of the daily challenges faced by local villages in providing food, and yet high expectations on the volunteers to engage community members and train them on the new laws and regulations. And in the WLAC workshop the girls were used to elevate the understanding of the journalists but there were implicit criteria for interaction, and the girls and journalists did not engage as equals.

Despite the instances when a specific HRE process could have been altered to ensure greater interaction and understanding, there appeared to be pre-existing power hierarchies, logistical and financial limitations that potentially restricted the capacity of NGOs to plan pedagogical strategies entailing in-depth analysis, engagement and learning with communities.

6 The dominant discourse

Human rights education as cultural translation

This chapter is a reflection and analysis of the evidence to see how it relates to the four interpretative orientations in HRE discourse: technical, interpretative, critical and counter-hegemonic. Is HRE discourse predominantly a fair reflection of the diversity of conceptions and approaches, or is it principally shaped by one or two orientations? Ultimately, what there appears to be is a predominant leaning towards a technical HRE discourse. Furthermore, this seems to rely upon the three-way division between the production, distribution and consumption of the discourse, which can operate as a form of control to manage dissent and resistance by directing it through state-sponsored mechanisms or institutions.

The chapter is divided into three sections. The first section draws upon the findings from Chapter 3, which mapped out the *production* of a global discourse of HRE; it analyses the way HRE discourse was increasingly institutionalised, via the systematic formation of an HRE concept and discourse, which was confined within the remit of the United Nations apparatus. This analysis shows how HRE evolved from disparate discussions and activities, outside the global structures, into an increasingly centralised and codified form. What then appears today as global HRE discourse is arguably a result of organised systems, which focused upon the international texts, language, practice and mechanisms of human rights. It is this discourse that is arguably used to regulate and control the choices and possibilities, action and agency of society.

The second section analyses the *distribution* of HRE discourse through NGOs between the global and the local, as well as institutions and society. It shows how, despite the plausible plural orientations presented in Chapter 2, a technical orientation has been able to thrive and dominate in contemporary HRE discourse. This, arguably, is primarily because of the apparent reluctance of HRE actors to address the complex and plural nature of human rights, which means they view human rights as facts, but often express this in either one of two ways: first, as inherent and universal rights where they speak about notions of universal dignity, justice and equality, but more often by reference to the principles outlined in international texts.

References to the Conventions and related instruments provide a unified and definitive perspective of human rights, which then avoids having to grapple with the real inconsistencies in human rights conceptions. In addition, this section shows that because of a predominantly technical conception, a significant concern is how to make international human rights principles contextually relevant, meaningful and accepted. The scholarly accounts of practice in Chapter 4 and the case study in Chapter 5 have shown how this was done principally through reflective inquiry. While processes of reflective inquiry appear to encourage participation and inclusivity, and give personal meaning to human rights, it can mask the way in which these types of processes are used to frame international human rights in ways that are contextually relevant through what I call *cultural translation*.

The third section is an analysis of the *consumption* of HRE discourse and how HRE processes in the research seemed to target particular social issues and groups, and how these choices involved the exercise of power over agendas and agency. In accepting the international discourse of human rights, HRE actors made certain assumptions about the production of knowledge: who has it, and who does not. This might explain why HRE processes are often targeted at sections of society with the least power. The findings from previous chapters illustrate that while HRE was viewed as a means of empowerment, this generally involved bringing people into the international discursive framework of human rights as 'human rights subjects'. Encouraging the articulation of experiences and suffering as expressions of human rights means they become viewed as demands and claims. As a result they are often channelled through state or inter-state sponsored mechanisms, such as the courts, government departments or the UN framework. In this way, HRE actors sometimes unconsciously exercise power and control through their conceptions and approach in HRE, which incidentally regulate the actions attached to individual and collective agency.

The production, distribution and consumption processes of HRE discourse have the capacity to entrench a technical orientation of HRE deep into the social fabric, which means that it then becomes difficult to see or go beyond this framework as a way of thinking about and addressing social experiences, issues and needs. This happens partly because of a generally unquestioning and uncritical conception and approach in HRE, which rarely acknowledges or gives precedence to the diversity of human rights.

The production of HRE discourse

Chapter 2 shows not only how theoretically HRE discourse consists of a diverse range of conceptions and approaches, but also how it can nevertheless plausibly be organised into an interpretative framework of four discursive orientations: technical, interpretative, critical and counter-hegemonic. It illustrates the way that approaches to HRE are intimately connected to conceptions of human rights, and how any one particular HRE orientation represents a unique set of interests that determines how we reflect on the world and make sense of our experiences within it.

According to this framework, if an individual sees human rights as facts, they will most likely prioritise the transmission of the content of human rights through

HRE processes that make them understandable and relevant. Viewed as interpretations, an individual will tend to focus upon the meaning-making and consensus-building processes that surround HRE, establishing a space where different individuals or groups of people could share their conceptions to deliberate and agree on common understandings either in context or universally. If human rights are seen as struggles, the priority of an HRE process will be the way it can be used to highlight injustice, and provide a forum for the many different voices of human rights experience and struggle, but without needing to reach agreement about common understandings. This distinguishes it from the former approach. Finally, if human rights are seen as nothing more than socio-historical constructions, an approach will be to critique the history and ideology of HRE as a way of understanding and showing how human rights have been socially and politically constructed, and the way that power has been exercised to serve particular interests.

The plurality of these plausible (and adopted) perspectives makes HRE difficult to regulate or manage on a global scale. An effective global system of governance relies upon universal agreement about the values and principles that shape international culture, values and beliefs. It explains why there has been such dedicated effort by the UN to constructing a global human rights discourse and framework. In what way, then, has HRE contributed to the construction of a singular global discursive orientation?

Chapter 3 showed that after 1945 there were few efforts to directly link concepts of human rights and education, and little if no institutional control over the content or process of educating in human rights. This lack of prescription allowed space for creativity, as well as the opportunity to broaden the scope of issues considered relevant. It was during this period that efforts were made by UNESCO to link education explicitly to concepts of human rights through various initiatives.

In the next few decades the relationship between human rights and education appears to have developed in a disorganised and sporadic fashion. This was until the 'Recommendation Concerning Education and International Understanding, Co-operation and Peace and Education relating to Human Rights and Fundamental Freedoms' in 1974. Even then there were no particular methodological guidelines at this stage, which meant that there was little, if any, institutional control or regulation over the political nature of the discourse that could emerge. This all came in the midst of the Cold War, when the idea of collective critique could have been a challenge to the capitalist ideological order.

However, the post-1994 period signified an important shift, when the term 'human rights education' emerged as a concept in itself, and as a specific programme that was removed from UNESCO and placed under the mandate of the OHCHR. The focus of HRE discourse shifted from issues on the world stage to human rights themselves, and HRE was explicitly linked to the aims of peace, democracy, development and social justice as they were stipulated by the UDHR. While the potential remit was broad, all the issues were clearly situated within the

UN framework: its role, the instruments and the institutions. HRE was being drawn further into the global political structures and policy-making framework.

The chronology in Chapter 3 showed the purpose of HRE was clearly stipulated in the Programme of Action for the UN Decade for HRE (1994–2004).[1] This stated that HRE was 'training, dissemination and information efforts aimed at building a universal culture of human rights through the imparting of knowledge and skills and the moulding of attitudes', and was firmly rooted in the provisions of the international human rights instruments.[2] The UN effectively centralised the production of HRE discourse, and by doing so was not only able to control its formation by focusing the language of HRE upon the definitions outlined in international instruments. It could also regulate the operation of the discourse by prescribing how human rights should be disseminated. The UN used its resources and influence, in order to build an HRE framework that could socialise international human rights further than national governments, and penetrate into society, to communities and individuals. Controlling the production and distribution of HRE discourse arguably enabled the UN to regulate and direct how human rights were understood and adopted in the language and action of individuals and communities.

The idea that institutions control the formation of discourse in order to regulate society was suggested by Michel Foucault, who claimed that discourse was 'a set of linguistic, polemic and strategic facts designed to produce and sustain an economy of truth'.[3] As a set of historically, socially and institutionally specific structure of statements, terms, categories and beliefs, discourse is the site where meanings are contested and power relations determined. It is the ability to control knowledge and meaning through disciplinary and professional institutions, as well as in social relations, that can illuminate the exercise of power in society.[4]

The way that power produces knowledge is therefore critical to understanding the formation of HRE discourse and, as Chapter 2 showed, the ways that in HRE discourse, technical, interpretative, critical and counter-hegemonic orientations coexist. Each and all occupy the HRE space at any one time, and provide the basis for an endless opposition between legitimacy and illegitimacy, struggle and submission.

HRE discourse is a central part of the struggle for knowledge, through which multiple relations of power function. Harnessing that power to serve particular

1 UN General Assembly (1996) *Plan of Action for the United Nations Decade for Human Rights Education, 1995–2004: Human rights education – lessons for life* (Appendix), in Human Rights Questions: Human Rights Questions, Including Alternative Approaches for Improving the Effective Enjoyment of Human Rights and Fundamental Freedoms, A/51/506/add.1 (12 December 1996).

2 Ibid., Appendix, para. 2.

3 M. Foucault, 'Truth and Juridical Forms', in M. Foucault, *Essential Works of Michel Foucault, 1954–1984, Vol. 3: Power*, ed. J.D. Faubion, Penguin, London, 1994, p. 3.

4 M. Marchand and J. Parpart, *Feminism/Postmodern Development*, Routledge, London, 1995, p. 3.

interests therefore becomes a significant, if not a predominant, role of discourse working within that space. In order to function effectively power relies upon an international discourse of human rights being accumulated, put into circulation and set to work.[5]

The construction of a global HRE discourse has therefore relied upon the subjugation of particular types of knowledge. This has occurred in two ways. The first has been by the institutionalisation and formalisation of HRE, so that historical knowledges are buried or masked. Chapter 3 showed that the idea of HRE appeared to surface with, and as part of, the Charter of the United Nations in 1945, wiping out any pre-existing knowledge, language and approaches to HRE. These were buried beneath the institutional UN structures and the systematic formation of a global HRE discourse.[6] Second, it occurred by subjugating a whole range of knowledges that were discounted or disqualified as non-conceptual or insufficiently elaborate to have a place; these were knowledges considered hierarchically naive or inferior; usually because they were judged below the level of scholarship or objectivity.[7] The way scholarly accounts of practice in Chapter 4 and the case study discussed in Chapter 5 appear to prioritise the language of international human rights norms and standards is evidence of this. Together, these processes of subjugation have enabled the construction and maintenance of a particular institutionalised form of HRE discourse.

But how have HRE actors responded to this? The next section discusses whether they have been approaching HRE, as required by the UN texts on HRE, by imparting knowledge and skills and moulding attitudes in a way which furthers a global human rights culture, or whether they have rejected the dominant technical orientation in favour of any one of the alternative theoretical orientations outlined in Chapter 2: interpretative, critical or counter-hegemonic.

The distribution of HRE discourse

HRE discourse appears on the surface to include reflective inquiry and deliberation in practice. This encourages participants to share experiences, problems and needs with each other and with the organisers. In this sense a belief by some that these processes value and validate the experiences and ideas of the people involved are justified. As a matter of practice, participants in HRE processes are often asked

5 M. Foucault, *Society Must Be Defended: Lectures at the Collège de France 1975–76*, Picador, New York, 2003, p. 24.

6 Ibid. In some ways I recognise that I am making the same error by tracking the development of a dominant global HRE discourse post-1948, but in developing a critique of this in particular it was an important starting point.

7 Ibid., pp. 7–8; by 'true' I take this to mean the same as Foucault, in which a particular phenomenon, in this case human rights, which appears and is accepted as fact and something beyond argument or questioning, rather than something that is socially or politically constructed and open to debate.

for their views on the issues being discussed and, in some cases, contribute to the agenda or organisation of the process itself.

While the language describing HRE practice appears to dismiss a didactic and one-way educational approach (banking style), the evidence suggests that it has not disappeared completely. Here, the existence of human rights tends not to be questioned and, as such, HRE processes are often preceded by a preconception of human rights as facts. There is frequent reference to international and regional human rights standards or to national laws in the individual explanations of HRE. Even when there are apparent attempts in the scholarly accounts to integrate participant ideas, interpretations or critiques into the process, the discourse of human rights, especially that of international human rights standards, is emphasised in the language and practice of HRE. Scholarship on human rights practice has a tendency to appear uncritical and unquestioning of the theoretical and philosophical underpinnings of HRE. Instead, readers are told the ways that communities and individuals were made aware of the content of international instruments, such as CEDAW or the CRC, or how they learn to reconceptualise their experiences in terms of the human rights language and provisions. The Tanzanian case study supports this and, while some interviewees described how they have tried to make processes participatory and build from individual experiences, they still appear to hold a preconceived notion of human rights as facts. These processes frequently encouraged participants to share their experiences in order to determine their needs and the context, rather than as a way of determining the meaning of human right themselves.

The apparent unquestioning of international human rights principles and language is generally coupled with limited efforts to engage in HRE practice in analytical or critical ways. There is very little evidence both in the scholarly accounts and observations of practice to suggest that the pluralistic and problematic nature of human rights is acknowledged or addressed. Instead, NGOs and individuals appear to be more concerned with the design and implementation of participatory *methods* and resources. One consequence of this is that HRE discourse involves processes of, what is termed here as, *cultural translation*.

Cultural translation

Cultural translation, as understood here, is one part of a broader process of transplantation of programmes and ideas from one context to another. It relies upon an 'elite' network of intermediaries who have a critical role in the 'emergence of a local rights consciousness amongst local communities and greater awareness of national and local issues amongst global activists'.[8] Cultural translation, as applied in HRE, has three parts. The first, and most important,

8 Consisting of politicians, human rights lawyers, activists, movement leaders, social workers and academics; see S.E. Merry, *Human Rights and Gender Violence: Translating International Law into Local Justice*, University of Chicago Press, Chicago, 2007, p. 134.

involves *framing*, through the construction of an interpretative package surrounding the core idea of human rights. The second involves adapting HRE to the structural conditions in the local context. The third part involves redefining the target population in terms of the context.

Framing and HRE discourse

As the first part of this definition of cultural translation, 'frames' are taken to consist of images, symbols and stories that draw upon specific local cultural narratives and conceptions. Frames are 'ways of packaging and presenting ideas that generate shared beliefs, motivate collective action, and define appropriate strategies of action'.[9] They can have powerful effects on the way situations are understood and on the tactics their supporters employ.[10] According to some social movement theorists framing is essential to mobilise consensus prior to collective action and necessary in order to orient and sustain this action.[11]

Frames help to render an event or issue meaningful, and function to organise experience and guide action. Sally Engle Merry claims that unwillingness on the part of the community to accept human rights is a problem of the resonance of a frame, rather than any fundamental problem with human rights itself. The resonance of any frame in any particular setting is claimed to be 'affected by its salience to targets of mobilization', and dependent on three factors.[12]

First is how central or essential the beliefs, values and ideas within the HRE frame are to the lives of the local population. Second is whether the frames are relevant to the personal, everyday experiences of the local population, or they are too abstract and distant to make them meaningful. Third is the extent to which the frame resonates with the local population's cultural narrative. In essence, then, resonance seems to be the idea that the more persuasive the methods of framing, the more palatable the idea.

Constructing a resonant frame as part of HRE therefore involves using symbols and discourse that are familiar to a particular target population. In which ways, then, is the HRE frame made resonant in local communities? Answering this requires identifying the different ways that the beliefs, values or ideas of the HRE frame are made central to the lives of communities, relevant and meaningful to personal and everyday experiences, and culturally resonant.

While framing of human rights can take place through a range of techniques, the scholarship on HRE practice illustrates that in many instances personal

9 Ibid., p. 136.

10 S. Khagram, J.V. Riker and K. Sikkink (eds), *Restructuring World Politics: Transnational Social Movements, Networks and Norms*, University of Minnesota Press, Minneapolis, 2002, pp. 12–13.

11 It originates from social movement theory in which social movement organisations (SMOs) are viewed as strategic creators of frames.

12 R.D. Benford and D.A. Snow, 'Framing Processes and Social Movements: An Overview and Assessment', *Annual Review of Sociology*, 26, 2000, p. 621.

experience is integrated into HRE processes. This is done, for example, by drawing on the life experiences of Khmer women in Cambodia,[13] the struggles of working and street children in Latin America[14] and the issues faced by a rural Zulu community in South Africa.[15] In these cases, human rights are introduced at a later stage of the process by HRE actors, either by showing how specific principles, instruments or laws, such as CEDAW, the CRC or the UDHR, could be used to address such issues, or by introducing the idea and language of human rights as a means through which participants could reconceptualise and frame their experiences. The objective, as expressed by some scholars, is to articulate international human rights instruments in a way that draws upon 'life experiences'[16] or to 'find relevance in cultures where these values are viewed as contradictory',[17] or 'simply to have human rights become a new metaphor reshaping' lives.[18]

International human rights instruments have also been re-created and presented in ways that make them more relevant and attractive to particular contexts. The most obvious way of doing this way to translate them into local languages; however, efforts often go further, such as the production of an image by a Cambodian artist being used on copies of the UDHR and other human rights instruments – in this way the indigenous image arguably became a symbol of human rights in Cambodia, rather than anything international. Other scholars describe how they produced special curriculums, or simplified versions of the UDHR so rural communities would understand it. It is through these types of techniques that those facilitating the HRE hope that human rights become culturally resonant.

A different approach is to introduce human rights standards first and then generate discussion with participants about how these standards are either present or lacking within that local context. In the case study there were several workshops where articles of the Maputo Protocol and the Tanzanian land laws were used to generate discussion about community experiences or issues. Participants do ask for clarification from the NGO staff about how the instruments or laws would address these particular issues, such as a widow's inheritance, gender-based

13 Chapter 4; see D Hicks's account of women in Cambodia in 'Conflict Resolution and Human Rights Education: Broadening the Agenda', in G.J. Andreopoulos and R.P. Claude (eds), *Human Rights Education for the 21st Century*, University of Pennsylvania Press, Philadelphia, 1992.

14 Chapter 4; see T. Holland's account of children in Latin America in 'Human Rights Education for Street and Working Children: Principles and Practice', *Human Rights Quarterly*, 20(1) 1998.

15 Chapter 4; see E. O'Brien's account of community HRE in South Africa in 'Community Education for Law, Democracy, and Human Rights', in Andreopoulos and Claude (eds), *Human Rights Education for the Twenty-First Century*.

16 Chapter 4, p. 79; see Hicks, 'Conflict Resolution and Human Rights Education', p. 82.

17 Felisa Tibbetts, HREA community listserve (hr-education@lists.org), as was highlighted in an online conversation in June 2011.

18 Holland, 'Human Rights Education for Street and Working Children', p. 181.

violence or land grabbing.[19] However, this approach is not as evident in the practical HRE scholarship, where HRE actors seem to favour the former approach and begin by discussing participants experiences. Nonetheless, examples of HRE discourse in both the scholarship and fieldwork, illustrate how effort is taken to establish a relationship between the daily lives and experiences of the population and the global human rights standards. It is arguable that in these ways human rights are made relevant and resonant in the local context.

Undoubtedly, the concept of framing and resonance in HRE is still problematic. This is because framing human rights can sometimes have the effect of obscuring how power relations shape the dominant discourse and affect the orientation of action and the use of speech.[20] Myra Marx Ferree suggests that framing channels 'what challengers will attempt to say and how they say it, as well as affecting how they are heard'.[21] In this sense the process of sharing personal stories or experiences is one particular method that can concentrate the power inequalities, and means that, unless it is carefully planned and implemented, it is open to possible abuse and misinterpretation.

This can be a particular problem where there is an evident lack of understanding or empathy between the story teller and the listener. This is apparent in the workshop for journalists in Tanzania with the interaction between the domestic workers and the journalists.[22] Observations led to a presumption that the unequal footing on which the girls, as storytellers, and the journalists, as listeners, entered the process in the first place undermined the girls' suffering and experiences. The girls become objects of information, in the sense that what they had to offer were personal accounts of human rights abuse. Their experiences are viewed as only one part of a broader HRE process, in which they play a minor part in the learning and action planning for the journalists and NGOs. In this sense they are not acknowledged as important and their knowledge not taken seriously. Instead, the journalists' learning appears more important. This might be because their role is to interpret, translate and communicate the girl's personal experiences and stories to a wider audience through the media. However, the journalists do not appear to display any significant level of engagement or empathy, which has the impact of a general sense of disinterest throughout the process.

In another meeting on land rights, one participant tries to explain the struggles faced by the community in finding food. It is a point apparently dismissed by the NGO staff member, who reverts to talking about training and processes.[23] In this

19 Chapter 6, Section 6.4.1. Observations from the Workshops.

20 M.M. Ferree, 'Resonance and Radicalism: Framing in the Abortion Debates of the United States and Germany, *American Journal of Sociology*, 109(2), 2003, p. 305.

21 M.W. Steinberg, 'The Talk and Back Talk of Collective Action: A Dialogic Analysis of Repertoires of Discourse among Nineteenth Century English Cotton Spinners, American Journal of Sociology, 15(3), 1999, pp. 740–741; and Ferree, 'Resonance and Radicalism', p. 305.

22 Chapter 6, Section 6.4.1.(C) WLAC Workshop for Journalists on GBV, pp. 225–226.

23 Chapter 5, LHRC series of meetings on land rights.

sense, local knowledge seems to have been more of a means to an end, a way of explaining the needs and issues human rights can resolve, rather than an explanation of human rights.

In addition, it is questionable whether a technical HRE frame can in fact be culturally resonant. Resistance can arise at local level when international and regional human rights standards were seen to conflict with local beliefs and culture. This is apparent when issues such as female genital mutilation and polygamy are discussed in some Tanzanian workshops, but also when those issues that touch upon patriarchal societal structures, such as the inheritance of property by women and ownership of land are raised, the men participating in the workshops appear to become outspoken and sometimes defensive.[24]

These have been issues at the forefront of activist lobbying and demands for changes in the law over a number of years. Although changes have recently been made through the Tanzanian land laws providing women the legal right to own land, it appeared from the workshops still to be challenged by some men.[25] The provisions of the Maputo Protocol support both land and inheritance rights of women.[26] On one level, then, there had been changes in the law; however, these changes are, as a consequence, likely to have an impact upon entrenched community and family structures, thereby provoking some resistance. One of the justifications therefore for continued community-based education processes is that raising awareness of legal rights can lead to social change through increased demands and claims. However, a technical approach to HRE with a purpose of raising awareness of legal rights does not address the historical, systemic or root causes that underlie the patriarchal structures or inequalities in wealth, so arguably leaves them unchallenged and intact.

This level of resistance is not as apparent in the practical HRE scholarship. This is possibly because the individuals writing the accounts are all proponents of HRE, but the critical accounts do discuss the potential resistance to the imposition of knowledge of human rights, especially if a one-way information transfer is employed.[27]

Awareness-raising in HRE is often justified by a common view that human rights and HRE are technical and specialised, and there is often an assumption that in their original declaratory form international human rights texts are too complex for the ordinary person to understand. This also reinforces the argument for HRE processes to involve cultural translation. A second justification for cultural translation is the need to (re)frame the stories of personal experience and suffering of individuals and groups in the language and terminology of international human rights norms and standards. Doing this means they can then be voiced and

24 Chapter 5, LHRC series of workshops on the Maputo Protocol.
25 Ibid.
26 Maputo Protocol.
27 Chapter 4, Critical Scholarship.

acted upon as demands and claims. Accounts of HRE practice describe how women are encouraged to see their needs and problems as rights under CEDAW, children to reframe their ideas in terms of the language of human rights, and rural communities to see their problems as human rights and take action in the form of legal demands and claims.[28]

Experiences and the knowledge of individuals and groups are often used to provide insight into contextual nature of the problems and issues they faced. This appears to be so external professionals can design training packages reframing the community issues in terms of human rights, then make and collate materials and resources to support the HRE activities. The claim that whole sections of society have little knowledge about human rights is further highlighted in the way that simplified versions of human rights texts are produced and presented in pre-packaged educational materials, which emphasise the purpose of making global norms relevant in the local context. Individual and group life experiences are used as a means through which to interpret human rights principles, to make them relevant and contextual; they are not seen as indicative of human rights narratives in themselves.

The use of these materials in mass HRE campaigns through the distribution of huge amounts of reading material or images is highlighted in some of the scholarly accounts and viewed as crucial in getting the human rights *message* across in communities. There is reference to step-by-step guides and the production of human rights educational resources, human rights handbooks, information leaflets and pamphlets, where the purpose is to break down international principles into simplified and understandable forms for the general population.[29]

Human rights stories are also often described as 'vignettes'[30] implying they are only a small illustration used as part of a broader script about international human rights. These vignettes claim to ensure that human rights standards are 'clarified in recognisable cultural settings'.[31] A consequence appears to be a preoccupation of the HRE community with processes of participation, which is 'viewed as motivating, humanizing and ultimately practical, since this form of learning is linked more strongly with attitudinal or behavioural change than with a pure lecturing approach'.[32]

While this enables individuals to reconceptualise their experiences as human rights demands and claims, the process of translation reinforces a technical orientation in which human rights are facts to be transmitted through HRE. Arguably this abstracts the authorship of human rights from their community setting and instead formalises and institutionalises the voices within a more

28 Chapter 4, p. 81.

29 Ibid., p. 80; Chapter 6, pp. 109–110.

30 R.P. Claude, 'Global Human Rights Education: The Challenges for NGOs', in Andreopoulos and Claude (eds), *Human Rights Education for the Twenty-First Century*, p. 399.

31 Ibid.

32 F. Tibbitts, 'Emerging Models in Human Rights Education', *International Review of Education, Special Edition on Human Rights Education*, 48(3–4), 2002, pp. 159–171.

institutionally legitimate form. By adopting the institutional language and form, HRE actors often ended up locating knowledge of human rights above and beyond the realm of the community or experience. Instead, it becomes a task delegated out to the educated elite trained in the language and practice of the international human rights framework.

In support of framing, some scholars argue that efforts to make human rights contextual are a way of giving voice and language to human suffering. They believe that the appropriation and translation of experience and suffering into human rights norms and standards provides individuals with a sense of human rights consciousness and a new identity as a rights holder, with which they can then experiment.[33] According to Mark Goodale because most people encounter human rights outside of the institutional architecture associated with the regimes of knowledge, it becomes both personal and translocal. This is because framing social issues in terms of human rights invites individuals 'to re-envision themselves beyond the boundaries of expected context'[34] and enables them to articulate problems and needs in a way that offers the expectation of change. Notwithstanding arguments that human rights must be translated into local webs of meaning based on religion, ethnicity, or place in order for them to appear both legitimate and appealing, such transformations appear to take place on a relatively superficial level.[35]

While human rights ideas are adapted they never become fully 'indigenised' and retain their underlying emphasis on individual rights embedded as legal principles and norms within the human rights system.[36] The trick, claims Merry, is in the ability of 'proponents to dress them in familiar costumes'.[37]

While the international human rights framework can provide people with a way of understanding and framing their own experiences (one of the core arguments offered in support of human rights), by opening up one avenue of legal pursuit, it can, at the same time, shut down the possibility of pursuing other modes of collective agency and action. The moral authority of human rights as pre-existing natural facts often gives way, as the research has shown, to a more legalistic discourse of human rights rooted in institutional standards and norms which claim universal equality before the law. And yet one of the problems with legal language is the way it replaces 'relationships with rules' and 'situational

33 M. Goodale and S.E. Merry, *The Practice of Human Rights: Tracking Law between the Global and the Local*, Cambridge University Press, New York, 2007.

34 M. Goodale, 'The Power of Right(s): Tracking Empires of Law and New Modes of Social Resistance in Bolivia (and Elsewhere)', in Goodale and Merry (eds), *The Practice of Human Rights*, p. 144.

35 See A. An-Na'im, 'Introduction', in A. An-Na'im, *Human Rights in Cross-Cultural Perspectives: A Quest for Consensus*, University of Pennsylvania Press, Philadelphia, PA, 1992, pp. 1–18.

36 Merry, *Human Rights and Gender Violence*, p. 137.

37 Ibid.

considerations with abstract principles',[38] as well as suggesting that any enforcement of rights claims always implies social justice.[39] Endowed with the status of the supreme arbiter of conflicts and disputes, the law is regarded as being above any actual social, political or cultural factors influencing those conflicts and disputes.[40]

Unquestionably then, framing is a strategic choice, but one which can too easily overlook the constraints and limits that the HRE discourse itself imposes upon the way that agency is exercised. The orientation of HRE does not only limit the choice of language and text, but also practice and action. Disguising human rights norms while they maintain their fundamental meaning can in the end serve to disarm and delegitimise the narratives and knowledge of those whom HRE discourse claims to empower. How the discourse is introduced into particular languages is therefore highly consequential, because this also influences what kinds of claims people can make by using their languages.[41]

Also important when understanding how frames are constructed are the kinds of documents and instruments that HRE actors have chosen for translation. The evidence suggests a two-way translation process: not only are international human rights texts translated into contextual terms, but also experiences and contextual issues are translated into human rights language. These choices can influence the ways that space becomes organised and used, which is discussed in the next section.

Structural conditions and the use of space

Social issues are often defined using legalistic and institutional language and human rights compartmentalised into individual legal problems to pursue through state-sponsored legal or regulatory structures. This means that individual and group dissent becomes moulded and action was guided towards pursuing claims through the legal system and courts, or using service providers such as hospitals, schools and shelters, and the civil society framework. These are usually institutional spaces that can direct and regulate the way in which individual or collective injustice was pursued.

For Michel Foucault, space guarantees the obedience of individuals through the architecture, function and hierarchies assigned to them. Discipline, he claims, is advanced from the organisation of individuals within this space; it gradually evolves through the overlapping, repetition, imitation and support between varieties of micro-processes which are distinguished from each other only by their

38 H. Englund, *Prisoners of Freedom: Human Rights and the African Poor*, University of California Press, Berkeley, CA, 2006, p. 48.

39 F.E. Kanyongolo, 'The Rhetoric of Human Rights in Malawi: Individualization and Judicialization', in H. Englund and F Nyamnjoh (eds), *Rights and the Politics of Recognition in Africa*, Zed Books, London, 2004, p. 75.

40 Englund, *Prisoners of Freedom*, p. 49.

41 Ibid., p. 60.

domain of application, but eventually produce a 'blueprint of a general method'.[42] The use of space is therefore an important feature within HRE discourse, and the way that it is organised, not only physically, in terms of organisations, actors and processes, but the manner in which it is occupied by interests, identities and hierarchies.[43] According to Foucault, the way space is used is essentially about the exercise of power. The formal organisation of space then appears not only to be about regulating how HRE discourse is distributed and communicated, but also a means of control over how people exercise their human rights within assigned and regulated spaces.

Evidence suggests that HRE discourse appears to operate in three spaces: the global (UN), the intermediate (NGO) and the local (community). How, then, is this transnational space organised and used? HRE discourse has become increasingly centralised and institutionalised in terms of both production of the content and the process. However, the distribution and translation of HRE discourse increasingly relies upon a network of intermediaries who can cross the global and local space, but also institutions and society divide. NGOs have become an important part of this intermediary network, especially in countries like Tanzania, where growth has mushroomed in the last 15 to 20 years.[44] These national NGOs theoretically have a choice: they can channel the institutional UN discourse of HRE into the fabric of society, or they can resist the global discourse and instead choose to focus upon more local indigenous knowledge and resources.

In reality, these choices are limited because of the precarious role of NGOs, which requires them to constantly navigate through a complex terrain of different interests, not only those of the state and society, but also their own organisational interests. Also, because most NGOs are reliant upon donor funding, their strategy is often influenced by the interests and agenda of donor organisations. The practice of NGOs in Tanzania therefore often consists of multiple and competing relations of power, the outcome of which is partly determined by the way that the HRE actors frame HRE discourse. The availability and conditions of donor funding implicitly determines the way that HRE space is organised and used in terms of the content, structure and timing, effectively limiting the choices available to what is stipulated but also practical.

HRE discourse in Tanzania is composed of different types of practice: from nationwide mass education campaigns on posters and through media, to the use of public spaces in markets and village centres, often used for public discussions or theatrical performances. Public consultations also take place between the government and society to discuss human rights issues raised in proposed changes

42 M. Foucault, *Discipline and Punish*, Penguin, London, 1977, p. 138.
43 Ibid.
44 See Chapter 5.

to legislation.[45] However, it is more common for HRE activities to take place within closed and formal settings, such as workshops or meetings, arranged for invited participants, rather than the general public.[46] These workshops tend to involve information and training about human rights principles or laws, which participants are then expected to take back and communicate to their local communities.

How these spaces are used in terms of the arrangement of the furniture, interactions of actors, and the way the information is delivered provides insight into the operation of power within. In Tanzania, distinctions between the NGO staff and participants are created in ways that are not uncommon to many other formal learning spaces, which give implicit messages about hierarchies of knowledge and power; for example, NGO organisers sitting behind a table at the front of the room (sometimes raised) or standing and walking around the room while talking or delivering material, and often hands being raised by participants wishing to speak.[47]

In Tanzania there is an elite group of human rights experts who are distinguishable from other activists. These work in NGOs mainly staffed by lawyers or legal experts, who often design and manage the human rights related projects and work, including HRE. In fact, some staff in these NGOs who have started their careers in different fields, such as teachers or sociologists, then retrained as lawyers. While these NGOs adopt a certain elite identity as both human rights and HRE experts, they are brought into the international discourse and framework in other subtle ways, including overseas training, the compilation of expert reports for international organisations, and by displaying literature about international human rights conventions or issues, sometimes in English. This elite status is also reinforced through the formal style of dress, office layout, air-conditioned environment and the language and terminology used. While the environmental factors are not so evident in the scholarly accounts of HRE practice, organisers are often located in places away from the locations where HRE workshops are delivered and, in some cases, designed and delivered by consultants bought in from overseas. This all reinforces the idea that HRE is something specialist exclusively for the educated professional to design and deliver, rather than anyone in general.

NGOs, however, are only one aspect of what appears to be an organised structure of regulation in Tanzania, which is designed and sustained on the basis of certain understandings about HRE expertise. This regulatory structure operates through nationwide networks of both salaried individuals and volunteers, most of the time called paralegals, but also known as village legal workers, community

45 For example I attended a public discussion at the Alliance Française with student members of Peace Clubs (GNRC) in November 2009. This was a consultation about the proposed Law of the Child Act. On the panel was a Minister from the Ministry of Community Development, Gender and Children (MCDGC).

46 Chapter 5, Observations from the Workshops.

47 Ibid.

justice facilitators or human rights monitors.[48] While these individuals principally come from and live in local communities, they are recruited and trained in a manner that distinguishes them from the rest of the population. This involves invitations to closed workshops, the adoption of a similar dress style and the use of human rights terminology, along with daily allowances for attending workshops. Over time they appear to increasingly associate themselves with the national NGOs or the HRE project, associations that are often reinforced by the apparent common practice of distributing various paraphernalia stamped with the organisations' name or logo, including pens and t-shirts, which the paralegals would regularly wear or use.

It is through these various processes that networks of volunteer HRE actors are given what Harri Englund calls a 'quasi professional identity';[49] a distinct identity that relies upon the 'disadvantaged and poor' being excluded from the group.[50] Distinguishing NGO staff and volunteers from the learners in the HRE process is a hidden lesson in HRE trainings, and volunteer HRE actors are provided with just enough knowledge of international human rights principles or laws to then be able to justify returning to their communities as HRE 'experts'.

This is reinforced by scholarship on HRE practice, which describes hierarchical systems of HRE where individuals become categorised as experts, specialists, trainers and volunteers. For example, three accounts of the HRE programme in Cambodia explain how it was implemented through an organised network of overseas professionals, national trainers and community-based volunteers (a national network of Buddhist Monks), who had the ability to reach even the most remote areas of society.[51] Despite this, the production of material and resources remained firmly in the hands and control of the staff in UNTAC.[52] Many of the other accounts show how the division of tasks and a hierarchical structure is not uncommon within HRE.

The organisation and use of HRE space therefore reinforces distinctions between those who have the knowledge (the NGOs and their legal staff), and those who do not (the rest of the population).

48 Many countries now have national networks of paralegal volunteers, often marketed as a strategic and cost efficient means of reaching communities. Usually these networks are one localised element of a global programme aimed at improving access to justice or provide them legal empowerment. Such programmes are usually spearheaded and financed by international institutions such as the World Bank and UN, and use networks of volunteers to transplant these international programmes at local level.

49 Englund, *Prisoners of Freedom*, p. 72.

50 Ibid.

51 Chapter 4, pp. 78–79.

52 Ibid., p. 78.

The consumption of HRE

The idea that HRE processes should be tailored to meet the specific requirements of a particular context is the third aspect of cultural translation. It is during the translation process that the target population becomes redefined.[53] For example, as Merry outlines, in China domestic violence occurs between family members, rather than just between a husband and wife or in a romantic relationship.[54] The law, she argues, has responded to this by moving gradually from protecting women in marriages to protecting women in households. This example raises a point of analysis about who identifies the issues and groups that HRE discourse addresses.

HRE processes are commonly organised and implemented by organisations or individuals, such as NGOs, international organisations like the UN or independent consultants viewed as specialists in HRE, who often come in from other areas. For example in Tanzania, NGOs based in Dar es Salaam conduct trainings with paralegals from rural areas, who then have the task of communicating the information to the rest of the population. Many of these staff have studied human rights at university and a number have been on regional or international training courses. Scholarship also shows how overseas, usually Western, specialists are either brought in by institutions, or volunteered as part of an HRE programme to assist the local organisations with planning and implementation.

HRE discourse is also shaped by external forms of control and agendas, such as international UN campaigns that drive both the national and funding agenda, such as gender-based violence (GBV), female genital mutilation (FGM) and HIV/AIDS; issues that are generally part of prominent international advocacy efforts.[55]

The presence of a core group of long-standing activist women, who have prominent roles in the leading national NGOs and international institutions, is one way that the international agenda influenced activism in Tanzania. This select group has been engaged in advocacy on the rights of women for the last 20 years and become involved in the early 1990s after attending the 'Third World Conference to review and appraise the achievements of the United Nations Decade for Women: Equality, Development and Peace' in Nairobi 1985, and the Fourth World Conference on Women in Beijing in 1995.[56] Some interviewees in

53 Merry, *Human Rights and Gender Violence*, p. 137.

54 Ibid.

55 An example from the fieldwork was the guidance given from a UN Committee to the Tanzanian government, advising them to draft and enact legislation in order to specifically address the rights and freedoms of children as per the UNCRC into single law. National NGOs had apparently been campaigning for a separate law since 1995 with little response, and yet within one year of the UN Committee's report, the Law of Child Act (2009) was in force.

56 This was information I gathered in the course of interviews during the fieldwork and through informal conversations. This group of women now headed NGOs, had senior positions in the UN and international institutions, or were academics.

the case study explained that after the conferences these women had returned to Tanzania with a sense of purpose and a way of advocating for the rights of women. Many NGOs in Tanzania that focused on women, including WLAC, TAWLA, TGNP, TAMWA and WILDAF, were established in the early 1990s after these conferences took place.[57] So, maybe there is some correlation between the focus of local activism, international interest and financial support.

However, the focus of international efforts and funding on particular aspects of human rights is possibly only one reason why some other issues dominate, while others are marginalised or ignored. NGO survival not only depends upon external funding but also on some level of state-sanctioned support in order to operate. This means they can easily become influenced by external agendas.

A number of concerns result. First, is that NGOs construct organisational strategies and programmes that meet the priorities of donor organisations or the state, rather than those of the community. While some of the practical scholarship on HRE implies that communities and individuals are approached as part of HRE programmes in order to understand their particular needs and problems, the strategies and programmes are often designed and implemented by HRE *professionals* and appear to involve the detail about the processes and making them participatory, but with the ultimate aim of raising awareness of the idea of human rights, rather than understanding it. While it is not clear that this process of *targeting* has been happening in Tanzania or in the scholarship, it can result in the flooding of particular issues by NGOs, on the one hand, like gender-based violence or HIV/AIDS, which is evident in Tanzania, while on the other, a neglect of other more systemic and complex problems, such as poverty or economic injustice. It can also have the effect of diverting attention away from the endemic and structural issues that cause national, regional and global social and economic inequalities, which means that without questioning, HRE discourse can be too easily absorbed into the other ideological agendas.

A second concern is how HRE can be used as an opening and opportunity to reach and educate the *target population* in line with these external agendas. An assumption about who has and who does not have knowledge of human rights is shaped by the orientation of the HRE organisations and individuals involved, and while many individuals express a belief in the inherent nature of human rights, it is often articulated in terms of international human rights norms and standards. This finding is supported by the frequent inclusion of international human rights principles or laws in the content of HRE processes and the instinctive reference

57 Women's Legal Aid Centre (WLAC), 1994, www.wlac.or.tz (accessed 20 November 2012); Tanzania Gender Networking Programme (TGNP), 1993, www.tgnp. org (accessed 20 November 2012); Tanzania Media Women's Association (TAMWA), 1987, www. global-womens-network.org/wiki/Tanzania_Media_Womens_Association,_(TAMWA), Dar_es_Salaam_Tanzania. (accessed 20 November 2012); Tanzania Women Lawyers Association (TAWLA), 1990, www.tawla.or.tz (accessed 20 November 2012); and Women in Law and Development in Africa(WLDAF), 1995, www.wildaftanzania.org (accessed 20 November 2012).

by interviewees to these standards to explain why they consider an issue to be wrong, like discrimination or gender-based violence.[58]

Arguably, it is easier to justify GBV as a human rights violation by making reference to the principles in CEDAW rather than engaging in lengthy debate about the socio-political or economic factors, such as those entrenched patriarchal social structures, poverty or a lack of state support. Alternatively, individuals may refer to universal principles and values because they validate and give their views, the international consensus-building processes within the UN being viewed as giving credence to what would otherwise be abstract and moral concepts. If human rights are understood as concrete principles inscribed and entrenched into international texts, it follows that knowledge of human rights is something one can learn by being educated about content of those texts, and directed towards the legal framework as a means of claiming these rights. From this perspective, a claim made by many HRE actors that people do not have knowledge of human rights could arguably be justified and correct.

HRE discourse is targeted at particular communities, groups or individuals and there appears to be an assumed link between the purpose of HRE and social struggles. Target populations appear to share some common characteristics: they are often poor, live in rural areas, lack access to basic services, and maintain strong cultural traditions and beliefs.[59] In relative terms, most examples of HRE processes and practice demonstrate at least a couple of these common traits, and HRE processes are generally targeted at populations distinct and different from that of the HRE actors, either in terms of where they came from (overseas or the city), by their dress (formal) or by their professional status (educated/lawyer).

There appears to be a common assumption that people, especially those who are rural, live in the countryside or villages and are poor, or groups such as women, do not know their human rights. In addition, there appears to be a presumed need for HRE and knowledge of international human rights in order to stop the cycle of abuse and violations that arguably occupy these communities. HRE strategies are commonly designed to reach deep into society and remote communities through organisations or networks of individuals. This reinforces the idea that ordinary people do not know or understand human rights. As such their knowledge is discounted as irrelevant until the point in time when it is translated into the language of human rights, and becomes strategically useful.

In the case study HRE processes tend to be targeted at rural communities rather than those in Dar es Salaam, and also particular populations within Tanzanian society.[60] An additional common tendency is also for HRE processes to focus upon groups within the population frequently viewed as marginalised or vulnerable, such as women and children, or particular ethnic groups.

58 Chapter 5, Conceptions of HRE.

59 This may not necessarily be true of HRE as an entity, but my focus was upon HRE in community settings and the evidence comes from this aspect.

60 Chapter 6, The Structure and Practice of HRE in Community-Settings.

Distinguishing and targeting groups within the population, who are viewed by HRE actors most in need of HRE, ensures that the distinction between those with knowledge and those without is maintained. This, in the words of Harri Englund, 'presupposes a categorical distinction between the advantaged and the disadvantaged. The former helps the latter to sustain itself, while the distinction itself remains virtually intact.'[61] Englund has described how he saw very little in the Malawian civic education project he studied that would 'actually have enabled the disadvantaged to lift themselves from their predicament'. The fact '[t]hat this troubling observation is largely unnoticed indicates how natural the distinction has become'.[62]

The justification for *targeting* certain groups is strengthened by the finding that HRE appears to be predominantly understood by HRE actors as a means of empowerment. Providing communities with awareness of human rights was seen to give them the ability to reframe their experiences, problems, issues and needs in terms of rights. Rights, in turn, are shown as principles with mechanisms attached and so can be acted upon and in some cases enforced through the legal framework. Empowerment can be viewed as 'moving out of constrained places and isolated spaces',[63] in that it widens the scope for action and multiplies potential sites for engagement, and enables an organic growth in 'confidence, in capacity, in wellbeing'.[64]

And yet, as Andrea Cornwall has argued, *empowerment* has increasingly become appropriated by mainstream development and become a way of bringing in, finding a place and lending opportunities to poor people – empowering them and inviting them to participate then becomes another way of relocating them within the prevailing order.[65] It has, in this respect, become an 'instrument for managed intervention' rather than a process through which people discover their own potential.[66] This is an interesting claim, which should raise a number of questions for HRE: who it targets, who it does not and why? It would appear from the research that more generally HRE discourse is targeted at sections of society that are often the most powerless. In this sense a lack of knowledge appears to be apparent because of an individual or group's lack of human rights.

This analysis suggests that if there was a more critical and questioning approach to HRE, then engagement with the poor and marginalised might be as equal knowledge-holders rather than as beneficiaries. Certainly, according to the interpretative framework in Chapter 2, if HRE actors adopted a more critical

61 Englund, *Prisoners of Freedom*, p. 71.
62 Ibid.
63 A. Cornwall, 'Making Spaces, Changing Places: Situating Participation in Development', Working Paper 170, Institute of Development Studies, 2002, p. 2. www.drc-citizenship. org/system/assets/1052734369/original/1052734369-cornwall.2002-making.pdf?1289311080 (accessed 30 November 2012).
64 Ibid.
65 Ibid., p. 3.
66 Ibid.

orientation the focus of HRE practice could shift from the idea of raising awareness of international human rights standards to trying to create space for the voices of these groups. Alternatively, a counter-hegemonic orientation would entail at least questioning the historical construction of human rights with a view to marking out spaces for resistance.

Instead, by identifying themselves as human rights subjects, individuals become inadvertently drawn into the state-sponsored or global justice mechanisms and, while arguably exercising agency, they can become managed by the regulated discourse of human rights and the framework in which it operated. Without questioning and critique, HRE discourse can too easily become implicated in the way that hegemonic systems of control exercise power over individual agency. The forging of distinctions between human rights *educators* and the rest of the population is a kind of cultural disposition, but one that does not exist in a political and economic vacuum, and in the end serves particular interests.

Conclusion

The production of a global and institutional HRE discourse is part of a gradual effort to control and determine not only what we understand as human rights, but the way in which we understand them and give meaning to them through encroaching processes of codification and classification. The role of intermediaries in HRE, as translators of international human rights principles and mechanisms, has therefore become crucial to furthering the UN's aim to build a human rights culture. Human rights do provide a radically different frame for thinking about power and inequality in society, and the power of HRE is often measured by its capacity to change the way that people think and act. This, however, ignores the way in which contemporary HRE discourse undermines the idea of collective agency, dissent and resistance as means of social change, by controlling the processes of knowledge production, distribution and consumption.

Cultural translation has become such an important feature in HRE practice and the primary concern is to make international human rights norms and standards relevant and accepted in the local context. While my research has shown the multifaceted and complex nature of human rights and HRE, a lack of questioning and critique results in the participatory methods of reflective inquiry they often adopt, obscuring the way that HRE can be a form of transnational social regulation.

The technical orientation in human rights is linked to a perceivable common conception that masses of individuals or groups are seen as lacking knowledge of and in need of education in human rights. HRE discourse is frequently targeted at some of the most disadvantaged and marginalised groups in society often by using organised networks of volunteers. In doing this there seems to be an assumed correlation between the idea of poverty or suffering and a lack of knowledge about human rights.

HRE discourse is principally seen as a means of empowerment; the idea being that knowledge of human rights can change the social situation because people then understand their rights and can take action to claim them. However, in adopting a predominantly technical orientation, HRE actors have underestimated the ways in which bureaucratic and structural forms can disarm threats, by constructing an HRE discourse that is ahistorical, apolitical and decontextual.[67] Rather than widening the scope for social transformation, the support and adherence to a technical, professionalised and institutional discourse of HRE has in fact narrowed the opportunities for this to take place.

A programme that focuses upon changes in behaviour and attitudes may educate individuals to some degree about and for human rights but it falls short of enhancing the capacity of the disadvantaged to confront the power relationships that underlie human rights violations.[68] While the power of HRE may be seen in its capacity to change the way people think and act, and to shift existing cultural practices, in the end cultural translation does not build upon local ideas or cultural resources as valid and important forms of knowledge.

The choice of orientation in HRE determines, in part at least, how individuals make sense of their own and other people's experiences, and the types of processes and action they chose to engage in as a result. Only certain languages are deemed valid and legitimate in HRE, and they are often the languages of regulation and control that fail to adequately capture the diversity and complexity of knowledge.[69] This introduces a second level of analysis, which considers my claim that it is this disposition in HRE and the notion of rights it sustains that are integral to a mode of governance that is transnational.

It is important, however, to remember how spaces of domination and deprivation can also be spaces for counter-hegemonic activity, radical possibility and resistance.[70] They can be spaces that people make and shape for themselves as opposed to those more formalised spaces where participation is invited or at least induced, and opportunities are extended by powerful agencies to take part in activities. This means, as Englund argues, that 'a certain radicalization of these projects seems inevitable in both intellectual and practical senses . . . because rethought human rights compel a confrontation with marginalization and impoverishment'.[71]

Like Foucault, it is important to advocate of situational possibilities, rather than grand theories or totalising perspectives and solutions, which potentially limit our political vision.[72] As one possible way forward, and in order to move beyond a technical and limited orientation, HRE discourse should invoke the multiple

67 A. Keet, *Human Rights Education: A Conceptual Analysis*, Lambert Academic Publishing, Saarbrücken, 2010.

68 Englund, *Prisoners of Freedom*, p. 96.

69 See P. McLaren and T. Tadeu da Silva, 'Decentering Pedagogy: Critical Literacy, Resistance and the Politics of Memory', in P. McClaren and P. Leonard (eds), *Paulo Freire: A Critical Encounter*, Routledge, London, 1993, p. 63.

70 Cornwall, 'Making Spaces, Changing Places', pp. 2–3.

71 Englund, *Prisoners of Freedom*, p. 201.

72 Ibid., p. 202.

discourses of resistance and action that are connected to pre-existing forms of indigenous knowledge and cultural resources of communities. This requires rethinking HRE discourse to one that is more concerned with unearthing the subjugated knowledges, and founded upon the characteristics of questioning and critique.

7 Conclusion

Learning from the edge: towards HRE as transformative praxis

> We only become what we are by the radical and deep-seated refusal of that which others have made us.[1]

By exploring HRE through the fourfold interpretative framework and using a form of ideology critique and genealogical approach, this book has pieced together a picture of HRE, how it has developed into a global discourse and penetrated the local context by controlling the production, distribution and consumption of the discourse through intermediary NGOs, predominantly using processes of cultural translation.

So far it has revealed that the discursive orientation of individuals determines, in part at least, how they make sense of both their own and others' experiences and the types of action they engage in as a result. And yet, despite this, dominant processes of knowledge production mean that only certain languages are deemed appropriate within HRE discourse. This process of regulation and control constrains the space for exploration and inquiry so ultimately fails to capture the diversity and complexity of knowledge and experience at the local level.

The purpose of this concluding chapter is therefore to explore how we can move forward from this static position. It takes into account the ways power has been exercised by dominant cultural groups to control HRE discourse and considers how, in light of this, we can move as a progressive collective towards a type of praxis that has the potential to be truly transformative. The first part of the chapter revisits Gramsci's analysis of culture, pedagogy and power, which offers the basis of the ideology critique taken in this book. Here, however, the analysis is focused more on Gramsci's thinking of pedagogy as a site of political struggle and the need to mobilise new intellectuals and cultivate democratic public spheres in the name of resistance. This leads to the second part of the chapter, which begins to explore the ways that these principles could be put into practice. What are the necessary characteristics and qualities for these organic intellectuals and how can they harness the dynamic and transformative potential of the public spaces?

1 J.P. Sartre, 'Preface', in F. Fanon, *The Wretched of the Earth*, Penguin, London, 2001, p. 15.

HRE as governance

While NGOs as HRE actors do appear to have a significant role in perpetuating the circulation of a dominant HRE discourse, the conclusion is that HRE discourse is a site of permanent struggle, and that efforts to control the production, distribution and consumption of HRE discourse are ultimately about the exercise of power. According to Foucault, the exercise of power is a question of regulating and controlling society through particular forms of governance. In this sense, the idea of government is broader than the traditional understanding about political structures or management of states. Instead it is taken to signify the ways in which the conduct of individuals and groups can be regulated, controlled and directed. It is about considered and calculated modes of action that are 'designed to act upon the possibilities of action of other people'.[2]

This fixation over the control of society is not new. Foucault describes it dating back to the sixteenth century when attention shifted from concerns about the nature of state control, to one concerned with introducing and maintaining the economy and order.[3] It is since this time that society has become a political target, and during this period that alternative forms of governance began to emerge through the development of disciplinary technologies in institutional spaces such as schools, prisons, workplaces and hospitals.

Chapter 1 showed how the lack of state investment in social and welfare institutions during the 1980s led to many services and institutions previously managed and financed by state resources becoming delivered increasingly by INGOs. As a consequence large sections of society previously under state control were progressively existing outside the state sector and therefore unregulated. It was a trend that pertained more to societies in developing countries, in particular rural communities, where there was a lack of access to basic services including schools, hospitals, welfare, employment, housing or legal services. The poor, disadvantaged and marginalised populations were therefore living outside the realm of governance considered so necessary in the maintenance of the global hegemonic order.

Increasingly central to the process of regulation were the intermediary HRE practitioners and NGOs, which arguably became entities through which global power structures could channel their human rights policies and strategies. The book has illustrated how NGOs were targeted and brought into the dominant HRE framework, using institutional donor funding and the promotion of participatory educational approach aimed at building a human rights culture. Chapter 6 showed how, in fact and in various ways, including adopting the

2 Michel Foucault, *Essential Works of Michel Foucault, 1954–1984, Volume 3: Power*, ed. J. Faubion, Penguin Press, London, 1994, p. 341.

3 M. Foucault, 'Afterwork: The Subject and Power', in H.I. Dreyfus and P. Rabinow (eds), *Michel Foucault: Beyond Structuralism and Hermeneutics*, Harvester Wheatsheaf, Hemel Hempstead,1982, pp. 212–213.

international language of human rights, NGOs began to regulate themselves as HRE subjects and became a key part of the global HRE framework. Processes of translation were a practical response and way of managing this HRE intermediary identity. It is the need to access and bring the unregulated populations within the global regulated framework that, I argue, offers one explanation for the construction of a codified and centralised HRE discourse within the UN framework.

Gramsci's claim is that the maintenance of a dominant hegemonic culture takes place not through the application of force, but through the forging of consent and the art of persuasion. Processes of cultural translation in HRE discourse are ultimately methods of persuasion, but there are other less apparent ways in which individuals and organisations have been co-opted into the global HRE discourse, such as funding and identity, which are ultimately about the exercise of power.

According to Foucault, power is dynamic; it operates through the social fabric, where it produces effects. It is also momentary, which means that in an instance of struggle between submission and resistance, power can be used to manage the possibilities of action. HRE discourse, then, is part of the transnational site of struggle that exists in a permanent relationship of provocation between domination and resistance. Literature about human rights has so often in the past been preoccupied with the distinction between universalism and cultural relativism, and this has distracted from the most important and determinate relationship in human rights, which is the way that power produces knowledge and knowledge produces power.

The plural and multiple perspectives and approaches that theoretically inform HRE, as illustrated in Chapter 2, are details that the international institutions and dominant discourses have attempted to bury and discount. Instead of acknowledging the diverse nature of knowledge and cultural resources that are attached to our understandings about life, knowledge of human rights has become unified and codified to such an extent that it becomes difficult to see beyond it, as an ethical framework for the way we live.

Within this institutional framework of HRE discourse and understanding, other pre-existing forms of knowledge and cultural resources are dismissed as meaningless. The experiences and knowledge of communities are instead used to give contextual meaning to human rights principles and open up ways of introducing the idea of human rights. For example, stories about women having suffered violence are used to open up discussion about equality or the provisions of CEDAW, and a way through which people can then reframe their experiences in terms of the global language of human rights. Reframing experiences in this global form is arguably a way of dislocating the language and experience of suffering or life from its community or cultural roots, and instead translating it into a global language considered valid and legitimate.

In the past, colonialism imposed new life systems through the 'cultural, educational, and linguistic priorities' of the coloniser 'antithetical to all things that were native'.[4] Colonial education abstracted the 'cultures, the center of their lives, and may have even de-patterned [the] mental dispositions'[5] of the African people, which then inscribed in their minds a feeling or acceptance of 'lower possibilities in their lives' as compared with others.[6] Not only was colonialism preoccupied with exploiting the psycho-social and natural resources of the colonised, but it was also

> bent on achieving a globally miseducated and, by extension, decultured world population that looks for protection and psychological sustenance from the European metropolis, and these two dimensions (i.e., the process of miseducation and deculturation) were the most potent weapons in achieving the socio-politically deconscientized and economically majority of our world.[7]

This raises the question of whether and how HRE discourse could perpetuate some of these historical and pre-existing inequalities by adopting an unquestioning and dominant discursive orientation? It should also be seriously troubling, especially given the evidence in this book, that there appears to be new contemporary forms of subjugation, operating through the imposition of structures of education, knowledge apparatus and cultural impositions. In accepting the institutional discourse of HRE, the conclusion is that proponents of the international human rights framework have underestimated the ways in which bureaucratic forms can disarm threats, and produce a global model for HRE that is ahistorical, apolitical and decontextual.[8] Rather than widening the scope for social transformation, the pursuit of a technical, professionalised and institutional approach to HRE has in fact narrowed the opportunities for this to take place.

That HRE is less about struggling communities but more a prescriptive and strategic political tool I argue is a direct consequence of two specific aspects: first, the acceptance and development of an institutional and bureaucratic framework of HRE; and second, the lack of reflexive engagement on the part of those involved in HRE on both the fundamental precepts of HRE and the changing nature of HRE in its relationship to the global setting. Taken together these gaps have enabled a dominant discourse to thrive in spaces that should have been used to challenge rather than sustain it, and instead 'constructing and

4 A.A. Abdi, 'De-Subjecting Subject Populations: Historico-Actual Problems and Educational Possibilities', in A.A. Abdi and L. Shultz (eds), *Educating for Human Rights and Global Citizenship*, State University of New York Press, 2008, p. 71.

5 Ibid., p. 72.

6 Ibid., p. 70.

7 Ibid., p. 69.

8 A. Keet, *Human Rights Education: A Conceptual Analysis*, Lambert Academic Publishing, Saarbrücken, 2010.

maintaining subjectivities that are necessary for reproducing existing social relations'.[9]

These spaces include the field of informal adult education. Considered politically and ideologically important, adult education has been a key site of struggle, and shaped by the distribution of political power in society. It was also historically one that opened up spaces for resistance through radical pedagogy. Given this, one would expect community-based HRE discourse to be an opportunity for dialogical processes of learning and modes of resistance. However, this does not appear to be the case. Notwithstanding the critical window of opportunity for HRE 'to provide a voice and language' to the world of human suffering, examples of HRE practice appear to show they are more often occupied by technical conceptions of human rights, which arguably undermine the often diverse and conflicting narratives discussed in Chapter 2.[10] A consequence has been to absolve HRE discourse of its radical political potential in some of these community-based settings, and resulted in it at times being used as a political opportunity to maintain unequal hierarchies of power rather than challenge them.

Despite the apparent preoccupation with human rights as facts and a technical discourse, HRE essentially remains a site of struggle in which intermediaries have a determinate role. Undoubtedly then, HRE discourse is not self-evident, it is socially and politically constructed. This means that it is individuals or organisations that determine the way in which HRE discourse is shaped and used, not only in terms of the way they articulate and communicate human rights, but also how they understand and determine the purpose of HRE through practice. Yet before we can begin to consider their role in social change dialogues, we must acknowledge how particular orientations in HRE discourse support regulatory global structures and weaken opportunities for agency and action.

Rethinking culture, pedagogy and power

Cultural pedagogy is central to any discourse on radical politics or social transformation. As Henry Giroux suggests, culture is 'the main pedagogical force to secure the authority and interests of the dominant group'.[11] Gramsci's account of the way that politics can bear down on everyday life through the might of its pedagogical practice, relations and discourses is evidenced in the way that culture of HRE has the power not only to shape groups and their identities but also conceptions of community and belonging. For progressive educators, Gramsci's understanding of culture as an instrument of politics and power is critical because

9 S. Macrine, P. Mclaren and D. Hill, *Revolutionizing Pedagogy: Education for Social Justice and Beyond Global Neo-Liberalism*, Palgrave Macmillan, New York, 2010, pp. 3–4.

10 U. Baxi, 'Concepts of Human Rights: The Three Worlds of Human Rights' in PDHRE, *Human Rights Learning: A People's Report*, PDHRE, New York, 2006, p. 18, www.pdhre.org/pdhre-report-2006.pdf.

11 H. Giroux. 'Rethinking Cultural Politics and Radical Pedagogy in the Work of Antonio Gramsci', *Educational Theory*, 49(1), 1999, p. 2.

it challenges theories of social and cultural reproduction, which overemphasise power as a force of domination. Instead, power is viewed as dynamic and productive and the site between domination and resistance. Gramsci illuminates the way that culture can be 'deployed, represented, address, and taken up in order to understand how power works to produce not only forms of domination, but also complicity and dissent'.[12] Politics is not something practised by governments and institutions, but rather it is part of, and embedded in, those everyday diverse spaces and places where 'cultural practices are deployed, lived and mobilised in the service of knowledge, power and authority'.[13]

From this perspective, in fact, pedagogy has less to do with methodology and more to do with politics and power. According to Giroux:

> Pedagogy is a moral and political practice that is always implicated in power relations and must be understood as a cultural politics that offers both a particular version of civic life, the future, and how we might construct representations of ourselves, others, and our physical and social environment.[14]

In order to find those pedagogical forms of resistance that can enable subordinated individuals and communities on the edge of the system to develop unimpeded in society we need to look beyond HRE to the ways that meaning and articulations are constructed. This does not mean searching for alternative forms of knowledge, but unearthing and bringing to the surface pre-existing knowledges which have been buried or discounted by mechanisms of domination and coercion. It calls for a mode of historical and reflective consciousness which confronts the 'social amnesia of generations in flight from their collective histories – the subjugated knowledge of the marginalized, the excluded, the disenfranchised, and immiserated groups'.[15] It is a process that Foucault called a form of 'counter-memory'.[16]

These surfaced knowledges, Foucault claims, need to be able to confront the technique or form of power that allow domination to take hold in the first place. At its extreme, this would entail tackling the structures of power and dominant apparatus of knowledge production. However, in its less extreme, it requires modes of critique which explore and question the way that discourse is produced, distributed and consumed through dominant cultural practices and norms. As progressive educators, this also demands reflection about the ways that our understandings, language and practice contribute to this predominant orientation in HRE discourse. Instead of always focusing on the other, Upendra Baxi suggests

12 H. Giroux, *On Critical Pedagogy*, Continuum, New York, 2011, p. 63.
13 Ibid.
14 Ibid., p. 71.
15 P. McLaren and T. Tadeu da Silva, 'Decentering Pedagogy: Critical Literacy, Resistance and the Politics of Memory', in P. McLaren and P. Leonard (eds), *Paulo Freire: A Critical Encounter*, Routledge, London, 1993, pp. 73–74.
16 M. Foucault, *Language, Counter-Memory and Practice: Selected Interviews and Essays by Michel Foucault*, ed. and trans. D. Bouchard, Cornell University Press, Ithaca, NY, 1980.

that the task for the HRE community is to learn about HRE, rather than presume to educate others, to 'learn to contest our own assumptions, in order then to contest the world'.[17]

In a process where meaning is produced, represented and consumed, the most critical dimension is a reflexive understanding of the interests embodied in the process itself, and how these interests might be transformed, challenged or sustained so as to promote rather than repress the dynamics of critical thought and action. In this sense, progressive educators must critically interrogate 'their inner histories and experiences', as a necessary element of understanding how their own experiences are 'reinforced, contradicted, and suppressed as a result of the ideologies mediated in the material and intellectual practices' that currently characterise HRE discourse.[18] According to Peter McLaren this is 'the first step with breaking with the logic and institutions of domination'.[19]

Critical pedagogy, according to McLaren, is 'an exchange that engages in the task of reframing, refunctioning, and reposing the question of understanding itself'.[20] Revolutionary pedagogy goes further in that it

> creates a narrative of agency, encounter, and conflict, in which subjectivity turns-back-on-itself, giving rise both to an affirmation of the world through naming it, and an opposition to the world through unmasking and undoing the practices of concealment that are latent in the process of naming itself.[21]

The task, then, is to engage in historical and reflective consciousness, where knowledge is recognised as something that cannot be constrained within the constructs of artificial boundaries, but is instead open-ended, dynamic and incomplete.[22] An approach not only requires the conditions to change subjectivity as constructed by a community's knowledge, wisdom and ethics, but also to change the political, economic and social foundations of the wider global society. This means that rather than viewing teaching as a technical practice, radical pedagogy in the broadest terms is a moral and political practice premised on the assumption that learning is not about processing received knowledge but about actually transforming it as a more expansive struggle for individual rights and social justice.

As such, any project of resistance should be able to illustrate how knowledge, values, interests and social relations are always implicated in the relations of power.

17 U. Baxi, 'Random Reflections on the Impossibility of Human Rights Education', 1996, para. 25, www.pdhre.org/dialogue/reflections.html (accessed 20 May 2012).

18 H. Giroux, *Theory and Resistance in Education: Towards a Pedagogy for the Opposition*, Bergin & Garvey, Amherst, 2001, p. 150.

19 P. McLaren, *Che Guevara, Paulo Freire and the Pedagogy of Revolution*, Rowman & Littlefield, Lanham, MD, 2000, p. 151.

20 Ibid., p. 185.

21 Ibid.

22 Ibid., p. 186.

This type of analysis provokes a deeper understanding which can be used both pedagogically and politically for broader systemic change and social transformation. The next part of the chapter explores some of the ways this may be possible

HRE as transformative praxis

Praxis is not simply action-based reflection; rather it is action that embodies certain qualities, which include a commitment to human well-being and the search for truth, and respect for others. It is the action of people who are free to choose how to act; this means having insight and a willingness to inquire into the ways that one's own experiences and location can shape that. The end of a particular scenario only emerges by deliberating about the appropriate means to a specific situation, which means that in praxis there can be no prior knowledge of the right means. Transformative praxis is therefore a process whereby as we think about what we want to achieve and set our intention, we alter the way in which we might achieve it; as we think about the way we might go about something, we change what we aim at.

Transformative praxis demands not only commitment and risk, but also an ethical obligation not only to bear witness to collective suffering but also be able to translate this into social action. Gramsci's work serves as a reminder that true democracy requires a particular type of person, those 'who feel responsible for something more than their own well-feathered corner', want to participate in shifting society and are willing to look deeply at themselves, their relationships with others and how this impacts upon society and the world. Organic intellectuals need to be reflective, critical and inquiring in order to address their own locations, assumptions and interests. Above all else they need to be in constant contact and dialogue with those in the context of their work, as educators, researchers or activists in order to surface the coercive practices and oppressive conditions through which groups and defined and differentiated.

According to Jiddhu Krishnamurti, education is not merely a matter of training the mind, because it does not bring about completeness. Intelligent revolt, on the other hand, comes with self-knowledge and through the awareness of one's own thought and feeling. It is only 'when we face experience as it comes and do not avoid disturbance that we keep the intelligence highly awakened'.[23] 'Intelligence is the capacity to grasp what is essential and to awaken this capacity, in oneself and in others, is education.'[24] This willingness of 'educators' to turn the lens back on themselves before reflecting on others and the situation is, first and foremost, at the core of transformative praxis.

One interpretation of transformative learning is that it is about inquiring into the ways we make meaning of our experiences. This is based upon the understanding that we all bring our own assumptions, beliefs, interests and bias that have been

23 J. Krishnamurti, *Education and the Significance of Life*, Victor Gollancz, London, p. 11.
24 Ibid., p. 14.

unconsciously absorbed through our lives and the world around us – family, community, school and culture. In this sense, transformation can occur only when we are able to recognise or at least question our own ways of seeing the world and challenge our assumptions. A process of transformative learning involves bringing unquestioned motivations and assumptions to the surface and questioning them. According to Mezirow it is this process that highlights the contradictions and enables us to move towards a more 'inclusive, permeable' and integrated perspective.[25]

A similar view is expressed by Edmund O'Sullivan, for whom transformative learning involves 'a deep structural shift in the basic premises of thought, feelings and actions' which 'dramatically and irreversibly alters our way of being in the world'.[26] This kind of shift requires not only having insight into our self and our location in the world, but also our interactions with others and our relationship to our immediate and broader environment, as well as the world. Transformative learning as a form of critical inquiry requires exploring and unpicking the relationships and hierarchies of power and how institutional systems can perpetuate inequality and identities based upon race, class or gender. But it is also about being aware that there is always the opportunity for alternative actions and an approach based upon a new and more ethical framework for living based upon ideas of equity and social justice.

Critical consciousness

Understanding the relationship between the self, the other and the situation enables us to explore a much wider connection between our own experiences and actions and the impact that these have upon others and the world. This is because our current day reality is not simple and straightforward; instead we live in a constantly shifting climate and tangle of interactions, competing perspectives and interpretations of and on the world. Society is a living system which continually re-creates itself.[27] It is dynamic and unpredictable, and representative of non-linear change processes that require understanding and working with the social field. This means that in some sense you need to be able to see it and feel it in order to then understand what it is about; to be embedded in the context and connected to your location and situation. Our understanding of how social change happens depends upon our level of awareness and quality of attention we give to the unfolding situation and respond to that.

However, more often than not our thinking is governed by habit, which means that we continue to do the things with which we are most familiar and comfortable.

25 J. Mezirow, *Transformative Dimensions of Adult Education*, Josey-Bass, San Francisco, 1991.

26 E. O'Sullivan, 'The Project and Vision of Transformative Education', in E. O'Sullivan, A. Morrell and M. O'Connor (eds), *Learning Toward an Ecological Consciousness*, Palgrave Macmillan, 2002.

27 P. Senge et al., *Presence: Exploring Profound Change in People, Organizations and Society*, Nicolas Brealey Publishing, Boston, 2005, p. 9

As long as our thinking is governed by habit and notions such as control, certainty, predictability and standardisation we will continue to reproduce a system that promotes inequity and injustice. It is the times of uncertainty, or when we are in a state of fear or anxiety that our actions are most likely to revert to what is habitual. Collective actions are no different and it is often the moments when taking a step back to observe is necessary that groups and organisations will continue to do the same things, because they fear the unknown and what could happen if they decided to do something different or take a new course.[28]

This type of reactive learning helps us to respond to events that we understand ourselves as having no part in creating. It is governed by habitual ways of thinking and doing, by continuing to see the world within familiar categories that we are comfortable with. Habit makes us discount different interpretations and options for action that do not match those we know and trust. In a consistent effort to defend our interests, we can easily end up in a continuous cycle of re-enacting habits that ultimately reinforce pre-established mental models and then we are surprised when they produce the same results.[29]

Instead, a new type of learning is needed, one about how we interact and in and on the world, where what is critical is the depth of awareness and consequent source of action. In reactive learning awareness never digs beneath the surface and instead is responding only to what we see immediately before us. The alternative is to cultivate a deeper awareness that penetrates more deeply to see the whole of 'what is' and our connection to this, which means that the source and effectiveness of our actions can noticeably shift.[30] We need a transformative praxis of HRE, one that is rooted firmly in critical pedagogy and concerned with understanding and overcoming the ways that a social system steeped in domination becomes legitimate through meanings and practices that prevent the development of an open, self-critical community of inquiring citizens. By linking critical inquiry to social action, the hope is to create the ideological and material conditions in which more equitable and just relationships can exist.[31]

The task, then, for individuals is to question the root of what they know and how this has been shaped by external relationships that shape what we know and how we know it. It requires a dialogical approach in which learning involves critical self-reflection and analysis of our experiences in order to understand the ways they are given meaning through external the external environment. Doing this also requires turning the lens inwards, a willingness to inquire into and understand oneself rather than relying upon ideologies, systems and beliefs. As Krishnamurti suggests, 'there is only radical transformation when we understand our own conditioning and are free of it'.[32]

28 Ibid., p. 10.
29 Ibid., pp. 21–22.
30 Ibid., p. 12.
31 Borg et al. (eds) *Gramsci and Education*, p. 43.
32 Krishnamurti, *Education and the Significance of Life*, pp. 24–28.

In a bid to transform existing conditions in society, we must first transform ourselves, and this means becoming more aware of our own thoughts, actions and feelings in each moment.[33] As Krishnamurti suggests: 'The government is what we are, religions and ideologies are but a projection of ourselves; and until we change fundamentally there can be neither right education nor a peaceful world.'[34]

Organic intellectuals

Central to social transformation is the role of the intellectuals. Intellectuals, in this sense, are not understood as traditional academics or experts who survive within the university or institutional settings. Instead, these are 'organic' intellectuals who are cultivated within and generated from those communities and groups at the edge of the system and society; those subordinated and marginalised groups that are often subjected to the harshest conditions of a society controlled and coerced by the dominant cultural groups. It is these individuals within civil society, who Gramsci anticipated nearly a century before, who can provide the leadership necessary to bridge the gap between critique and politics, theory and action, traditional education and everyday life. According to Gramsci, 'the role of the engaged intellectual was a matter of moral compassion and practical politics aimed at addressing the gap between theory and practice'.[35]

These individuals adopt the role of influential agitators and leaders in those everyday spaces and public spheres on the margins. In this sense, transformative praxis is political and not only about nurturing progressive intellectuals and educators, but more importantly about broadening and shifting the conditions for the production, distribution and consumption of knowledge and the range of sites and spaces where learning for social transformation can occur.

Dialogue and unfolding spaces

Dialogue, according to Freire, 'is the encounter between men, mediated by the world in order to name the world'.[36] It is viewed by many as essential if we are to transform the world and is not simply a means or method that educators use, but a process of cultivating relationships and awareness with others in everyday spaces. The importance of a conversation as a way of reaching an understanding is linked to the work of Gadamer who suggests dialogue as 'a process of two people understanding each other' who are fully open and willing to listen to and appreciate the others point of view.[37] However, according to David Bohm a dialogue can take place between any number of people, even one, if it has the right spirit.[38] His

33 Ibid., p. 70.
34 Ibid., p. 83.
35 Giroux, *On Critical Pedagogy*, p. 64.
36 Freire, *Pedagogy of the Oppressed*, p. 69.
37 H.-G. Gadamer, *Truth and Method*, Sheed & Ward, London, 1979, p. 347.
38 D. Bohm, *On Dialogue*, Routledge, New York, p. 7.

picture of a true dialogue is of a 'stream of meaning flowing among and through us and between us'.[39] It is a creative process that makes possible a flow of meaning within a group, which may lead to some new understanding.

In dialogue, knowledge is not viewed as something fixed or that needs to be understood; rather it emerges as part of the interaction. In order to do this there needs to be a willingness to question and put our own assumptions and pre-conceptions to the test, to suspend judgement and try to understand a 'horizon' that is not our own.[40] The only objective is to 'learn from the other'; it doesn't matter if we agree or not with what is being said, as Bernstein suggests, it is 'only by fully grasping its claims upon one can it be critically encountered'.[41] In this way we can begin to see things from another perspective that may ultimately challenge our own inhabited beliefs and assumptions. It is this cyclical process through the process of dialogue where we continually re-visit and re-assess our assumptions through which the 'horizon of the present is being continually formed'. It is an ongoing and continual process of 'fusion' whereby 'the old and new grow together to make something of living value, without either being explicitly distinguished from the other'.[42]

When we come together to talk or otherwise do something in common, are we each aware of the fear and pleasure sensations that block our ability to listen freely? However, if we each can pay attention to those sensations while at the same time also attending to what is being communicated, then together we might be able to create something new.

According to Bohm dialogue is a process through which to unearth and surface the ways that many of our opinions and assumptions have been instilled over time through 'cultural understandings, histories and habits'.[43] He believed that when we create free space, what might seem like chaos will eventually unfold and emerge as some kind of collective pattern or agreement that is focused more upon the 'we' rather than 'me'. For Bohm a lot of what is professed to take place in the name of dialogue, is not dialogue, in the true sense and instead involves discussions, trade-offs and negotiations. This is because the people involved in them are not really open to questioning their fundamental assumptions or willing to challenge themselves or open to a whole new way of thinking, being and doing.

However, what can often happen is that troubling assumptions become unstuck and provoke emotional and knee-jerk responses. Dialogue requires really digging

39 Ibid.

40 Gadamer introduced the idea that we all have our own 'horizons of understanding': This is the 'range of vision that includes everything that can be seen from a particular vantage point' (*Truth and Method*, p. 143). It is with the judgements and understandings that we engage ourselves in what is being said.

41 R.J. Bernstein, *The New Constellation. The Ethical-Political Horizons of Modernity/Postmodernity*, Polity, Cambridge, 1991, p. 4.

42 Gadamer, *Truth and Method*, p. 273.

43 Bohm, *On Dialogue*.

into the underlying factors which sit behind the assumptions, so that we are inquiring into the thought process and how it occurs collectively. What normally happens is that we don't usually pay attention to thought as a process but focus on the thoughts themselves. It is the process that requires our attention and can help us to establish a common consciousness.

Buber believes that real educators teach most successfully when they are not consciously trying to teach at all, but when they act spontaneously out of their own life. In fact opportunities for change to emerge out of the blue, with little formal planning, and rely upon a decision to step forwards towards the emerging opportunity rather than retreat. This depends upon the quality of attention rather than initiation.[44]

There is no purpose or agenda in dialogue; in fact, very often we don't have to do anything at all; there is no authority or hierarchy. Instead, it is a kind of empty and free space where people are free to talk about anything.[45] The idea is not to win an argument or exchange opinions; rather it is about suspending judgement and listening to others in an effort to see what that means. It is a process of collective inquiry that can lead to a common consciousness where each person has a voice, partaking in the formation of meaning of the group and in it. Because we are constantly in the space of being and becoming, nothing is fixed, and instead we are part of a dynamic process of interconnected experiences and events through which reality unfolds.

Both Freire and Burbles[46] see dialogue as a type of social relation between participants but, in addition to skills such as critical inquiry and reflection, entails certain emotions and values. These include love, humility, hope, trust, respect and appreciation.

Reframing HRE discourse in these ways would mean that people can reclaim their 'right to redefine issues, attach meanings to both past and actual events, and use local resources' with respect to their own indigenous needs and expectations rather than those of the global power structures'.[47] Local forms of knowledge and cultural resources should be integrated into HRE discourse in a positive way. Rather than being viewed, as they often are, as obstacles to a human rights culture, they should be viewed as meaningful and important. This does not entail romanticising them, but requires one recognising the strength and agency of local ideas and resources that different communities use in problem-solving and can share with others. While not detracting attention away from the daily violations and suffering that takes place in the world, there is also much to learn from

44 A. Hodes, *Encounter with Martin Buber*, Rowman & Littlefield, Lanham, MD, 1972, pp. 136–137, 140.
45 Ibid.
46 N. Burbules, *Dialogue in Teaching: Theory and practice*, Teachers College Press, New York, 1993.
47 A.A. Abdi, 'De-Subjecting Subject Populations: Historico-Actual Problems and Educational Possibilities', in A.A. Abdi and L. Shultz, *Educating for Human Rights and Global Citizenship*, State University of New York Press, Albany, NY, 2008, pp. 76–77.

localised stories of agency, resistance and change, which apply to a particular set of circumstances.

Rethinking HRE discourse may not actually result in something called 'human rights education', but may require pursuing other ethical discourses beyond the scope of the term itself. It should include considering, as Sefra Dei suggests, 'the sites and sources of local peoples resisting and empowering themselves through their own creativity and resourcefulness' as an educational strategy, and how we can revitalise the buried knowledges and resources as a way of reclaiming relevant past cultural values in order to deal with contemporary problems.[48] In this way HRE discourse should move beyond problematising, characterising and targeting the poor, disadvantaged and marginalised lack of knowledge as justification for intervention and practice. Instead their knowledge, wisdom and experiences should be recognised, respected and valued as offering insight into ways of life from which we can learn.

This acknowledgement of difference is not a call to cultural relativism; rather it is recognition that we live in a complex society demarcated by differences in culture, traditions, gender, class, language and ethnicity. Indigenous discourses must remain plural and diverse, and must not be appropriated by global power frameworks in an attempt to instigate further unified and regulated discourses that ultimately undermine the complexity of knowledge. To advocate that there is a one size fits all solution to society's problems ignores the diversity of those problems and lacks appreciation of the complexities faced. The risk of overemphasising your immediate location without historical or reflective consciousness about other perspectives of the world means that you can easily be drawn into a form of *essentialism*. Using your location as a point of reference and knowing your world in-depth should be used in order to relate to other locations. The challenge, as Paulo Freire states, is always to transcend without losing touch of that place.[49]

These unearthed discourses should not be privileged or reified and remain subject to critique, even in the acknowledgement of the ways that these have been subjugated and displaced by historical and social conditions of hegemony. However, these alternative discourses could offer the opportunity to resist the predominant HRE discourse by opposing the power structures that regulate it. Consciously engaging in different forms of HRE discourse in radical ways opens up the opportunities for alternative languages, practice and learning.

48 S. Dei, *Teaching Africa: Towards a Transgressive Pedagogy*, Springer, Dordrecht, 2012, p. xxiii.
49 L. Pepi, *Presence of Mind: Education and the Politics of Deception*. Westview, Boulder, CO, p. 50.

Conclusion

An important part of the critique in this book has been acknowledgement that there is power in knowledge and the theorising of HRE beyond the artificially constructed boundaries. One of the main things it has shown is how the institutionalisation and centralisation of HRE discourse has gradually eroded diverse ways of knowing and interpreting human rights by regulating the production, distribution and consumption of HRE discourse as a means of social control; something that has been perpetuated by a lack of questioning and critique. The hope is to provoke some level of reflection about how HRE discourse can perpetuate systemic inequality rather than challenge it and how we as progressive educators, should engage with or rethink HRE in future.

It is now over 20 years since the start of the UN Decade for Human Rights Education which means it is an opportune time for those to take a step back, ask serious questions about the ways we interact with communities and articulate ideas about knowledge and whose interests it serves. This reassessment not only requires a shift in HRE practice but also more importantly in the intrinsic mentality and critical consciousness of the 'educators'. This shift is not one that can emerge quickly or without complications; developing any radical pedagogy that attacks the global knowledge apparatus and power structures is susceptible to being labelled dangerous, subversive and political. Perhaps it is, but for individuals and organisations that believe in and are committed to the transformative potential of HRE discourse, it is a challenge *we* need to face.

Appendix 1

Methodologies used during the research

Methodology	*Description*	*Record*
Semi-structured interviews with NGOs and international organisations (34)	20 interviews with Tanzanian NGO staff 5 interviews with International NGOs/funders 4 interviews with UN institutions 1 interview with overseas government agency 2 interviews with Tanzanian academics 2 interviews with Tanzanian government ministries/departments	Conducted in English Recorded Contemporaneous notes Transcribed by researcher
Semi-structured interviews with CSOs and workshop participants (8)	8 interviews	Conducted in Kiswahili and translated* Contemporaneous notes
Unstructured interviews/guided conversations with young people (5)	5 interviews	Conducted in Kiswahili and translated Contemporaneous notes
Group interviews after workshops (translated and notes taken) (2)	2 group interviews with some workshop participants (10–15 individuals)	Conducted in Kiswahili and translated Contemporaneous notes
Focus group discussions (2)	1 focus group discussion with staff at the LHRC 1 focus group discussion for organisations at UNESCO	Mainly conducted in English and contemporaneous notes taken by a volunteer**
Short questionnaires in Kiswahili (5 questions)	116 distributed to workshop participants	Written answers translated from Kiswahili to English

Methodology	*Description*	*Record*
Participant observation	Based in Tanzania for 12 months and situated in an NGO Participated in community events: gender festival/ public consultations on the Child Act/NGO consultation on the Child Act	Reflective fieldwork notes
Workshop observation	Series of 3 observations of sites of HRE discourse Series of 4 workshops on the Maputo Protocol: Dodoma, Manyoni, Mpwapwa and Morogoro 3 meetings on land rights in Kiteto District 3-day workshop for journalists on gender-based violence	Workshops conducted in Kiswahili with parallel translation to English Contemporaneous notes and reflective notes
Primary sources	Material from workshops	
Secondary sources	Books and reports Website information	

Appendix 2

Total interviews conducted in Tanzania

	Interviewee	*Type*	*Recorded*	*Date*
1	Senior staff/lawyer	Tanzania NGO	Yes	29.10.09
2	Manager/lawyer	Tz NGO	Yes	24.11.09
3	Programme officer/lawyer	Tz NGO	Yes	25.09.09
4	Senior staff/lawyer	Tz NGO	Yes	28.08.09
5	Programme officer/lawyer	Tz NGO	No	10.09.09
6	Coordinator	Tz NGO	Yes	05.10.09
7	Senior staff	Tz NGO	Yes	22.09.09
8	Senior staff/lawyer	Tz NGO	Yes	18.09.09
9	Senior staff/lawyer	Tz NGO	Yes	23.09.09
10	Programme coordinator/ lawyer	Tz NGO	Yes	23.09.09
11	Staff/lawyer	Tz NGO	No	01.02.10
12	Programme manager	Tz NGO/funder	Yes	23.04.10
13	Programme administrator	Tz NGO/funder	Yes	23.04.10
14	Senior staff	Tz NGO	No (notes)	27.11.09
15	Senior staff	Tz NGO	Yes	22.01.10
16	Senior staff	Tz NGO	Yes	29.11.09
15	Programme officer	Tz NGO	Yes	
16	Programme officer	Tz NGO	Yes	
17	Senior staff	Tz NGO	No (notes)	11.03.10
18	Programme coordinator	Tz NGO	No (notes)	09.04.10
19	Programme coordinator	INGO	Yes	03.11.09
20	Programme officer	INGO	Yes	03.11.09
21	Academic	University	Yes	08.12.09
22	Academic	University	Yes	
23	International country coordinator	INGO	Yes	21.04.10
24	International country coordinator	INGO	No (notes)	27.04.10
25	Tz staff member	INGO	No (notes	27.04.09
26	Programme officer	State agency	Yes	30.11.09
27	Programme coordinator	UN institution	Yes	23.04.10
28	HRE consultant	UN institution	Yes	23.04.10
29	Programme coordinator	UN institution	Yes	27.11.09

	Interviewee	*Type*	*Recorded*	*Date*
30	Head of Tz office	UN institution	Yes	28.04.10
31	Head of programme	Government	Yes	25.04.10
32	Head of programme	Government	Yes	27.05.10
33	Workshop participant (LHRC Dodoma)	Community paralegal	No (notes)	09.02.10
34	Workshop participant (LHRC Dodoma)	Community	No (notes)	09.02.10
35	Workshop Participant (LHRC Dodoma)	Community	No (notes)	09.02.10
36	Workshop participant (LHRC Manyoni)	CSO member	No (notes)	10.02.10
37	Workshop participant (LHRC Manyoni)	CSO member	No (notes)	10.02.10
38	Workshop participant (LHRC Manyoni)	CSO member	No (notes)	10.02.10
39	Workshop participant (LHRC Manyoni)	CSO member	No (notes)	10.02.10
40	Workshop Participant (LHRC Mpwapwa)	Community	No (notes)	11.02.10
41	Child	–	No (notes)	11.04.10
42	Child	–	No (notes)	11.04.10
43	Child	–	No (notes)	11.04.10
44	Child	–	No (notes)	11.04.10
45	Child	–	No (notes)	11.04.10

Appendix 3

Interviews used and content referred to in Chapter 5

Interview Code	*Interviewee*	*Organisation*	*Dates*	*Time/Length*
1	Programme manager	Tz NGO	04 April 2010	1 hr 1 min.
2	Senior staff	Tz NGO	24 November 2009	1 hr 18 min.
3	Senior manager	Tz NGO	29 October 2009	1 hr 46 min.
4	Consultant	International organisation	23 April 2010	1 hr 26 min.
5	Senior manager	Regional NGO	18 September 2009	1 hr 19 min.
6	Country representative	Int NGO	21 April 2010	58 min.
7	Executive director	Tz NGO	22 January 2010	33 min.
8	Academic	University of Dar es Salaam	08 December 2009	54 min.
9	Head of research	Government department	24 April 2010	53 min.
10	Coordinator	Tz CSO	05 October 2009	1 hr 7 min.
11	Executive director	Tz NGO	23 September 2009	1 hr 1 min.
12	Executive director	Tz CSO	13 November 2009	1 hr 13 min.
13	Governance officer	International organisation	30 November 2009	58 min.
14	Gender programme officer	Tz NGO	25 September 2009	40 min.
15	Programme officer	INGO	30 November 2009	1 hr 31 min.
16	Head of department	Government ministry	27 May 2010	1 hr 3 min.
17	Lawyer	Tz NGO	23 September 2009	44 min.

Interview Code	*Interviewee*	*Organisation*	*Dates*	*Time/Length*
18	Programme manager	INGO	03 November 2009	1 hr 31 min.
19	Programme manager	International organisation	27 November 2009	1 hr 1 min.
20	Programme manager	Tz NGO	October 2009	30 min. approx. – not recorded

Note: Referenced according to corresponding interview codes, i.e. Interview 1, 4 April 2010

Bibliography

Abdi, A.A., 'De-Subjecting Subject Populations: Historico-Actual Problems and Educational Possibilities', in A.A. Abdi and L. Shultz, *Educating for Human Rights and Global Citizenship*, State University of New York Press, Albany, NY, 2008, pp. 65–80.

Abdi, A.A. and L. Shultz, *Educating for Human Rights and Global Citizenship*, State University of New York Press, Albany, NY, 2008.

Alhadeff-Jones, M., 'Learning to Challenge Time in Adult Education: A Critical and Complex perspective', in B. Merrill (ed.), *Proceedings of the 40th Annual Standing Conference on University Teaching and Research in the Education of Adults (SCUTREA)*, Warwick: Warwick University, 2010.

Alston, P., *The EU and Human Rights*, Oxford University Press, Oxford, 1999.

Andreopoulos, G.J and R.P Claude (eds), *Human Rights Education for the Twenty-First Century*, University of Pennsylvania Press, Philadelphia, PA, 1997.

An-Na'im, A., *Human Rights in Cross-Cultural Perspectives: A Quest for Consensus*, University of Pennsylvania Press, Philadelphia, PA, 1992.

Appadurai, A., 'The Right to Research', *Globalization, Societies and Education*, 4(2), 2006, pp. 167–177.

Apple, M.V., 'Curricular Form and the Logic of Technical Control', *Economic and Industrial Democracy*, 2, 1981, pp. 293–319.

Apple, M.V., W. Au and L.A. Gardin, *The Routledge International Handbook of Critical Education*, Routledge, New York, 2009.

Asad, T., 'On Torture, or Cruel, Inhumane or Degrading Treatment', in A. Kleinman, V. Das and M. Lock (eds), *Social Suffering*, University of California Press, Berkeley, CA, 1997, pp. 285–308.

Bajaj, M., 'Human Rights Education: Ideology, Location, and Approaches', *Human Rights Quarterly*, 33, 2011, pp. 481–508.

Bajaj, M., *Schooling for Social Change: The Rise and Impact of Human Rights Education in India*, Continuum, London, 2011.

Ball, S., 'Intellectuals or Technicians: The Urgent Role of Theory in Educational Studies', *British Journal of Educational Studies*, 43(3), 1995, pp. 255–271.

Baxi, U., 'Random Reflections on the [Im]possibility of Human Rights Education', 1996, www.pdhre.org/dialogue/reflections.html (accessed 20 May 2012).

Baxi, U., 'Human Rights Education: The Promise of the Third Millennium?', in G. Andreopoulos and R.P. Claude (eds), *Human Rights Education for the Twenty–First Century*, University of Pennsylvania Press, Philadelphia, PA, 1997, pp. 142–154.

Baxi, U., 'Conceptions of Human Rights and Human Rights Education', in U. Baxi and K. Mann (eds), *Human Rights Learning: A People's Report*. PDHRE, New York, 2006.

Baxi, U., *The Future of Human Rights*, 3rd edn, Oxford University Press, New Delhi, 2008.

Baxi, U., 'Concepts of Human Rights: The Three Worlds of Human Rights', in U. Baxi and K. Mann (eds), 'Human Rights Learning: A People's Report', PDHRE, New York, 2006, www.pdhre.org/report (accessed 11 January 2011).

Baxi, U., 'Human Rights and Human Rights Education: Arriving at the Truth', in Baxi, U. and K. Mann (eds), 'Human Rights Learning: A People's Report', PDHRE, New York, 2006, www.pdhre.org/report (accessed 11 January 2011).

Baxi, U. and K. Mann (eds), *Human Rights Learning: A People's Report*, PDHRE, New York, 2006, www.pdhre.org/report (accessed 11 January 2011).

Beitz, C., 'Human Rights as a Common Concern', *American Political Science Review*, 95(2), pp. 269–282.

Benford, R.D. and D.A. Snow, 'Framing Processes and Social Movements: An Overview and Assessment', *Annual Review of Sociology*, 26, 2000, pp. 611–639.

Bentzon, A.W. et al. (eds), *Pursuing Grounded Theory in Law: South–North Experiences in Developing Women's Law*, Mond Books, Harare, 1998.

Bernstein R.J., *The New Constellation: The Ethical-Political Horizons of Modernity/Postmodernity*, Polity, Cambridge, 1991.

Betron, M., 'Gender-Based Violence in Tanzania: An Assessment of Policies, Services, and Promising Interventions', USAID Health Policy Initiative, 2008, www.mcdgc.go.tz/data/PNADN851.pdf.

Bohm, D., *On Dialogue*, Routledge: New York, 1996.

Borg, C., J.A. Buttigieg and P. Mayo (eds), *Gramsci and Education*, Rowman & Littlefield, Lanham, MD, 2002.

Bowles, S. and H. Gintis, *Schooling in Capitalist America*, Basic Books, New York, 1976.

Bowles, S. and H. Gintis, 'Education as a Site of Contradictions in the Reproduction of the Capital–Labor Relationship: Second Thoughts on the "Correspondence Principle"', *Economic and Industrial Democracy*, 2, 1981, pp. 223–243.

Bowm, L., 'Adult Education in the Third World', in M. Tight (ed.), *Adult Learning and Education*, Croom Helm, Beckenham, 1983.

Brown, W., *States of Injury: Power and Freedom in Late Modernity*, Princeton University Press, Princeton, NJ, 1995.

Brown, W., 'The Most We Can Hope For . . .: Human Rights and the Politics of Fatalism', *South Atlantic Quarterly*, 103(2–3), 2004, 451–463.

Bourdieu, P. and J.C. Passeron, *Reproduction in Education, Society and Culture*, 2nd edn, Sage, London, 1990.

Buck-Morss, S., *The Origins of Negative Dialectics*, Free Press, New York, 1977.

Burbules, N., *Dialogue in Teaching: Theory and practice*, New York, Teachers College Press, 1993.

Campbell, H. and H. Stein (eds), *The IMF and Tanzania*, SAPES, Harare, 1991.

Caney, S., *Justice Beyond Borders: A Global Political Theory*, Oxford University Press, Oxford, 2005.

Cardenas, S., 'Adaptive States: The Proliferation of New Human Rights Institutions', Carr Center for Human Rights Policy Working Paper T.-01-04, 2004, http://content.knowledgeplex.org/kp2/cache/kp/24.pdf (accessed 20 November 2012).

Cardenas, S., 'Constructing Rights? Human Rights Education and the State', *International Political Science Review*, 26(4), 2005, pp. 363–379.

Carter, J., 'The American Road to a Human Rights Policy', in S. Power and G. Allison (eds), *Human Rights: Moving from Inspiration to Impact*, Palgrave Macmillan, New York, 2000, pp. 49–61.

Chachage, C.. and A. Cassam (eds), *Africa's Liberation: The Legacy of Nyerere*, Pambazuka Press, Kampala, 2010.

Chachage, S.L. and M. Mbilinyi (eds), *Against Neo-Liberalism: Gender, Democracy and Development*, Tanzania Gender Networking Programme and E & D Publishers: Dar es Salaam, 2003.

Chabal, P., *Africa: The Politics of Suffering and Smiling*, Zed Books, London, 2009.

Claude, R.P., 'Global Human Rights Education: The Challenges for NGOs', in G. Andreopoulos and R.P. Claude (eds), *Human Rights Education for the Twenty-First Century*, University of Pennsylvania Press, Philadelphia, PA, 1997, pp. 394–415.

Cohen, L. and L. Manion, *Research Methods in Education*, 5th edn, Routledge, London, 2000.

Conteh, M.B., 'Human Rights Teaching in Africa: The Socio-Economic and Cultural Context', in A Eide and M. Thee (eds), *Frontiers of Human Rights Education*, Universitetsforlaget, Oslo, 1983, pp. 53–81.

Cornwall, A., 'Making Spaces, Changing Places: Situating Participation in Development', Working Paper 170, Institute of Development Studies, Brighton, 2002.

Cowan, J., 'Culture and Rights After *Culture and Rights*', in, M. Goodale (ed.), *Human Rights: An Anthropological Reader*, Wiley-Blackwell, Chichester, 2009.

Dale, R., E. Esland and M. MacDonald (eds), *Schooling and Capitalism*, Routledge, London, 1976.

Dei, S., *Teaching Africa: Towards a Transgressive Pedagogy*, Springer, Dordrecht, 2012.

Dembour, M.B., *Who Believes in Human Rights? Reflections on the European Convention*, Cambridge University Press, New York, 2006.

Dembour, M.B., 'What Are Human Rights? Four Schools of Thought', *Human Rights Quarterly*, 32, 2010, pp. 1–20.

Dias, C., 'Human Rights Education as a Strategy for Development', in G.J. Andreopoulos and R.P. Claude (eds), *Human Rights Education for the Twenty-First Century*, University of Pennsylvania Press, Philadelphia, PA, 1997, pp. 51–63.

Donnelly, J., *Universal Human Rights in Theory and Practice*, Cornell University Press, Ithaca, NY, 2003.

Dorsey, E., 'Charter Making and Participatory Research', in G. Andreopoulos and R.P. Claude (eds), *Human Rights Education for the Twenty-First Century*, University of Pennsylvania Press, Philadelphia, PA, 1997, pp. 119–141.

Douzinas, C., *The End of Human Rights: Critical Legal Thought at the Turn of the Century*, Hart, Oxford, 2000.

Douzinas, C., *Human Rights and Empire: The Political Philosophy of Cosmopolitanism*, Routledge-Cavendish, Abingdon, 2007.

Dow, U., S. Stumbras and S. Tatten, 'Looking at Women's Empowerment Initiatives from a Grassroots Level', in G. Andreopoulosand R.P. Claude (eds), *Human Rights Education for the Twenty-First Century*, University of Pennsylvania Press, Philadelphia, PA, 1997, pp. 455–468.

Durkheim, E., 'On Education and Society', in J. Karabel and A.H. Halsey (eds), *Power and Ideology in Education*, Oxford University Press, New York, 1992.

Eide, A., 'Dynamics of Human Rights and the Role of the Educator', in A. Eide and M. Thee (eds), *Frontiers of Human Rights Education*, Universitetsforlaget, Oslo, 1983, pp. 105–116.

Eide, A. and M. Thee (eds), *Frontiers of Human Rights Education*, Universitetsforlaget, Oslo, 1983.

Ely Yamin, A., 'Empowering Visions: Towards a Dialectical Pedagogy for Human Rights', *Human Rights Quarterly*, 15(4), 1993, pp. 640–685.

Englund, H., *Prisoners of Freedom: Human Rights and the African Poor*, University of California Press, Berkeley, CA, 2006.

Englund, H. and F. Nyamnjoh, *Rights and the Politics of Recognition in Africa*, Zed Books, London, 2004.

Esteva, G. and M.S. Prakash, *Grassroots Postmodernism*, Zed Books, London, 1998.

Fairclough, N., *Discourse and Social Change*, Polity Press, Cambridge, 1992.

Fanon, F., *The Wretched of the Earth*, Penguin, London, 2001.

Faulkner, R., 'My Fight for Women's Rights', *Guardian*, 13 November 2009, www.guardian.co.uk/world/2009/nov/13/tanzania-women (accessed 17 January 2012)

Ferree, M.M., 'Resonance and Radicalism: Framing in the Abortion Debates of the United States and Germany, *American Journal of Sociology*, 109(2), 2003, pp. 304–344.

Foucault, M., *Essential Works of Michel Foucault, 1954–1984, Vol. 3: Power*, ed. J.D. Faubion, Penguin, London, 1994.

Foucault, M., *The Archaeology of Knowledge*, Harper & Row, New York, 1976.

Foucault, M., *Discipline and Punish*, Penguin, London, 1977.

Foucault, M., *Language, Counter-Memory and Practice: Selected Interviews and Essays by Michel Foucault*, ed. and trans. D. Bouchard, Cornell University Press, Ithaca, NY, 1980.

Foucault, M., *Power/Knowledge: Selected Interviews and Other Writings, 1972–1977*, Pantheon Books, New York, 1980.

Foucault, M., 'Afterword: The Subject and Power', in H. Dreyfus and P. Rabinow (eds), *Michel Foucault: Beyond Structuralism and Hermeneutics*, Harvester Wheatsheaf, Hemel Hempstead, 1982.

Foucault, M., 'Truth and Juridical Forms', in *Essential Works of Michel Foucault, 1954–1984, Vol. 3: Power*, ed. J.D. Faubion, New Press, New York, 2001.

Foucault, M., *Society Must be Defended: Lectures at the Collège de France, 1975–1976*, Picador, New York, 2003.

Freire, P., *Education for Critical Consciousness*, Continuum, New York, 1974.

Freire, P., *Pedagogy of the City*, Continuum, New York, 1993.

Freire, P., *Pedagogy of the Oppressed*, rev. edn, Penguin, London, 1996.

Freire, P., *Pedagogy of Freedom: Ethics, Democracy and Civic Courage*, Rowman & Littlefield, Lanham, MD, 1998.

Freire, P., 'Literacy and the Possible Dream', in P. Mayo (ed.), *Gramsci, Freire and Adult Education: Possibilities for Transformative Action*, Zed Books, London, 1999.

Frowein, J.A and R. Wolfrum, *Max Planck Yearbook of United Nations Law*, Vol. 5, Kluwer International, The Netherlands, 2001.

Gadamer, H.-G. (1979) *Truth and Method*, London: Sheed & Ward Gierycz, D., 'Education on the Human Rights of Women as a Vehicle for Change', in G.J. Andreopoulos and R.P. Claude (eds), *Human Rights Education for the Twenty-First Century*, University of Pennsylvania Press, Philadelphia, PA, 1997, pp. 96–118.

Giroux, H. 'Rethinking Cultural Politics and Radical Pedagogy in the Work of Antonio Gramsci', *Educational Theory*, 49(1), 1999, 1–19.

Giroux, H., *Theory and Resistance in Education: Towards a Pedagogy for the Opposition*, Bergin & Garvey, Amherst, 2001.

Giroux, H., *On Critical Pedagogy*, Continuum, New York, 2011.

Goodale, M., 'Locating Rights, Envisioning Law Between the Global and the Local', in M. Goodale and S.E. Merry (eds), *The Practice of Human Rights: Tracking the Law Between the Global and the Local*, Cambridge University Press, New York, 2007, pp. 1–38.

Goodale, M., 'The Power of Right(s): Tracking Empires of Law and New Modes of Social Resistance in Bolivia (and Elsewhere)', in M. Goodale and S.E. Merry, *The Practice of Human Rights: Tracking the Law Between the Global and the Local*, Cambridge University Press, New York, 2007, pp. 130–162.

Goodale, M., *Human Rights: An Anthropological Reader*, Wiley-Blackwell, Chichester, 2009.

Goodale, M. and S.E. Merry (eds), *The Practice of Human Rights: Tracking the Law Between the Global and the Local*, Cambridge University Press, New York, 2007.

Gramsci, A., *Selections from Prison Notebooks*, ed. Q. Hoare and G. Nowell-Smith, International Publishers, New York, 1971.

Gunther, K., 'Human Rights and Political Culture', in P. Alston (ed.), *The EU and Human Rights*, Oxford University Press, Oxford, 1999, pp. 117–146.

Habermas, J., *Legitimation Crisis*, Beacon Press, Boston, 1976.

Haugaard, M., *Power: A Reader*, Manchester University Press, Manchester, 2002.

Heaney, T.W. and A.I. Horton, 'Reflective Engagement for Social Change', in J. Mezirow and Associates (eds), *Fostering Critical Reflection in Adulthood: A Guide to Transformative and Emancipatory Learning*, Jossey-Bass, San Francisco, 1990, pp. 74–98.

Henkin, L., 'Human Rights: Ideology and Aspiration, Reality and Prospect', in S. Power and G. Allison (eds), *Realizing Human Rights: Moving from Inspiration to Impact*, Palgrave Macmillan, New York, 2000.

Hicks, D., 'Conflict Resolution and Human Rights Education', in G. Andreopoulos and R.P. Claude (eds), *Human Rights Education for the Twenty-First Century*, University of Pennsylvania Press, Philadelphia, PA, 1997, pp. 80–95.

Hodes, A. (1972) *Encounter with Martin Buber*, Rowman & Littlefield, Lanham, MD.

Holland, T., 'Human Rights Education for Street and Working Children: Principles and Practice', *Human Rights Quarterly*, 20(1) 1998, pp. 173–193.

Howard, R.E. and J. Donnelly, 'Liberalism and Human Rights: A Necessary Connection', in M. Ishay (ed.), *The Human Rights Reader: Major Political Essays, Speeches and Documents from the Bible to the Present*, Routledge, New York, 1997.

Huddleston, T., 'The Person Nyerere', in C. Legum and G. Mmari (eds), *Mwalimu: The Influence of Nyerere*, Africa World Press, London, 1995.

Ignatieff, M., *Human Rights as Politics and Idolatry*, Princeton University Press, Princeton, NJ, 2001.

Ishay, M., *The Human Rights Reader: Major Political Essays, Speeches and Documents from the Bible to the Present*. Routledge, New York, 1997.

Ishumi, A.G. and T.L. Maliyamkono, 'Education for Self-Reliance', in C. Legum and G. Mmari, *Mwalimu: The Influence of Nyerere*, James Currey, London, 1995.

Kanyongolo, F.E., 'The Rhetoric of Human Rights in Malawi: Individualization and Judicialization', in H. Englund and F. Nyamnjoh (eds), *Rights and the Politics of Recognition in Africa*, Zed Books, London, 2004, pp. 64–83.

Karabel, J., 'Revolutionary Contradictions: Antonio Gramsci and the Problem of Intellectuals', *Politics and Society*, 1976, 6(2), pp. 123–172.

Karabel, J. and A.H. Halsy (eds), *Power and Ideology in Education*, Oxford University Press, New York, 1977, pp. 340–355.

Keet, A., *Human Rights Education: A Conceptual Analysis*, Lambert, Saarbrücken, 2010.

Keller, A., A.L. Horn, S.K. Sopheap and G. Otterman, 'A Cambodian Human Rights Education Programme for Health Professionals', in G. Andreopoulos and R.P. Claude (eds), *Human Rights Education for the Twenty-First Century*, University of Pennsylvania Press, Philadelphia, PA, 1997, pp. 345–358.

Khagram, S., J.V. Riker and K. Sikkink (eds) *Restructuring World Politics: Transnational Social Movements, Networks and Norms*, University of Minnesota Press, Minneapolis, MN, 2002.

Kijo-Bisimba, H. and C.P. Maina, 'Mwalimu Nyerere and the Challenge of Human Rights', in C. Chachage and A. Cassam (eds), *Africa's Liberation: The Legacy of Nyerere*, Pambazuka Press, Kampala, 2010, pp. 149–159.

Kiondo, A.S. and C. Mogella, 'Historical Development of the Civil Society in Tanzania', in A.S. Kiondo and J.E. Nyang'oro (eds), *Civil Society and Democratic Development in Tanzania*, MWENGO, Harare, 2006, pp. 19–32.

Kiondo, A.S. and J.E. Nyang'oro (eds), *Civil Society and Democratic Development in Tanzania*, MWENGO, Harare, 2006.

Kleinman, A., V. Das and M. Lock, *Social Suffering*, University of California Press, Berkeley, CA, 1997.

Krishnamurti, J., *Education and the Significance of Life*, Victor Gollancz, London, 1992.

Krug, E.G., L.L. Dahlberg et al. (eds), *World Report on Violence and Health*, WHO, Geneva, 2002.

Lattas, A., 'Essentialism, Memory and Resistance: Aboriginality and the Politics of Authenticity', *Oceania*, 1993, pp. 2–67.

Legum, C. and G. Mmari, *Mwalimu: The Influence of Nyerere*, James Currey, London, 1995.

Lema, E., I. Omari and R. Rajani (eds), *Nyerere on Education/Nyerere Kuhusu Elimu: Selected Essays and Speeches, 1954–1998*, HakiElimu and E. & D. Ltd, Dar es Salaam, 2005.

Lichtenstein, P.M., 'Radical Liberalism and Radical Education: A Synthesis and Critical Evaluation of Illich, Freire, and Dewey', *American Journal of Economics and Sociology*, 44(1), 1985, pp. 39–53.

Livingstone, D.W., 'On Hegemony in Corporate Capitalist States: Materialist Structures, Ideological Forms, Class Consciousness and Hegemonic Acts', *Sociological Inquiry*, 46(3 – 4), 1976, pp. 235–250.

Long, N. and A. Long, *Battlefields of Knowledge*, Routledge, London, 1992.

Lukes, S., *Power: A Radical View*, Macmillan, London, 1974.

Lukes, S., 'Five Fables About Human Rights', in M.R. Ishay (ed.), *The Human Rights Reader: Major Political Essay, Speeches, and Documents from the Bible to the Present.* Routledge, New York, 1997.

MacIntyre, A., *After Virtue*, Duckworth, London, 1981.
McLaren, P., *Che Guevara, Paulo Freire and the Pedagogy of Revolution*, Rowman & Littlefield, Lanham, MD, 2000.
McLaren, P. and P. Leonard, *Paulo Freire: A Critical Encounter*, Routledge, London, 1993.
McLaren, P. and T. Tadeu da Silva, 'Decentering Pedagogy: Critical Literacy, Resistance and the Politics of Memory', in P. McClaren and P. Leonard (eds), *Paulo Freire: A Critical Encounter*, Routledge, London, 1993.
Macrine, S., P. Mclaren and D. Hill, *Revolutionizing Pedagogy: Education for Social Justice and Beyond Global Neo-Liberalism*, Palgrave Macmillan, New York, 2010.
Magendzo, A., 'Problems in Planning Human Rights Education for Re-emerging Latin American Democracies', in G. Andreopoulos and R.P. Claude (eds), *Human Rights Education for the Twenty-First Century*, University of Pennsylvania Press, Philadelphia, PA, 1997, pp. 468–483.
Mahon, M., *Foucault's Nietzschean Genealogy: Truth, Power, and the Subject*, State University of New York Press, New York, 1992.
Manji, F. and P. Burnett (eds) *African Voices on Development and Social Justice: Editorials from Pambazuka News*, Pambazuka, London, 2005.
Marchand, M. and J. Parpart (eds), *Feminism/Postmodern/Development*, Routledge, London, 1995.
Marks, S.P., 'Human Rights Education in UN Peace Building: From Theory to Practice', in G.J. Andreopoulos and R.P. Claude (eds), *Human Rights Education for the Twenty-First Century*, University of Pennsylvania Press, Philadelphia, PA, 1997, pp. 35–50.
Marshall, J.D., 'Foucault and Educational Research', in S. Ball (ed.), *Foucault and Education: Disciplines and Knowledge*, Routledge, London, 1990, pp. 11–28.
Martin, J.P., C. Gitta and T. Ige, 'Promoting Human Rights Education in a Marginalized Africa', in G.J. Andreopoulos and R.P. Claude (eds), *Human Rights Education for the Twenty-First Century*, University of Pennsylvania Press, Philadelphia, PA, 1997, pp. 436–454.
Marx, K. and F. Engels, *Selected Works*, Vol. 2, Moscow Foreign Languages Publishing House, Moscow, 1962.
Marx, K. and F. Engels, *Selected Works*, International Publishers, New York, 1968.
Marx, K. and F. Engels, *The Communist Manifesto*, trans. S. Moore, Pluto Books, London, 1998.
May T., *Between Genealogy and Epistemology*, Pennsylvania State Press, University Park PA, 1993.
Mayo, M., *Imagining Tomorrow: Adult Education for Transformation*, NIACE, Leicester, 1997.
Mayo, P., *Gramsci, Freire and Adult Education: Possibilities for Transformative Action*, Zed Books, London, 1999.
Mayo, P., 'Flying Below the Radar? Critical Approaches to Adult Education', in M.V. Apple, W. Au and LA Gardin (eds), *The Routledge International Handbook of Critical Education*, Routledge, New York, 2009.
Mbilinyi, M., 'Tanzania Gender Networking Programme: Economic Justice and Livelihoods of Marginalized Women in the Context of the Global Economic Crisis and the Scramble for African Resources', plenary paper for Gender Festival, 9 September 2009.

Mbilinyi, M., 'Reflecting with Nyerere on People-Centred Leadership', in C. Chachage and A. Cassam (eds), *Africa's Liberation: The Legacy of Nyerere*, Pambazuka Press, Kampala, 2010, pp. 77–92.

Meintjes, M., 'Human Rights Education as Empowerment: Reflections on Pedagogy, in G. Andreopoulos and R.P. Claude (eds), *Human Rights Education for the Twenty-First Century*, University of Pennsylvania Press, Philadelphia, PA, 1997, pp. 64–79.

Menon, N., *Recovering Subversion: Feminist Politics Beyond the Law*, University of Chicago Press, Chicago, 2004.

Merrill, B. (ed.), *Proceedings of the 40th Annual Standing Conference on University Teaching and Research in the Education of Adults (SCUTREA)*, Warwick, Warwick University, 2010.

Merry, S.E., *Human Rights and Gender Violence: Translating International Law into Local Justice*, Chicago University Press, Chicago, 2007.

Mezirow, J., 'How Critical Reflection Triggers Transformative Learning', in J. Mezirow and Associates (eds), *Fostering Critical Reflection in Adulthood: A Guide to Transformative and Emancipatory Learning*, Jossey-Bass, San Francisco, 1990, pp. 1–21.

Mezirow, J. and Associates (eds), *Fostering Critical Reflection in Adulthood: A Guide to Transformative and Emancipatory Learning*, Jossey-Bass, San Francisco, 1990.

Mutua, M., 'Savages, Victims, and Saviours: The Metaphor of Human Rights', *Harvard International Law Journal*, 42(1), 2001, pp. 201–245.

Mutua, M., *Human Rights: A Political and Cultural Critique*, University of Pennsylvania Press, Philadelphia, PA, 2002.

Mwakikagile, G., *Nyerere and Africa: The End of an Era*, 5th edn, New Africa Press, Dar es Salaam, 2010.

Myamba, F.P., 'Domestic Violence Rights Movement in Tanzania: An Exploration', PhD Thesis, Western Michigan University, 2009.

Name, C., 'How Should Human Rights and Development Respond to Cultural Legitimation of Gender Hierarchy in Developing Countries', *Harvard International Law Journal*, 41, 2000, pp. 391–395.

Neacsu-Hendry et al, 'Implementing Human Rights Education in Three Transitional Democracies: Romania, Slovakia, and Albania', in G.J. Andreopoulos and R.P. Claude (eds), *Human Rights Education for the Twenty-First Century*, University of Pennsylvania Press, Philadelphia, PA, 1997, pp. 484–516.

Nelson, P.J. and E. Dorsey (2008) *New Rights Advocacy: Changing Strategies of Development and Human Rights NGOs*, Georgetown University Press, Washington DC, 2008.

Nyang'oro, J.E., 'Civil Society, Democratic Governance and Political Development in Tanzania: An Introduction', in A.S. Kiondo and J.E. Nyang'oro, *Civil Society and Democratic Development in Tanzania*, MWENGO, Harare, 2006, pp. 7–18.

Nyerere, J.K., *Freedom and Unity*, Oxford University Press, Dar es Salaam, 1966.

Nyerere, J.K., *Freedom and Development: A Selection from Writings and Speeches*, Oxford University Press, Oxford, 1973.

Nyerere, J.K., 'Adult Education and Development', Opening Speech to the International Adult Education Conference, Dar es Salaam (21 June 1976), in E. Lema, I. Omari and R. Rajani (eds), *Nyerere on Education/Nyerere Kuhusu Elimu: Selected Essays and Speeches, 1954–1998*, HakiElimu and E. & D. Ltd, Dar es Salaam, 2005, pp. 133–144.

Nyerere, J.K., 'Education for Liberation' (20 May 1974), in E. Lema, M. Mbilinyi, and R. Rajani (eds), *Nyerere on Education/Nyerere Kuhusu Elimu: Selected Essays and Speeches, 1954–1998*, HakiElimu and E. & D. Ltd, Dar es Salaam, 2005, pp. 122–132.

Nyerere, J.K., 'Education for Self-Reliance' (March 1967)', in E. Lema, I. Omari and R. Rajani (eds), *Nyerere on Education/Nyerere Kuhusu Elimu: Selected Essays and Speeches, 1954–1998*, HakiElimu and E. & D. Ltd, Dar es Salaam, 2005, pp. 67–88.

Nyerere, J.K., 'Musoma Resolution: Directive on the Implementation of "Education for Self-Reliance"' (November 1974), in E. Lema, I. Omari and R. Rajani (eds), *Nyerere on Education/Nyerere Kuhusu Elimu: Selected Essays and Speeches, 1954–1998*, HakiElimu and E. & D. Ltd, Dar es Salaam, 2005, pp. 100–112.

Nyerere, J.K., 'The Objective of Adult Education' (31 December 1969), in E. Lema, I. Omari and R. Rajani (eds), *Nyerere on Education/Nyerere Kuhusu Elimu: Selected Essays and Speeches, 1954–1998*, HakiElimu and E. & D. Ltd, Dar es Salaam, 2005, pp. 85–90.

Nyerere, J.K., 'The Situation and Challenges of Education in Tanzania' (22 October 1984), in E. Lema, I. Omari and R. Rajani (eds), *Nyerere on Education/Nyerere Kuhusu Elimu: Selected Essays and Speeches, 1954–1998*, HakiElimu and E. & D. Ltd, Dar es Salaam, 2005, pp. 145–158.

O'Brien, E., 'Community Education for Law, Democracy, and Human Rights', in G.J. Andreopoulos and R.P. Claude (eds), *Human Rights Education for the Twenty-First Century*, University of Pennsylvania Press, Philadelphia, PA, 1997, pp. 416–435.

Okafor, O.C. and S.C. Agbakwa, 'Re-imagining International Human Rights Education in our Time: Beyond Three Constitutive Orthodoxies', *Leiden Journal of International Law*, 14, 2001, pp. 563–590.

Paci, M., 'Education and the Capitalist Labor Market', in J. Karabel and A.H. Halsy (eds), *Power and Ideology in Education*, Oxford University Press, New York, 1977, pp. 340–355.

Pepi, L., *Presence of Mind: Education and the Politics of Deception*, Westview, Boulder, CO, 1999.

Perry, M.J., 'The Morality of Human Rights: A Nonreligious Ground?', *Emory Law Journal*, 54, 2005, pp. 97–150.

Power, S. and G. Allison, *Realizing Human Rights: Moving from Inspiration to Impact*. Palgrave, New York, 2000.

Raz, J., *The Morality of Freedom*, Oxford University Press, Oxford, 1986.

Reardon, B.A., 'Human Rights as Education for Peace', in G.J. Andreopoulos and R.P. Claude (eds), *Human Rights Education for the Twenty-First Century*, University of Pennsylvania Press, Philadelphia, PA, 1997, pp. 21–34

Reimann, K.D., *International Politics, Norms and the Worldwide Growth of NGOs*, paper prepared for the 43rd Annual Convention of the International Studies Association, New Orleans, 24–27 March 2002, http://isanet.ccit.arizona.edu/noarchive/kimreimann.html#_ftn1 (accessed 15 March 2012).

Said, E., *Representations of the Intellectual: The 1993 Reith Lectures*, Vintage, New York, 1996.

Sen, A., *The Idea of Justice*, Allen Lane and Harvard University Press, London, 2009.

Senge P. et al. (2005) *Presence: Exploring Profound Change in People, Organizations and Society*, Nicolas Brealey Publishing, Boston.

Shapin, S. and B. Barnes, 'Science, Nature and Control in Interpreting Mechanics Institutes', in R. Dale, E. Esland and M. MacDonald (eds), *Schooling and Capitalism*, Routledge, London, 1976.

Shariff, F., 'Dilemmas of Subaltern Ethnographic Research: The Politics of Identity and Power in the Field', paper presented at the 'Ethnographic Futures' conference, Keele University, 6–7 September 2007.

Shivji I., *The Concept of Human Rights in Africa*, Codesria, London, 1989.

Shivji, I., 'Constructing a New Rights Regime: Promises, Problems and Prospects', *Social Legal Studies*, 8, 1999, pp. 253–274.

Shivji, I., *Silences in NGO Discourse: The Role and Future of NGOs in Africa*, Fahamu, Oxford, 2006.

Smillie, I. and H. Helmich, in collaboration with T. German and J. Randel, *Stakeholders – Government–NGO Partnerships for International Development*, OECD Development Centre, Paris; Earthscan, London, 1999.

Speed, S., 'Resistance in Zapatista Juntas de BuenGobierno', in M. Goodale and S.E. Merry (eds), *The Practice of Human Rights: Tracking the Law Between the Global and the Local*, Cambridge University Press, New York, 2007, pp. 163–192.

Steinberg, M.W., 'The Talk and Back Talk of Collective Action: A Dialogic Analysis of Repertoires of Discourse among Nineteenth Century English Cotton Spinners', *American Journal of Sociology*, 15(3), 1999, pp. 736–780.

Stewart-Harawira, M., 'Traditional Peoples and Citizenship in the New Imperial Order', in A.A. Abdi and L. Shultz (eds), *Educating for Human Rights and Global Citizenship*, State University of New York Press, New York, 2008, pp. 159–175.

Suarez, D. and F. Ramirez, 'Human Rights and Citizenship: The Emergence of Human Rights Education', CDDRL Working Paper No. 12, Stanford IIS, 19 August 2004, http://iis-db.stanford.edu/pubs/20682/ramirez_suarez_6.25.2004.pdf (accessed 19 January 2011).

Symonides, J., 'UNESCO's Contribution to the Progressive Development of Human Rights', in J.A. Frowein and R. Wolfrum (eds), *Max Planck Yearbook of United Nations Law*, 5, 2001, pp. 307–340.

Thompson, J.L., *Adult Education for a Change*, Hutchinson, London, 1980.

Tibbitts, F., 'Emerging models in Human Rights Education', *International Review of Education, Special Edition on Human Rights Education*, 48(3–4), 2002, pp. 159–171.

Valen-Sendstad, A., 'Theories of Human Rights in Relation to Understandings of Human Rights Education: The Relevance to Diversity', PhD thesis submitted to the School of Education, University of Birmingham, 14 April 2010.

Wetherall, M., 'Debates in Discourse Research', in M. Wetherall, S. Taylor and S.J. Yates (eds), *Discourse Theory and Practice: A Reader*, Sage, London, 2001, pp. 380–399.

Wetherall, M., S. Taylor and S.J. Yates (eds), *Discourse Theory and Practice: A Reader*, Sage, London, 2001.

Williams, R., *Culture and Society, 1780–1950*, Chatto & Windus, London, 1958.

Williams, R., *Marxism and Literature*, Oxford University Press, London, 1977.

Wink, J., *Critical Pedagogy: Notes from the Real World*, Pearson, Upper Saddle, NJ, 2011.

Youngman, F., *Adult Education and Socialist Pedagogy*, Radical Forum on Adult Education Series, Croom Helm, Beckenham, 1983.

Reports

Global Non-Violent Action Database, 'Masai Women Protest Land Seizure in Tanzania, 2009', http://nvdatabase.swarthmore.edu/content/maasai-women-protest-land-seizure-tanzania-2009 (accessed 23 March 2012).

Legal and Human Rights Centre, 'Through a Crucible of Human Rights Struggles in Tanzania', LHRC, Dar es Salaam, 2006.

Legal and Human Rights Centre, 'Tanzania Human Rights Report', LHRC, Dar es Salaam, 2009.

ORGUT, Technical Assistance to the SULEDO Forest 01/02/2008-30/06/2009, ORGUT, www.orgut.se/referenceinfo.aspx?rid=890 (accessed 1 November 2012)..

SIDA, 'Land Rights and Villagers: Experiences of Securing Access to Land', Lamp Booklet Series, www.orgut.se/files/lamp/lands.pdf (accessed 1 November 2012).

Social Research Association Ethical Guidelines, 2003, www.the-sra.org.uk/documents/pdfs/ethics03.pdf (accessed 30 August 2012).

Socio-Legal Studies Association Statement Principles of Ethical Research Practice (SLSA), 2009, www.slsa.ac.uk/images/slsadownloads/ethicalstatement/slsa%20ethics%20statement%20_final_%5B1%5D.pdf (accessed 30 August 2012).

SULEDO Village Forest Land Reserve: Access to Land and Other Natural Resources for Improving People's Livelihoods. Third European Development Forum on Rural Development. Presentation, 30 March 2011.

TACAIDS and World Bank, 'Effective Reporting on HIV and Aids', 2007.

TGNP, 'Tanzania Gender Networking Programme Gender Festival 2011, Gender, Democracy and Development: Land, Labour and Livelihoods! Guidelines and Concept Note for Performances and Presentations', 2011, www.tgnp.org/images/stories/2011/Gender%20Festival%202011%20presentation%20guidelines%20%20concept%20note.pdf (accessed 20 May 2012).

UNDP, Human Development Index (HDI), 2011, http://hdrstats.undp.org/en/countries/profiles/TZA.html (accessed 20 May 2012).

University of Warwick, Research Code of Practice (regularly updated), http://www2.warwick.ac.uk/services/rss/researchgovernance_ethics/research_code_of_practice/120228_research_code_of_practice.pdf (accessed 30 August 2012).

USAid, 'The 2009 NGO Sustainability Index for Sub-Saharan Africa', 2009, www.usaid.gov/our_work/democracy_and_governance/technical_areas/civil_society/angosi/ANGOSI_Reports/2009/2009_African_NGO_Sustainability_Index_TZ.pdf (accessed 20 May 2012).

Women's Legal Aid Centre, 'Annual Report', WLAC, Dar es Salaam, 2006, www.wlac.or.tz/annual.php accessed (17 January 2012).

World Bank–Civil Society Relations, 'Fiscal 1999 Progress Report', World Bank, Washington, DC, 1999.

International and regional instruments

Charter of the United Nations, 1945.

Universal Declaration of Human Rights, 1948.

International Convention on the Elimination of All Forms of Racial Discrimination, 1965.
International Covenant on Civil and Political Rights, 1966.
International Covenant on Economic, Social and Cultural Rights, 1966.
Convention of Elimination of All Forms of Discrimination against Women, 1979.
African Charter for Human and People's Rights, 1981.
Protocol of San Salvador, 1988.
Convention on the Rights of the Child, 1989.
Protocol to the African Charter on Human and People's Rights on the Rights of Women (Maputo Protocol) 2003 (into force 2005).

United Nations documents

OHCHR, Human Rights Education and Human Rights Treaties, www.ohchr.org/Documents/Publications/HRTreaties2en.pdf (accessed 17 January 2011).
OHCHR, 'Vienna Declaration and Plan of Action', adopted by the United Nations General Assembly on 23 July 1993, A/CONF./157/23, www.unhchr.ch/huridocda/huridoca.nsf/(symbol)/a.conf.157.23.en (accessed 1 February 1993).
OHCHR, 'Human Rights Questions: Human Rights Questions, Including Alternative Approaches for Improving the Effective Enjoyment of Human Rights and Fundamental Freedoms', A/51/506/add.1, 12 December 1996, www.unhchr.ch/huridocda/huridoca.nsf/(Symbol)/A.51.506.Add.1.En?OpenDocument.
OHCHR, Legislative History of the Convention of the Rights of the Child, Vol. 2, 2007, www.ohchr.org/Documents/Publications/LegislativeHistorycrc2en.pdf (accessed 21 November 2012).
OHCHR Report on achievements and shortcomings of the decade and on future United Nations activities in this area, http://daccess-dds-ny.un.org/doc/UNDOC/GEN/G04/112/36/PDF/G0411236.pdf?OpenElement (accessed14 February 2011).
OHCHR, 'Final evaluation of the implementation of the first phase of the World Programme for Human Rights Education', A/65/322 at www2.ohchr.org/english/issues/education/training/evaluationWPHRE.htm (accessed 16 November 2012).
OHCHR, 'Draft plan of action for the second phase (2010–2014) of the World Programme for Human Rights Education', A/HRC/15/28, 2010, http://www2.ohchr.org/english/bodies/hrcouncil/docs/15session/A.HRC.15.28_en.pdf.
UNESCO, Resolution 1.341, 7th session of the UNESCO General Conference, 1952, in, UNESCO, 'Celebration of the 60th Anniversary of the Universal Declaration of Human Rights', 2007, http://unesdoc.unesco.org/images/0015/001542/154277e.pdf (accessed 26 June 2012).
UNESCO, 'Recommendation Concerning Education for International Understanding, Co-operation and Peace and Education Relating to Human Rights and Fundamental Freedoms', adopted by the General Conference at its eighteenth session, Paris, 19 November 1974, www.unesco.org/education/nfsunesco/pdf/Peace_E..pdf (accessed 20 January 2011).
UNESCO, 'International Congress on Teaching of Human Rights', Final Document, *Universal Human Rights*, Vol. 1, No. 3 (Jul–Sept 1979), pp. 89–98.
UNESCO, 'The World Plan of Action on Education for Human Rights and Democracy' (Montreal Declaration), Canada, 1993, www.unesco.org/webworld/peace_library/UNESCO/HRIGHTS/342-353.HTM#one (accessed 19 January 2011).

UNESCO, 'Declaration and Integrated Framework of Action on Peace, Human Rights and Democracy', 1995, www.unesco.org/education/nfsunesco/pdf/REV_74_E..PDF (accessed 2 February 2011).

UNESCO Associated School Project Network (ASPnet): Historical Review 1953–2003, 50th Anniversary International Congress, Quality Education for the 21st Century, 3–8 August 2003, http://unesdoc.unesco.org/images/0013/001305/130509e.pdf (accessed 18 January 2011).

UNESCO and OHCHR, 'Plan of Action: World Programme for Human Rights Education (WPHRE), First Phase', UNESCO, New York and Geneva, 2006, http://unesdoc.unesco.org/images/0014/001478/147853e.pdf (accessed 2 February 2011).

United Nations, Beijing Declaration and Platform for Action, Fourth World Conference on Women, 15 September 1995, www.un.org/womenwatch/daw/beijing/pdf/BDPfA%20E.pdf, (accessed 21 November 2012).

United Nations, Resolution concerning the Universal Declaration of Human Rights, Records of the General Conference, 3rd Session, Resolution 8.1, 11 December 1948.

United Nations, Comment of the General Assembly on the United Nations Declaration of Human Rights, 10 December 1948, www.un.org/en/documents/udhr/index.shtml (accessed 12 January 2011).

United Nations, General Comment No. 6 on effective national machinery and publicity adopted by the Committee on the Elimination Against Women in 1988.

United Nations, General comment under Article 44, paragraph 1 (b) of the Convention on the Rights of the Child, (CRC/C./58).

United Nations, 'Past Peacekeeping Operations', at www.un.org/en/peacekeeping/operations/past.shtml (accessed 30 March 2012).

United Nations, 'A United Nations Priority', www.un.org/rights/HRToday/declar.htm (accessed 12 January 2011).

United Nations, 'Final Act of the International Conference on Human Rights', Tehran, 22 April to 13 May 1968, U.N. Doc. A/CONF. 32/41, Part XX, http://untreaty.un.org/cod/avl/pdf/ha/fatchr/Final_Act_of_TehranConf.pdf (accessed 8 February 2011).

United Nations, 'Agreements on a Comprehensive Political Settlement of the Cambodia Conflict', United Nations, Paris, 23 October 1991.

United Nations, 'An Agenda for Peace: Preventative Diplomacy, Peace-making and Peace-keeping', 1992, www.un.org/Docs/SG/agpeace.html (accessed 30 March 2012).

United Nations Declaration on Human Rights Education and Training, 19 December 2011, Resolution 66/137, http://www2.ohchr.org/english/issues/education/training/UNDHREducationTraining.htm (accessed 27 June 2012).

United Nations General Assembly, Resolution 217A (III) on the Universal Declaration of Human Rights, 10 December 1948, http://daccess-dds-ny.un.org/doc/RESOLUTION/GEN/NR0/043/88/IMG/NR004388.pdf?OpenElement (accessed 17 November 2012).

United Nations General Assembly Resolution, 'Human Rights Education Decade', A/RES/48/127 of 20 December 1993, www.un.org/documents/ga/res/48/a48r127.htm (accessed 17 November 2012).

United Nations General Assembly Resolution, 'United Nations Decade for Human Rights Education', A/RES/49/184 of 23 December 1994, www.un.org/documents/ga/res/49/a49r184.htm (accessed 17 November 2012).

United Nations General Assembly Resolution, 'United Nations Decade for Human Rights Education', A/RES/50/177 of 22 December 1995, www.un.org/documents/ga/res/50/a50r177.htm (accessed 17 November 2012).

United Nations General Assembly Resolution A/res/59/113 of 17 February 2005.

United Nations General Assembly, 'Plan of Action for the United Nations Decade for Human Rights Education, 1995–2004: Human rights education – lessons for life', in UNHCHR, 'Human Rights Questions: Human Rights Questions, Including Alternative Approaches for Improving the Effective Enjoyment of Human Rights and Fundamental Freedoms', A/51/506/add.1, 12 December 1996, www.unhchr.ch/huridocda/huridoca.nsf/(Symbol)/A.51.506.Add.1.En?OpenDocument (accessed 21 November 2012).

Tanzanian legislation

Constitution of the United Republic of Tanzania 1977.

Law of the Child Act, Act No. 21 of 2009,

Parliament of Tanzania website: http://polis.parliament.go.tz/PAMS/docs/21-2009.pdf (accessed 20 November 2012).

Land Act (Cap 113) 1999, Parliament of Tanzania, http://rita.go.tz/laws/History%20Laws/Land%20(law%20of%20Prorerty%20and%20Conveyancing)%20Ordinance,%201923%20(cap.%20114).pdf (accessed 21 November 2012).

Village Land Act (Cap 114) 1999, Parliament of Tanzania, http://polis.parliament.go.tz/PAMS/docs/5–1999.pdf (accessed 21 November 2012).

Law of Marriage Act (1971), Act No. 5 of 1971, Parliament of Tanzania, http://polis.parliament.go.tz/PAMS/docs/5–1971.pdf (accessed 21 November 2012).

Index

For Product Safety Concerns and Information please contact our EU representative GPSR@taylorandfrancis.com Taylor & Francis Verlag GmbH, Kaufingerstraße 24, 80331 München, Germany